Our Elders Understand Our Rights: Evolving International Law Regarding Indigenous Peoples

By Sharon Helen Venne

Theytus Books Ltd.
Penticton, British Columbia

Canadian Cataloguing in Publication Data

Venne, Sharon Helen, 1951-
  Our elders understand our rights

Includes bibliographical references.
ISBN 0-919441-66-1

1. Indigenous peoples--Legal status, laws, etc. I. Title.
K3247.V46 1998   341.4'81'08997   C98-910900-3

Editor: Louise Wallace
Assistant Editor: Lil Sheps
Layout & Design: Marlena Dolan
Cover Design: Marlena Dolan
Cover Art Courtesy of Stephanie Eneas
Tattoo Artist: Percy Lemaigre
Cover Photograph: Eric Simard - Eric's Photo Lab, Smmerland BC

Theytus Books Ltd.
RR#2, Site 50, Comp. 8
Penticton, B.C. V2A 6J7

*The publisher acknowledges the support of the Canada Council,
Department of Canadian Heritage and the Cultural Services Branch of
the Province of British Columbia in the publication of this book.*

Printed in Canada

Dedicated to the Cree and Blood Elders who never forgot that we are part of Nations and to my son's grandchildren's grandchildren so they will not forget.

TABLE OF CONTENTS

Introduction

Discovering Peoples in International Law

Introduction   1

Doctrine of Discovery   2
    Columbus Comes to America   2
    Papal Bulls   3
    Vitoria and Las Casas   5
    Council of the Indies   6
    Effect of Doctrine of Discovery   8

Sources of International Law   10
    Custom   11
    Treaties   13
    International Law on Treaties   14
    Jus Cogens   15
    General Principles of Law   16

Secondary Sources   17

Conclusion   19

Modern International Organizations

Introduction   28

League of Nations   29

International Labour Organizations   30
    Contribution to International Law   31
    Action on Indigenous Peoples   32

Non-UN Organizations   34
    Organization of African Unity   35
    Organization of American States   37

World Bank   39

United Nations   42
    General Assembly   42
    International Court of Justice   44
    Commission on Human Rights   47

UN High Commissioner for Human Rights   48
Sub–Commission on the Prevention   50
of Discrimination
and Protection of Minorities   50
Role of Special Rapporteurs   50
Working Group on Indigenous People   51

Conclusion   53

Indigenous Peoples and Minorities in International Law

Introduction   68

Rights of Peoples   68
ILO Convention 107   69
UN Charter   71
Cristescu Study   75
Studying Minorities and Peoples   76
Espiell's Study   77
Caportorti Study   79
Deschenes Study   79

Indigenous Peoples at the UN   83
First Optional Protocol   83
International Court Cases   86
Defining Indigenous Peoples and Rights   86
Cobo's Study   87
ILO Convention 169   88
Working Group's Draft Declaration   92

Conclusion   94

Key Provisions of the Draft Declaration on the Rights of Indigenous Peoples

Introduction   107

Background to the Declaration   107
Continuing UN Charter Activities   108
Participation by Indigenous Peoples   109

The Draft Declaration   112
Right to Self–Identification   116
Self–Determination   119
Rights to Land and Resources   122

Conclusion   128

The Response of The UN to the Draft Declaration

Introduction   135

Drafting of the Declaration   138
    Development of International Rights Standards   138
    Participation by Indigenous Peoples   144
    The Sub–Commission   153
    Commission on Human Rights   154
    Inter–Sessional Working Group   158

Preparing for the General Assembly   160

Conclusion   163

Bibliography
    General UN Documents   172
    International Labour Organization   174
    World Bank   176
    Working Group on Indigenous Peoples   176
    Other Instruments   178
    International Court of Justice   179
    Human Rights Committee Cases   179
    Secondary Sources
        Books   180
        Articles   190

Appendix I
    Draft Declaration on the Rights of Indigenous Peoples   205

Appendix II
    Draft of the Inter–American Declaration on the Rights of   217
    Indigenous Peoples

Abstract

This book argues that the rights of Peoples in international law extends to Indigenous Peoples who are colonized. Following Columbus, the doctrine of discovery was developed by Eurocentric states to deny that Indigenous Peoples are subjects of international law. Rather, the doctrine relegates Indigenous Peoples to being objects, a position that Indigenous Peoples never accepted.

The first three chapters of this book explore and analyze international law and the various international organizations, including two regional bodies, which have developed in the twentieth century are explored in relation to their response to Indigenous and Peoples' issues. The UN–specialized agency system is only one place where international law norms can be affected. This book documents one such process.

The last two chapters focus on the development of the Draft Declaration on the Rights of Indigenous Peoples and its passage through the UN system. The Draft Declaration is analyzed as a unique international instrument not only in its contents but also in the manner in which it was drafted in public with the full participation of Indigenous Peoples. The Draft Declaration process allowed Indigenous Peoples to move from being observers to subjects in the evolving international law norms on their rights.

Acknowledgements

There are many people who supported and contributed to writing this book.

To the Elders of the Cree and Blood Peoples who keep alive our laws and governments of our Nations and for their patience in teaching us to seek redress for the wrongs of colonization in the international community.

To the Blood Tribe Post Secondary Program for their encouragement and help in the final production of this book. Your support was greatly appreciated.

To the Chiefs and Headmen of the Dene Nation, Lubicon Cree, Joseph Bighead and Opetchesaht and to the many friends especially the Old Women of our Mother–the earth, the Black Swan, Crows, Bears and Eagles for keeping me spiritually strong and focused.

To Professor Linda Reif who read and re–read with her green pen the many drafts of the book and her encouragement to continue writing to finish. Her strength helped me to realize the universal strength of women working together.

To Professor Catherine Bell for serving on my committee, I am grateful. To Dr. Tom Keating, a further thanks for serving on my committee.

To the University of Alberta John A. Weir Memorial Library Staff especially Michael Storozuk who helped me negotiate computer generated card catalogues from around the world and Janice MacLean of inter–library loans who ordered books, articles and cases from far off places. To the library staffs at the Palais des Nations in Geneva and the University of Colorado law library in Boulder, Colorado, thanks for everything.

Finally, to Adam, who relinquished his time on the computer for his mother to work. Adam, thank you for helping me to understand the significance of the future.

Introduction

The goal of Indigenous Peoples is to act and be treated as subjects—and not as objects—in international law. International law has persistently viewed Indigenous Peoples as objects since the European Middle Ages. Not until the middle of the twentieth century have Indigenous Peoples begun to obtain recognition and achieve progress in changing our legal status from objects to subjects through direct participation in international organizations. International law norms—particularly in the area of rights—have been evolving rapidly since the establishment of such international organizations as the League of Nations, the United Nations and regional bodies representing nation–states roughly associated with a geographic location, such as a continent. Such organizations have been encouraged by Indigenous Peoples to grapple with inherent contradictions in international law regarding the recognition of Indigenous Peoples as peoples and the implementation of their rights. Contradictions derive from commitments in the charters that outline the mandate of the international organizations—charters with the status and obligations of treaties—in contrast to an aspect of international law developed in the European Middle Ages.

When an envoy of the Spanish sovereign arrived on the shore of the Indigenous Americas in 1492, his apparent discovery of resource–rich lands suitable for European settlement resulted in the development of international law norms about peoples previously unknown to Europeans. Successive Spanish sovereigns sought support from jurisprudential intellectuals and another major international power at the time, the Papacy, to determine whether lands of Indigenous Peoples in the Americas could be acquired legally for colonization. The resulting norm, known as the doctrine of discovery, subverted the principles of international law by denying Indigenous Peoples legal status as peoples—for a time, not even as human beings—and, thereby, rejecting rights of Indigenous Peoples that were and are applicable to other peoples. While the doctrine of discovery was developed as a result of the desire for European states to acquire the lands of the Indigenous Americas, it has been applied to deny Indigenous Peoples their legal status as subjects and to deny their rights worldwide.

Indigenous Peoples have never accepted the doctrine of discovery and were not invited to participate in or consent to the development of the international law norms that changed their legal status and denied their rights. Prior to the doctrine of discovery, Indigenous Peoples had determined their way of life and exercised their customary laws collectively as peoples. In the twentieth century, the treaties establishing international organizations direct them to attend to the rights of peoples, especially to the rights to free themselves from colonization and return to being self–determining. Thus, international organizations generally recognize that Indigenous Peoples are peoples and have rights but they have been reluctant to implement those rights. Indigenous Peoples have been active in persuading international organizations to clarify legal points and reasoning about their legal status and rights. Among their accomplishments are the announcements of both an international year and a decade to celebrate Indigenous Peoples, the establishment within the United Nations Commission on Human Rights of a Working Group on Indigenous Peoples and the drafting of a Declaration on the Rights of Indigenous Peoples.

International organizations have been established by state governments to improve relations between nation–states and to advance and continue the development of international law. International organizations generally have been studious in the ares of rights, although evolving international law tends to follow advice from member state governments. Although peoples and not governments exercise the right to self–determination, state governments seem resistant to peoples within their states implementing this right. State governments also seem reluctant to recognize collective or group rights, as Indigenous Peoples have customarily exercised them. Despite restrictions by nation–states to limit the effectiveness of their efforts, Indigenous Peoples continue to participate in the evolution of international law norms and rights standards by international organizations to gain greater recognition for their legal status and rights.

Chapter 1 of this book introduces the doctrine of discovery and sources of international law: that is, state custom, nation–to–nation treaties, general principles of law and certain secondary sources such as legal scholarship and opinions delivered by the International Court of Justice. This introduction demonstrates how Indigenous Peoples became objects of international law.

Chapter 2 discusses modern international organizations in relation to Indigenous Peoples and their rights. Particular attention is paid to the United Nations and its human rights bodies.

Chapter 3 examines specific work undertaken by international organizations to study and clarify the legal status and rights of minorities and Indigenous Peoples and to recommend legal mechanisms to protect these rights. This work began with the debates in the League of Nations over the right of minorities in European states to decolonize themselves and embrace self–determination. Part of the League that survived the transformation to the United Nations, the International Labour Organization (ILO), developed Convention 107 as an international standard that asserts assimilation for Indigenous Peoples into their resident states rather than recognize their rights. A draft declaration by the Organization of American States (OAS) is contrasted with the African Charter, an international rights treaty that considers the societies implementing the Charter.

Chapter 3 also provides a survey of selective studies by UN Special Rapporteurs on the rights of minorities and Indigenous Peoples and closes with a discussion of two UN processes to develop legal instruments as international law standards: the ILO revision process that produced Convention 169 and the establishment of the Working Group on Indigenous Peoples that produced the Draft Declaration on the Rights of Indigenous Peoples.

Chapter 4 focuses on the Draft Declaration on the Rights of Indigenous Peoples. The context in which international rights standards are being developed is presented, as well as the role and scope of the participation by Indigenous Peoples. ILO Conventions 107/169 and the OAS draft were developed without such participation thus affirming state practices of treating Indigenous Peoples as objects of law. The content of the Draft Declaration is reflective of the extensive participation by Indigenous Peoples in the drafting process. Attention is given to the major rights for which there was consistent consensus among participating Indigenous Peoples: self–identification and self–determination following decolonization, collective land rights and collective resource rights.

Chapter 5 assesses the processes through which international law norms and standards on the rights of Indigenous Peoples are evolving. The chapter documents the drafting of the Draft Declaration by the Working Group on Indigenous Peoples, and the response by representatives of state governments sitting on UN bodies further up the internal UN hierarchy as the Draft Declaration was submitted to them. The dynamic of these processes reflects the impact that contrasting interests of Indigenous Peoples and state governments have on the quasi–legal procedures of international organizations. Finally, other initiatives by Indigenous Peoples are presented as evidence of their worldwide efforts to revise international law norms and standards with regard to their legal status and rights.

Since the doctrine of discovery was developed five hundred years ago, Indigenous Peoples worldwide have been denied their legal status as subjects of international law. Their customary laws and collective rights have never been recognized by nation–states. Nevertheless, Indigenous Peoples are seeking direct involvement —acting as subjects—to amend the procedural rules and operations of international organizations to effect changes in international law norms and standards. Indigenous Peoples are seeking ways to have international law amended to recognize them so that they can take their rightful place among the community of nations.

1

Discovering Peoples in
International Law

Introduction

Did Christopher Columbus discover America? Can something that is not
lost be discovered? Despite the obvious answer to this fundamental question, it is widely held that Columbus did discover America. The United
States of America has a national holiday to celebrate the occasion. But
Columbus did not discover America; he sailed his ships into waters
occupied and used by Indigenous Peoples. This reality is not generally
included in history books: "Until the late 1970s, mainstream historians
propagated the view that everything significant about America began in
1492 or thereafter and that the story of America was of the triumph of
European peoples bringing civilization and prosperity."[1] The writing of
history is dominated by the Eurocentric[2] view of the world:

> One of the most powerful beliefs of our time concerning the world
> history and world geography . . . is the notion that European civi-
> lization—"The West"—has had some unique historical advantage,
> some special equality of race or culture or environment or mind or
> spirit, which give this human community a permanent superiority
> over all other communities, at all times and down to the present. [3]

Likewise, this world view has also dominated the formulation of
European legal systems which in turn are the basis for customary international law.[4] From this perspective, development of these legal systems
nullify the legal values of peoples who do not share this world view,
including the Indigenous Peoples of the Americas. Historical and legal
writings about America that are based on the belief that Columbus discovered the lands of millions of Indigenous People deny the rights of
these people.

Spanish and other European exploration led to the development of
the doctrine of discovery and its acceptance in international law. This
chapter outlines this development and its acceptance. The right of

1

Indigenous Peoples in the Americas to continue determining their way of life was denied though acceptance of the doctrine of discovery, and this denial persists to the present day. However, in recent decades, Indigenous Peoples have become active in promoting recognition of their rights in international law. International law has evolved with contributions from a variety of sources—custom, treaty and general principles of law—increasingly from within international organizations set by the nation-states. Because the recent efforts of Indigenous Peoples have been within these international organizations, this chapter introduces the sources of international law and the following chapter introduces the organizations in which Indigenous Peoples are trying to effect recognition of their rights.

Doctrine of Discovery

Columbus Comes to America

A convenient starting point for an analysis of the rights of Indigenous Peoples is a discussion of its effect on international law and its development. One approach is to examine some of the international standards drawn from the Eurocentric world view that have been applied to Indigenous Peoples. From earliest contact, Indigenous Peoples have been treated as objects of international law rather than as subjects—that is, active participants. In order to understand the situation of Indigenous Peoples within the context of international law, there is a need to examine the history of interaction between Indigenous Peoples of the Americas and the states that colonized their lands.[5]

Columbus arrived on the shores of the Indigenous America in 1492. When Columbus sailed from Europe, he had made:

> an agreement with Ferdinand and Isabella whereby he was granted, along with certain honors and privileges, a tenth part of the "pearls, precious stones, gold, silver, spices, and other things and merchandise whatsoever, of whatever sort," to be found in the lands that "should be discovered and gained."[6]

Columbus came to Indigenous America as an invader and a colonizer without regard for the original inhabitants of the lands he "discovered":

> Columbus's presumption that he could lawfully claim these "discoveries" for the Spanish Crown was based on the fact of the

natives' divergence from Christian European cultural norms of religious belief and civilization.[7]

The belief in the inherent superiority of the European current at the time allowed the initial claim to be made, but the legal basis for the legitimacy of this claim is doubtful.

The arrival of Columbus set in motion the development of the Eurocentic legal norms in relation to human beings living in Indigenous America:

> When European sovereigns asserted that they had various sorts of rights in the New World, these rights were in the nature of a territorial sovereignty or "dominion." This conclusion was based on the assumption that a single code of international law regulated the struggle for empire . . . not between rival sovereigns in their capacities as personal lords of the new territories or as holders of some "crown," but between representatives of nation-states. Discovery conferred title; all European powers accepted that principle because it was in their interests to do so. [8]

Questions were raised in Spain and in other European countries, particularly Portugal, concerning Spain's claims. Portugal's worries were not for the legal status of the Indigenous Peoples but rather for the rights to the land and resources that could come under the jurisdiction of Spain. Portugal's concerns related to previous Papal Bulls—as Romanus Pontifex—whereby the Pope had given Portugal possession of the Canary Islands and all lands west of Portugal in the Atlantic Ocean.[9] It was an accepted convention at the time for popes and states to do this. The sovereign of Portugal believed that Spain did not possess authority to discover lands to the west. The right of Columbus to "discover" revolved around the Spanish sovereign's authority to empower Columbus to discover and claim new lands and peoples. To claim Indigenous America, the Spanish sovereigns circumnavigated the restrictions placed upon them by both secular and religious laws.

Papal Bulls

Queen Isabella and King Ferdinand—the rulers of Spain delegating responsibility to Columbus—did not depend solely upon their authority as sovereigns to assert rights to Indigenous lands in America; they appealed to the Pope for his help in establishing their legitimacy. The Pope, taking his cue from the Spanish lawyers:

who drafted the Crown's proposed bulls, had convinced Rome that random discovery of peaceful non-Christians not in apparent gross violation of natural law permitted the Pope to exercise his guardianship responsibilities by placing such peoples under the tutelage and direction of the discovering Christian princes.[10]

The Pope then issued a number of papal bulls to deny the rights of Indigenous Peoples. The Spanish Crown readily mixed the secular with the religious in order to assert their jurisdiction against other European crowns.

Pope Alexander tried granting legitimacy to the colonizing orders of Queen Isabella and King Ferdinand by enacting certain papal bulls that restricted Portugal's claims and supported the Spanish Crown's claims:

> At the Spanish Crown's request, Pope Alexander issued three successive bulls . . . Alexander's bulls resolved both legal problems raised by Columbus's voyage—the rights of Spain in relation to the barbarous peoples of the islands discovered and the rights of Spain in relation to Portugal—firmly in favour of the Spanish Crown.[11]

The first Spanish Papal Bull, issued in 1493 and known as Inter Caetera divinai,[12] helped to give legitimacy to the colonization of Indigenous America by declaring that non-Christians could not own land in the face of claims made by the Christian sovereigns. The *Inter Caetera divinai* Papal Bull outlined the criteria that would be applied to Indigenous Peoples for the next five hundred years by declaring that:

> The Pope could place non-Christian peoples under the tutelage and guardianship of the first Christian nation discovering their lands as long as those peoples were reported by the discovering Christian nation to be "well disposed to embrace the Christian faith."[13]

The sovereign and the church collaborated to deny the rights of Indigenous Peoples using the "doctrine of discovery" as their basis. It is noteworthy that these papal bulls were enacted without consulting or achieving the consent of the Indigenous Peoples of the Americas.

By 1493, the patterns were set for the next five hundred or so years in the Americas and other places where European colonizers relocated, displaced and dispossessed Indigenous Peoples from their lands and resources. No state in Europe contested the doctrine of discovery. Every subsequent European state that moved onto the lands of Indigenous peoples used the doctrine of discovery to assert their jurisdiction. Indigenous Peoples were moved along with the flora, fauna, water and land. They had no protection against slavery,[14] torture,[15] murder[16] and other horrendous acts committed against the Indigenous inhabitants by the European colonizer. During the colonization period—lasting five hundred years—Indigenous lands changed hands from one sovereign to another[17] without consideration of the rights of the Indigenous inhabitants. The colonizer states treated Indigenous Peoples in national law as they were being treated in international law—as objects rather than subjects—and denied the Peoples their right to continue determining their way of life.

Vitoria and Las Casas

"Are Indigenous Peoples not human beings with the same rights as other humans" became an issue of public debate within fifty years of Columbus's voyages and the development of the doctrine of discovery to support Spain's seizure of Indigenous lands. Bringing the debate before the members of the Spanish public were two prominent thinkers: Francisco de Vitoria[18] and Bartolome de Las Casas.[19] Both were members of the Dominican Order. Las Casas, who spent a number of years in Spanish colonies of Indigenous America, returned to Spain and wrote about his experiences, thereby bringing the horror of colonization to the Spanish public. These two Dominicans looked at colonization not only in accordance with the canons of church law, but they also examined the nature and dignity of the Indigenous Peoples being exploited and used. Las Casas and Vitoria argued for the rights of the Indigenous Peoples of the Americas based on international law norms. Marks explains what drew him as a modern legal scholar to the writings of Vitoria and Las Casas:

> First, their analyses, carried out at the very beginning of European colonial expansion into the New World, had relevance to the modern day situation of minority Indigenous peoples . . . The issues addressed were very similar, and their analyses were clear, forthright, and well-informed. They seemed to offer some potential for a better understanding of current problems and dilemmas in the development of International protection of Indigenous rights. Secondly, I was struck by the scant, and it seems somewhat superficial, treatment which has been accorded Vitoria and Las Casas by modern writers.[20]

Scholars of international law have largely ignored the sixteenth century Spanish juri-theologians when considering the legal rights of Indigenous Peoples. This denial of the rights of Indigenous Peoples in the Americas gave rise to the role of the sovereign and state in the subsequent development of customary international law. Las Casas saw firsthand the result of the denial of these rights, for he wrote: "It was the general rule among Spaniards to be cruel, not just cruel, but extraordinarily cruel so that harsh and bitter treatment would prevent Indians from daring to think of themselves as human beings or having a minute to think at all."[21] Not only were the Indigenous Peoples not to think of themselves as humans—that is, as Peoples—the rest of humanity was to exclude Indigenous Peoples from legal systems in which they ought to have rights as human beings.

Francisco de Vitoria and Bartolome de Las Casas viewed the Indigenous Peoples of the Americas as human beings with rights. Their rights could not be ignored, they said, in the sovereigns' effort to take Indigenous lands and resources. Vitoria's lectures, delivered in 1532, developed three fundamental arguments in relation to the rights of Indigenous Peoples within the framework of customary international law:

> 1. The inhabitants of the Americas possessed natural legal rights as free and rational people.
> 2. The Pope's grant to Spain of title to the Americas was "baseless" and could not affect the inherent rights of the Indian inhabitants.
> 3. Transgressions of the universally binding norms of the Law of Nations by the Indians might serve to justify a Christian nation's conquest and colonial empire of the Americas.[22]

The "transgressions" Vitoria refers to in the third point were based on stories circulating in Spain at the time that Indigenous People ate human flesh. As a result of hearing this information, Vitoria concluded that "human sacrifices violated the natural law."[23] In his writing, Las Casas rebuts Vitoria's third point by making the following distinction: "Although they are not excusable before God, they are indeed totally so before human beings."[24] In the end, Las Casas believed that his God must make the judgment, not other men. Despite their differences over Vitoria's third point, the publication of Las Casas's and Vitoria's materials and reports pertaining to the atrocities committed in the so-called New World prompted the sovereign of Spain to set up an investigation— by the Council of the Indies—to determine the moral and legal rights of discovery.

Council of the Indies

The Spanish king established the Council of the Indies to meet in Valladolid during the fall of 1550. Struggling to promote the legitimacy of his arguments in support of its activities in Indigenous America, the

Spanish sovereign wanted to "attempt to resolve the continuing contention in Spain over the morality and legality of the wars of conquest against the Indians . . . before a Council of 14 comprising eminent juries and theologians."[25] Two eminent jurists were selected to present each side of the argument. Las Casas defended the Indigenous Peoples as human beings with rights. Juan Gines de Sepulveda supported the Spanish conquest and subjugation of the Indigenous Peoples, including the *conquistador's* right to treat Indigenous People as animals. Sepulveda based his case largely on the teachings of the Bible.[26] Indigenous Peoples did not attend the Council of the Indies; they were not invited. The Council's decision was that Indigenous Peoples were to be converted to Christianity. Any unbaptized Indigenous person could be killed by Christians. A spiritual battle for the souls of Indigenous Peoples emerged as an objective for states to continue to deny legal rights to Indigenous inhabitants of colonized lands.

The sixteenth-century debates that culminated at the Council of the Indies at Valladolid have four important implications for Indigenous Peoples within international law. First, it was the earliest attempt by the European mind to deal with the rights of peoples who were not European. Second, the debates were engaged in with great seriousness since the issues were considered to be significant. Third, the most interesting component was not about the biology of Indigenous Peoples— whether they were indeed humans—but rather "whether the Indians were to be accorded the status of legitimate humans in the eyes of the church and state."[27] Fourth was the treatment of Indigenous Peoples as objects of the debate without inviting them to be active participants. At the outcome, Indigenous Peoples were considered to be biological human beings but "were not seen as legitimate peoples in the eyes of the Spanish."[28] Sixteenth-century Spanish intellectuals would not accept that other peoples could have their own culture and customary law. In the end, the Spanish sovereign countenanced the verdict of the Council of the Indies which did not admit that Indigenous Peoples were to be granted legal status.

Following Valladolid, the Spanish and other European sovereigns continued to deny that any rights to the Indigenous Peoples of the colonized Americas. Indigenous Peoples continue to challenge the international law system to this day, as pointed out by Falk in his essay on the "Rights of Peoples":

> The jurisprudential starting point of the rights of peoples is a direct assault upon positivist and neo-positivist views of international law as dependent upon State practice and acknowledgment. In this regard, the rights of peoples can be associated with pre-positivist conceptions of natural law which at the very birth of inter-

national law were invoked by Victoria [sic] and others on behalf of Indians being cruelly victimized by the Spanish *conquistadors*.[29]

The sixteenth-century debates resulted in a net loss for Indigenous peoples: biologically human but without rights as Peoples. The "doctrine of discovery" interpreted to mean that Indigenous Peoples were not entitled to rights—human or otherwise—lies at the heart of international law norms relating to Indigenous Peoples to this day.

Effects of Doctrine of Discovery

With the doctrine of discovery[30] as a guiding principle—despite its lack of legal legitimacy—European countries began to carve up the world of the Indigenous Nations.

> A major challenge confronting Indigenous Peoples, therefore, as they seek to extend international legal recognition and protection of the collective group rights necessary for their survival, is to deprive this state resistance of its strenuously asserted legitimating foundation in a rule of law. That rule of law, of course, is maintained by the Doctrine of Discovery, which, at its medievally derived and racist foundation, is fundamentally at odds with the universal principles of the equality and human dignity of all peoples reflected in contemporary human rights law and standards.[31]

The existence of lands and peoples previously unknown to Europeans was not considered a challenge to the idea of a Christian family of nations which had motivated several papal bulls in the fourteenth and fifteenth centuries. The Papal Bull *Romanus Ponifex*,[32] in particular, while referring to the lands overseas, denied that Indigenous Peoples had rights to their lands, allowing Spain and Portugal to assert conquest.

After the war in Indigenous America against the French and their Indigenous allies (1755-1763), the British monarch, George III, reconfirmed boundaries between the colonies and the Indigenous territories in the Royal Proclamation of 1763.[33] Nearly one-third of the text is devoted to British relations with Indigenous Nations, many of whom were allied to the British victors. The Proclamation refers to Indigenous Peoples as "Nations," as distinct societies with their own forms of political organization with whom treaties had to be negotiated. It also enshrines protection of Indigenous lands by the British Crown, and a process for seeking Indigenous consent through a treaty process to allow for European settlement. Finally, the Royal Proclamation clearly spells out that Indigenous Nations have an inalienable right to their lands.[34] The Royal Proclamation was to bind the British Crown and its colonial agents to the rules to be followed in relation to Indigenous Peoples and their lands. In fact, the Proclamation was a codification of the norms of customary international law for the British Crown to enter into treaties with Indigenous Nations in the Americas. International law requires that a sovereign enter into formal agreements with another people's sovereign prior to entering lands occupied by those peoples.[35] However, entering into treaties with Britain did not ensure a place for Indigenous Peoples within the family of nations under the international law in the face of the doctrine of discovery.

The doctrine of discovery allowed competing European powers to define their respective spheres of influence. Joseph Story wrote that in the nineteenth century as a conventional rule, discovery might "properly govern all the nations which recognized its obligations, but it could have no authority over the Aborigines of America, whether gathered into civilised communities or scattered in hunting tribes of the wilderness."[36] According to Lindley, discovery was:

> adapted to regulate the competition between European Powers themselves, and it had no bearing upon the relations between those Powers and the natives. What the discoverer's state gained was the right, as against other European powers, to take steps which were appropriate to the acquisition of the territory in question. What those steps were would depend on whether there was already a native population in possession of the territory.[37]

Consequently, discovery only gave an inchoate title. Lindley compares three schools of thought[38] on how to incorporate Indigenous Peoples into the family of nations. The conclusion reached is that Indigenous sovereignty is recognized (e.g. by Vitoria, Grotius), conditionally recognized (e.g. by Vattel, Martens), or negated (e.g. by Westlake, Oppenheim):

> Comparing these three schools of thought, we see that, extending over some three and a half centuries, there had been a persistent preponderance of juristic opinion in favour of the proposition that lands in the possession of any backward peoples who are politically organized ought not to be regarded as if they belonged to no one. But that, and especially in comparatively modern times, a different doctrine has been contended for and has numbered among its exponents some well-known authorities; a doctrine which denies that International Law recognizes any rights in primitive peoples to the territory they inhabit, and, in its most advanced form, demands that such peoples shall have progressed so far in civilization as to have become recognized as members of the Family of Nations before they can be allowed such rights.[39]

Treaty making was a double-edged sword for the colonizer state. In order to claim international legitimacy, the state must be able to claim the land but through what means? Could a state claim to occupy the lands through a treaty process and at the same time deny the existence of the rights of the Indigenous Peoples as international subjects? This is exactly the case whereby Indigenous Peoples continually nip at the heels of state legitimacy:

> Europe during the Discovery era refused to recognize any mean-
> ingful legal status or rights for indigenous tribal peoples because
> "heathen" and "infidels" were legally presumed to lack the ratio-
> nal capacity necessary to assume an equal status or to exercise
> equal rights under the West's medievally derived colonizing law.
> Today, principles and rules generated from this Old World dis-
> course of conquest are cited by the West's domestic and interna-
> tional courts of law to deny indigenous nations the freedom and
> dignity to govern themselves according to their own vision.[40]

Sources of International Law

Despite the arguments put forward by Las Casas, the Council of the Indies at Valladolid rejected the application to Indigenous Peoples of cus-tomary norms of international law. International law had become the sys-tem of law governing relations between states.[41] Usually, in law, there is a body such as a state parliament that enacts and enforces the law. This is not the case under international law. In international law, state practice became the basis for development of the legal principles. Positivists argue that international law: "would be more properly labeled 'interna-tional comity' or 'positive morality.'"[42] The norms of international law were established by the tacit consent of states and accepted state custom constitutes the original source of international law. The modern interna-tional community of states is a recent development based upon:

> the ideas of territorial sovereignty, nationality, and the legal equal-
> ity of states, [which] is generally regarded as dating from the
> Treaties of Westphalia of 1648. The English term "International
> Law" itself was not used until another century and a half when it
> was coined by the English jurist, Jeremy Bentham.[43]

The issues relating to European acquisition of Indigenous lands in America without the consent of the Peoples bear directly on the development of norms that would become international law. Eurocentric insistence that excluded the customary law of non-European peoples had developed long before Westphalia.

Before the sixteenth century, public debates over principles by which people should govern their relations with other people drew heavily on Roman law and the canons of Catholic law. This foundation puts the development of norms for international law in relation to Indigenous Peoples into its Eurocentric and state-based perspective: "International law ... stretches back beyond the Peace of Westphalia of 1648, often taken as its starting point, to a time when organized states were not the predominant or sole actors in international law."[44] Norms for international law, if applied to the rights of Indigenous Peoples "discovered" in the fifteenth century might have challenged the foundation of sovereign, state and papal authority—a challenge, as Falk argues, to "two fundamental statist notions—that of territorial sovereignty and that of a unified 'nationality' juridically administered by governmental organs."[45] Rather than challenge the foundation of their own nations, the Council of the Indies chose to change the direction of the law of nations toward the customary law that became the accepted standard for nation-states. Indigenous Peoples were denied their rights because the nations to which they belong as Peoples were unrecognized under norms of international law evolving at that time.

The direction in which the norms of international law has been evolving through five hundred years after Valladolid has been to recognize the rights of the sovereign (later, the state) over the rights of Peoples. James Brown Scott, who analyzed Vitoria's writings, attributes to debates surrounding the "discovery" of America: "the expansion of international law until it has become a universal rule of conduct."[46] Despite the initial flurry for the recognition of Indigenous Peoples' rights within a natural law framework—as argued by Vitoria and Las Casas—the community of states over the ensuing five centuries has been organizing international law around the rights of states to the exclusion of Indigenous Peoples. In the early forms of international law, only European Christian princes had rights, which were not extended to other peoples or other types of government. Sovereigns—and later states—were considered to be the sole legitimate subjects of international law. This section outlines sources of international law as they have been evolving.

Custom

The primary focus for norms and principles of international law has been to protect and govern relations between nation-states. Within the conventional formulation of international law, there are two sources: custom (that is, sovereign or state practice) and treaties.[47] Each source will be reviewed for its scope and breadth.

Custom, as accepted practice by a sovereign or state, is one of the main sources of what has become international law. Custom was "enforced not by the use of the axe or scimitar, the knout, or the bayonet, but by the public opinion of the community."[48] Gradually, accepted practice between sovereigns became extended as custom between states. Custom can be defined as any practice or standard accepted into the law that is generally agreed on by states:

> The elements of custom are four-fold: duration, uniformity and consistency of practice, generality of practice and opinio juris [which is the requirement that nations must engage in the identified uniform and general practice out of a sense of legal obligation, as opposed to courtesy, fairness or morality][49] *et necesessitates.*[50]

Affiliations and obligations between states—based on these elements—began to form the basis of international law.

Custom as a source of international law entails determining state practice. The challenge in using custom to develop norms is assessing when state practices have acquired the status of accepted inter-state practice moving toward a customary practice. It is a matter of fact. In order to determine the facts for such an assessment, Brownlie suggests reviewing the following:

> diplomatic correspondence, policy statements, press releases, the opinions of official legal advisers, official manuals on legal questions, comments by governments on drafts produced by International Law Commission, state legislation, international and national judicial decisions, recitals of treaties and other international instruments, a pattern of treaties in the same form, the practice of international organs, resolutions relating to legal questions in the United Nations General Assembly.[51]

Reviewing the facts is critical in ascertaining state practice. In many circumstances, materials may not be available for review if they are subject to the laws of state secrecy.[52] By reviewing a wide variety of state practices within various forums, a general view of the state practice can be perceived. Within the interactions, a kernel of the norm will be formed based on the evidence of custom practised by states. As states interact on a number of levels, custom is more difficult to determine and the norms that can be binding on the states are likewise difficult to impose. In the *North Sea Cases*, there was no doubt left as to the conditions needed to prove *opinio juris*:

> the acts concerned ... must also be such, or be carried out in such

a way, as to be evidence of a belief that this practice is rendered obligatory by the existence of a rule of law requiring it. . . . The States concerned must therefore feel that they are conforming to what amounts to a legal obligation.[53]

The state feels that it must comply with the accepted practice as a matter of law or face some form of sanctions. *"The North Sea Cases* suggest that a customary rule requires both material practice and *opinio juris*, and that there is a close affinity between the two."[54] It appears that *opinio juris* must be widespread among more than a few states but not necessarily found in every state.[55] Custom over the last five hundred years has developed against the rights of Indigenous Peoples. Inter-state practice moved towards an accepted international law norm that Indigenous Peoples were not to be recognized as "Peoples." Indigenous Peoples challenge customary international law norms which have evolved to support the interests of nation-states, especially those settling and exploiting Indigenous lands.

Treaties

Another source of international law is treaty[56] law, whereby contracting parties, by expressed agreement, can establish norms and practice. While treaties are not a source of law in a strict sense, they are a source of oblig-ation. Treaties negotiated and ratified between states have no prescribed form.[57] States agree to bind themselves through the articles of a treaty.[58] The signing of a treaty by a state is an indication to other nations of its intention to be bound by the terms of the treaty. However, the signing does not necessarily mean that the treaty has formed part of the norms of international law:

> It must be emphasized that, whereas custom is the original source of international law, treaties are a source the power of which derives from custom. For the fact that treaties can stipulate rules of international conduct at all is based on the customary rule of law of nations, that treaties are binding upon the contracting parties.[59]

It is possible to have a treaty negotiated but not consented to by a state until it is signed and ratified as formal acceptance under international law by the state's legal mechanisms. There is a difference between "consent to be bound" and "entry into force" of a treaty.

> A multi-lateral treaty frequently states that it will be open for sig-nature at a particular place from a certain future date for a stated time. At the end of the negotiating conference, there will be a sign-

ing ceremony but these signatures will only adopt the final act of the conference, which will include the authentic text of the treaty. A signature to adopt a text is not a substitute for a signature to express consent to be bound by the treaty. . . . The first few signatory states may not in fact be bound by the convention qua treaty law for some time. They are not, however, without obligations, for, as Article 18 of the Vienna Convention requires, once a state has expressed its consent to be bound it must "refrain from acts which would defeat the object and purpose" of the treaty.[60]

Since the advent of the United Nations, there has been an attempt to draft universal standards and codes of conduct based on the treaty process. For example, in the area of human rights, two United Nations Covenants (treaties) are binding only on states after they have become contracting parties. Any state that becomes a member of the United Nations agrees to be bound by the Charter of the United Nations, which is itself a treaty. The relevance of this practice to the rights of Indigenous Peoples is discussed in the final three chapters of this thesis.

International Law on Treaties

International law norms related to treaties were codified in 1969 by the Vienna Convention on the Law of Treaties.[61] The Convention contains the following definition of a treaty which is regulated by the Vienna Convention: "Treaty means an international agreement concluded between States in written form and governed by international law, whether embodied in a single instrument or in two or more related instruments."[62] The Vienna Convention is an example of the way in which international law norms have been codified and developed through a multilateral treaty. A suggestion for setting standards in international law is contained in Article 9(2) of the Vienna Convention, wherein states provide for the adoption of a treaty at an international conference by a two-thirds majority of the states present and voting.[63] The Article also allows the states at the conference to change the rules of adoption. However, in keeping with the customary international law norms, such an adoption cannot be binding without the consent of the states: "The adoption and authentication of the text does not by itself create legal obligations and rights. A Treaty comes into being only after the negotiating State/States and organization/organizations consent to be bound by it."[64] The Vienna Convention took aspects of the customary international law norms and extended their provisions to allow for multilateral adoption of the treaty. So many international and regional conferences adopted multilateral treaties and programs of action that a variation of the Article was developed for the following amended rule:

In cases of procedural disagreements, "the adoption of the text shall take place by the vote of two-thirds of the participants present and voting". This rule is also flexible in the sense that if the participants decide to apply a different rule (not to apply the two-thirds majority rule) they may do so by the same majority.[65]

As is evident, states can determine the rules of procedures for international conferences and meetings by determining the application of rules codified in the Vienna Convention. Once a treaty has been adopted, it is then signed and ratified by individual states, entering into force on a specific date.

The International Court of Justice (ICJ) has provided a forum for the interpretation of international law norms and the making of pronouncements on the application of various conventions and treaties. The ICJ[66]—composed of persons of different nationalities with high moral characters and various judicial backgrounds—is competent to review international disputes by the determination and application of the rules of international law. The members of the ICJ were provided with an opportunity to review the rules of international law including multilateral treaties as a source of international law norms. For example, in the *North Sea Cases*,[67] the ICJ reviewed a multilateral convention on the continental shelf and the application of customary international law and multilateral treaties:

> What conclusions can we draw from the judgment of the Court in the North Sea continental shelf case? First, and perhaps most important, the Court has in terms recognized the possibility most customary international law may be generated by treaty.[68]

A multilateral treaty may not only codify existing custom, it may also act as a catalyst for the later development of custom which takes form according to the written terms of a treaty provision.

Jus Cogens

A significant change made by the acceptance of the Vienna Convention relates to the creation of peremptory international norms that are binding on all states and can only be changed by the development of a different peremptory norm. The *jus cogens*[69] rule has been set out under Article 53[70] of the Vienna Convention:

> A treaty is void, if at the time of its conclusion, it conflicts with the preemptory norm of general international law. For the purposes of the present Convention, a peremptory norm of general international law is a norm accepted and recognized by the international

community of states as a whole as a norm from which no derogation is permitted and which can be modified only by a subsequent norm of general international law having the same character.

Article 53 states that a treaty is void if the articles conflict with peremptory norms of general international law. This is a restriction on a state's ability to enter freely into a treaty with another state: "The test of a *jus cogens* rule is the legality of establishing a contrary legal regime and not the legality of violating it which is the test of the legal rules at large."[71] The extraordinary aspect of this article goes to the heart of the sovereignty of a state. Under this Article, a state cannot enter into a treaty which conflicts with the preemptory norms of general international law. The difficulty with *jus cogens* involves its scope within international law. During the discussions on its adoption, there were legal scholars who called into question whether *jus cogens* could exist within international law. The rule of international law which constitutes *jus cogens* is that the rule must have been accepted relatively universally by the politically dominant nations.[72]

General Principles of Law

The third source of international law is "general principles of law." The Statute[73] of the ICJ under Article 38(1)(c) permits the ICJ to apply "general principles of law[74] recognized by "civilized nations." The main application has been "either the general principles of legal liability and of reparation of breaches of international obligations or the administration of international justice."[75] The aspects of which general legal principles should be applied are not specified. Neither is it clear whether the judges are to look to state practice or to an international order. Customary law is based on state practice and the *opinio juris*, whereas general principles of law rest on the common attitudes and approaches of different municipal legal systems.

Judge McNair in the *South-West Africa Case*[76] reviewed the general principles of law recognized by civilized nations and wrote:

> The way in which international law borrows from this source is not by means of importing private law institutions "lock, stock and barrel," ready made and fully equipped with a set of rules. It would be difficult to reconcile such a process with the application of the "general principles of law." In my opinion, the true view of the duty of international tribunals in this matter is to regard any features or terminology which are reminiscent of the rules and institutions of private law as an indication of policy and principles rather than as directly importing these rules and institutions. [77]

The ICJ in this case decided not to import a private law institution into the international law as a means of determining general principles. There had been an attempt by states to put private law into context as evidence of a norm rather than as a source of public international law. The aspect of the statute related to "civilized" nations seems to have been dealt with as a recognition of various legal regimes of the independent states without defining "civilized". In conclusion, Article 38(1)(c) gave the ICJ the ability to apply general principles of law as evidence of state practice.

Through customary practices, treaties and evidence of general principles, international law norms have developed to bind states to certain means of action. Over the years, there has been a diminution in the relevance of papal bulls and sovereign preferences. However, there has been a rise in the importance of state practice and obligation as expressed by moral suasion. This development of standards by modern international organizations drawing on the treaty process, state customs and judgments of the ICJ have contributed to the essence of change in the evolution of international law norms.

Secondary Sources

As well as these three primary sources of international law, there are other secondary or subsidiary sources which can be drawn upon: judicial decisions at the ICJ, decisions of other international tribunals and domestic courts, legal commentaries and law making through the international organizations like the United Nations and the specialized agencies associated with the United Nations. In addition, through time, new instruments adopted by various international bodies could form part of the international law.

With the addition of Article 38(1)(d),[78] the framers of the ICJ Statute provides another consideration for appraising evidence of the international law norms discussed above. Legal writings are not considered to be a source of international law, but as evidence of what international law is. Article 38 sets out some of the evidence that could be applied by the ICJ. While not a source of international law, the importance of the writings of publicists was recognized in 1908 by Oppenheim who wrote:

> The writers on international law, and in especially [sic] the authors of treaties, have in a sense taken the place of judges and have to pronounce whether there is an established custom or not, whether there is a usage only in contradistinction to a custom, whether a recognized usage has now ripened into a custom, and the like.[79]

It was understood that the binding character of these principles was not derived from state practice or from consent of states however expressed, but from the acknowledgment by the framers of the legislation in establishment of the ICJ.

Other aspects under Article 38(1)(d) which merit consideration as subsidiary sources of public international law are national and international judicial decisions: "Judicial decisions are not strictly speaking a formal source, but in some instances at least they are regarded as authoritative evidence of the state of law and the practical significance of the label 'subsidiary means.'"[80] The amount of material that the ICJ can review is a considerable addition to conventional sources of evidence for international law.

One of the most influential recent institutions for the development of international law standards is the International Law Commission,[81] established by the UN General Assembly. This Commission drafted the Vienna Convention and developed other international instruments that have in turn started generating secondary sources of international law. Instruments created by international bodies are not formal sources of law but are authoritative. Under international law, they are persuasive in the sense that they make up elements of state practice leading to custom or to the further elaboration of a treaty obligation. Within an international organization, the instrument may be merely persuasive or recommendatory, or it may be legally binding on a state member and, therefore, a source of international law. Thus, the UN is "engaged in law-making through treaty as well as custom."[82] Law making by the specialized agencies follows the same patterns of making customary international law by way of custom and treaty as follows:

> 1. International law-making by treaty or treaty-like processes within the Specialized Agencies and deviations from treaty law which do not eliminate them from the category of treaty law.
> 2. International law-making by legislative or quasi-legislative acts which are entirely outside treaty law.
> 3. The generation of Specialized Agencies or usage and customary rules as adopted in their internal practices.[83]

There is a great complexity of UN procedures and rigor in the evolution of the standards which will be reviewed in the next chapter.

CONCLUSION

International law has come full circle in its application. Initially, the rights of peoples were recognized through the natural law forms that flowed from interaction between human beings. It was the norm that the public could accept. The system of public international law underwent a significant change with the alleged discovery of Indigenous America by Europeans. Some members of the European public did not want to accept that the Indigenous Peoples had no rights. This public reaction forced the Spanish sovereign to convene the Council of the Indies to resolve the issue. When the evidence was placed before the Council—rather than undermine their own sovereignty—the Council decided to deny international rights to the Indigenous Peoples. The state or the sovereign overrode the legal arguments presented by Las Casas who supported the rights of the Indigenous Peoples of the Americas. The doctrine of discovery formed the foundation of colonizing states to usurp the rights of Indigenous inhabitants. The sovereignty of the state formed the basis of the development of international law norms for the next five hundred years.

There were two recognized sources of international law: custom and treaty-making. The Vienna Convention codified customary law on treaties and their interpretation. With the adoption of the Statute of the ICJ, another source for international law was acknowledged: the general principles of law recognized by "civilized" nations. Finally, there exist secondary sources of international law based upon the judicial decisions of the ICJ, decisions of other international tribunals and domestic courts, legal commentaries and law-making through the international organizations like the UN and the specialized agencies. Papal bulls no longer have the influence over state and international law that they did. This is evidence of a shift in relative importance of one source of international law. International law continues to evolve. It is the work of international organizations like the UN and the specialized agencies—as discussed in the next chapter—where international norms are being developed that affect the rights of Indigenous Peoples.

With the advent of the establishment of the UN and the development of specialized agencies to deal with particular areas of interest, international law norms are being developed and implemented quickly through processes within and outside the state system. It is in this atmosphere that the rights of Indigenous Peoples are being addressed. Indigenous Peoples are challenging their legal status as objects rather than subjects of international law. When the world's attention is turned to this issue by Indigenous Peoples, the need to correct historical injustices perpetuated by international law norms confronts the state framework:

A growing number of legal theorists argue that the current international legal regime, controlled by sovereign states, has a limited life span. . . . Unless there is a means created for Indigenous peoples to participate in international legal processes. . . . the current denial of Indigenous sovereignty will continue to be perceived as the result of a system that has not involved them and only serves the interest of states.[84]

The Spanish sovereign had wanted to deflect attention from the colonization of Indigenous America, but only managed to delay judgment. The wrongs have not been remedied: justice is still waiting to be done five hundred years later.

Footnotes

1. John C. Mohawk and Oren R. Lyons eds., *Exiled in the Land of the Free, Democracy, Indian Nations and the U.S. Constitution* (Santa Fe: Clear Light Publishers, 1992) at 3 [hereinafter Lyons, Exiled].

2. There are problems associated with the word "Eurocentric". One observer points out that: "In most discourse it is thought of as a sort of prejudice, an "attitude," and therefore something that can be eliminated from modern enlightened thought in the same way we eliminate other relic attitudes such as racism, sexism, and religious bigotry. But the really crucial part of Eurocentrism is not a matter of attitudes in the sense of values and prejudices, but rather of science, and scholarship, and informed and expert opinion": J.M. Blaut, *The Colonizer's Model of the World Geographical Diffusionism and Eurocentric History* (New York: Guilford Press, 1993) at 9 [hereinafter Blaut, *Colonizer's Model*]. It is my view that the lack of protection for rights of Indigenous Peoples stems from Eurocentrism.

3. Ibid. at 1.

4. Customary international law is discussed *infra* under "Sources of International Law."

5. It is impossible to summarize the entire history of Indigenous Peoples and the effects of colonization on them. However a number of authors have attempted to write aspects of the history of colonization: see: Greta Bird, Gary Martin and Jennifer Nielson eds., *Majah—Indigenous Peoples and the Law* (Annandale, New South Wales: The Federation Press, 1996); Vine Deloria Jr., *Red Earth, White Lies—Native Americans and the Myth of Scientific Fact* (New York: Scribner, 1995); Lyons, Exiled, supra note 1; David E. Stannard, *American Holocaust—The Conquest of the New World* (New York: Oxford University Press, 1992) [hereinafter Stannard, *American Holocaust*]; Blaut, *Colonizer's Model*, supra note 2; Andrew Armitage, *Comparing the Policy of Aboriginal Assimilation: Australia, Canada and New Zealand* (Vancouver: University of British Columbia Press, 1995); Katherine Pettipas, *Severing the Ties that Bind—Government Repression of Indigenous Religious Ceremonies on the Prairies* (Winnipeg: The University of Manitoba Press, 1994); Sarah Carter, *Lost Harvests: Indian Reserve Farmers and Government Policy* (Montreal & Kingston: McGill-Queen's University Press, 1990); Brian Dippie, *The Vanishing American: White Attitudes and the U.S. Indian Policy* (Middleton:

Wesleyan University Press, 1982); Norma Sluman and Jean Goodwill, *John Tootoosis: A Biography of a Cree Leader* (Ottawa: The Golden Dog Press, 1982); Brian E. Titley, *A Narrow Vision: Duncan Campbell Scott and the Administration of Indian Affairs in Canada* (Vancouver: University of British Columbia Press, 1986); Francis Jennings, *The Founders of America From the Earliest Migration to the Present* (New York: W.W. Morton and Company, 1993) [hereinafter Jennings, *Founders*]; Francis Jennings, *The Invasion of America: Indian, Colonialism and the Cant of Conquest* (Chapel Hill: University of North Carolina Press, 1975) [hereinafter Jennings, *Invasion*] and George Sioui, *For an American Autohistory—An Essay on the Foundations of a Social Ethic* (Montreal & Kingston: McGill- Queen's University Press, 1992).

6. Gustavo Gutierrez, *Las Casas—In Search of the Poor of Jesus Christ* (Maryknoll, New York: Orbis Books 1993) at 22 [hereinafter Gutierrez, *Las Casas*].

7. Robert A. Williams Jr., "Columbus's Legacy: Law as an Instrument of Racial Discrimination against Indigenous peoples' Right of Self-Determination" (1991) 8 *Arizona Journal of International and Comparative Law*. Williams writes: "His description of the Indigenous tribal peoples he encountered on his first voyage is markedly similar in tone and content to the description of the Canary Islanders contained in the 1436 letter of King Duarte of Portugal to Pope Eugenious IV. In that letter, the Portuguese monarch had sought to legitimate his colonizing desires in Africa by noting the infidel Canarians' 'nearly wild' and barbarous customs and manners" (at 64).

8. Lester S. Geoffrey, *Aboriginal Land Rights: Some Notes on the Historiography of English Claims in North America* (August 1988) Ottawa: Canadian Arctic Resource Committee at 12-13.

9. There is extensive literature on these papal bulls and their effect: see James Muldoon *The Americas in the Spanish World Order, The Justification for Conquest in the Seventeenth Century* (Philadelphia: University of Pennsylvania Press, 1994): "Grotius composed the Mare liberum as part of an effort to deny the legitimacy, on the basis of Alexander's VI's bulls, of Castilian and Portuguese possession of the newly discovered lands. . . . Further on, Grotius argued that any claim to domination of the New World based on the papal grant was invalid because the pope 'has no authority over infidel nations, for they do not belong to the Church. Consequently, Castilian and Portuguese claims to possession of the New World and to a monopoly of trade with these lands was insupportable in law " [hereinafter Muldoon, *Justification*]. See, also: James Muldoon, Popes Lawyers, and Infidels: *The Church and the Non-Christian World, 1250-1550* (Philadelphia: University of Pennsylvania Press, 1979) and Williams in the next note.

10. Robert A. Williams Jr., *The American Indian in Western Legal Thought: The Discourses of Conquest* (Oxford: Oxford University Press, 1990) at 80 [hereinafter Williams, *Conquest*].

11. Ibid. at 79.

12. Muldoon, *Justification*, supra note 9 writes: "Alexander VI's *Inter Caetera*, the bull that divided responsibility for the conversion of the inhabitants of the newly discovered lands between the Castilians and the Portuguese" (at 22).

13. Muldoon, *Justification, supra* note 9 at 80.

14. On Columbus's failure "to discover the expected quantities of gold, the Admiral now offered the sovereigns another source of wealth: the sale of slaves." Gutierrez, *Las Casas, supra* note 6 at 23.

15. Stannard scrutinizes some of the atrocities that accompanied the invasion of the Americas by the Europeans and the inhumanity inflicted on the Indigenous inhabitants.

Stannard writes: "Just twenty-one years after Columbus's first landing in the Caribbean, the vastly populous island that the explorer had re-named Hispaniola [present day Haiti and Dominican Republic] was effectively desolate; nearly 8,000,000 people—those Columbus chose to call Indians—had been killed by violence, disease, and despair . . .for years now historical demographers have been uncovering, in region upon region, post-Columbian depopulation rates of between 90 and 98 percent with such regularity that an overall decline of 95 percent has become a working rule of thumb. What this means is that, on average, for every twenty natives alive at the moment of European contact— when the lands of the America teemed with numerous tens of millions of people—only one stood in their place when the bloodbath was over" (Stannard, *American Holocaust, supra* note 5 at x.)

16. "Europeans did not find a wilderness here," he writes, "rather, however involuntarily, they made one . . . The so-called settlement of America was a resettlement, reoccupation of a land made waste by the diseases and demoralization introduced by the newcomers" (Jennings, *Invasion, supra* note 5 at 146).

17. See, Sharon Venne, "Treaty 6 Indigenous Perspective" in [1996] forthcoming publication, University of British Columbia Press for a discussion on the transfer of the Hudson's Bay lands from the company to the newly formed state of Canada [hereinafter Venne].

18. For more information on Francisco de Vitoria, see: James Brown Scott, *The Spanish Origin of International Law : Francisco de Vitoria and his Law of Nations,* (Oxford: Clarendon Press, 1934) [hereinafter Scott, *Vitora*].

19. For more information on Bartolome de Las Casas, see: the review by G.C. Marks, "Indigenous peoples in International law: The Significance of Francisco de Vitoria and Bartolome de Las Casas" [1993] *Australian Year Book of International Law* 1 [hereinafter Marks, Significance]. See also, Muldoon, *Justification, supra* note 9, and Williams, Conquest, *supra* note 10.

20. Marks, Significance, *supra* note 19 at 1.

21. Bartolome de Las Casas, *History of the Indies,* quoted in Jennings, *Founders, supra* note 5 at 101.

22. Vitoria's observations can be found in Williams, *Conquest, supra* note 10 at 97.

23. Gutierrez, *Las Casas, supra* note 6 at 169.

24. Gutierrez, *Las Casas, supra* note 6 at 174. Marks observes: "Las Casas demonstrated the widespread existence of sacrifice throughout history and in many cultures. He noted, from Plutarch, that the Roman did not usually punish barbarian sacrifice because they knew it was done from custom and law. The essential point Las Casas was making was not that human sacrifice is necessarily correct or moral, but rather that intervention, beyond the level of peaceful suasion, cannot be justified: it would be an infringement of jurisdictional boundaries" (Marks, Significance, *supra* note 19 at 32-33).

25. Marks, Significance, *supra* note 19 at 22.

26. "One of the important points argued at great length was the interpretation of the four-teenth chapter of St. Luke, wherein the Lord commended his servant, 'Go out into the high-ways and hedges, and compel them to come in, that my house may be filled. Sepulveda maintained that this command justified war against the Indians in order to bring them into the Christian fold. . . . Two of Sepulveda's distinct but interrelated arguments were that

Spain was justified in making war on the Indians because Spain had a mandate to bring the Indians, at whatever the cost to the Indians, into the Christian fold. [Sepulveda] further argued that the Spanish colonial policy that was enslaving and destroying millions of Indians was not cruel but was instead beneficial to the Indians" John C. Mohawk, "Indians and Democracy: No One Ever Told Us" in Lyons, *Exiled, supra* note 1 at 14.

27. John C. Mohawk, "Indians and Democracy: No One Ever Told Us" in Lyons, *Exiled, supra* note 1 at 50.

28. John C. Mohawk, "Indians and Democracy: No One Ever Told Us" in Lyons, *Exiled, supra* note 1 at 51.

29. Richard Falk, "The Rights of Peoples (In Particular Indigenous Peoples)", in James Crawford, ed., *The Rights of Peoples* (Oxford: Clarendon Press, 1988), at 19 [hereinafter Falk, Peoples].

30. For a general discussion of the doctrine of discovery see: Williams, *Conquest, supra* note 10 at 325- 327.. *See, also: Mark F. Lindley, The Acquisition and Government of Backward Territory in International Law—Being a Treatise on the Law and Practice Relating to Colonial Expansion,* (New York: Negro Universities Press, 1926) at 179-132 reviewed the doctrine of discovery with an analysis of why the doctrine was so widely accepted among European sovereigns: "It was a principle of peace and repose, of perfect equality of benefit in proportion to the actual and supposed expenditures and hazards attendant upon such enterprises; it received a universal acquiescence, if not ready approbation" at 130 [hereinafter Lindley, *Backward Territory*].

31. Williams, *Conquest, supra* note 10 at 333.

32. Papal Bull of 8 January 1455. For a general discussion of the application of the Papal Bull, see: Muldoon, *Justification, supra* note 9 at 135-142 and Williams, Conquest, supra note 10 at 71-74.

33. "As reflected in the Proclamation of 1763, this imperial discourse accepted the necessity of peaceful purchase of frontier Indian lands under strict imperial supervision in order to avoid costly, needless wars. Despite this problematic approach to Indian Affairs, imperial policy ultimately rested on the ancient legitimating formation of the superior rights of Christian Europeans in lands held by the normatively divergent, non-Christian peoples" Williams, *Conquest, supra* note 10 at 229; see, also: Venne, *supra* note 17.

34. The Proclamation says in part: "And whereas it is just and reasonable, and essential to our Interest, and the Security of our Colonies, that the several Nations or Tribes of Indians with whom we are connected, and who live under our Protection, should not be molested or disturbed in the Possession of such Parts of Our Dominions and Territories as, not having been ceded to or purchased by Us, are reserved to them, or any of them, as their Hunting Grounds. - We do therefore, with the Advice of our Privy Council, declare it to be our Royal Will and Pleasure, that no Governor or Commander in Chief in any of our Colonies of Quebec, East Florida, or West Florida, do presume, upon any Pretence whatever, to grant Warrants of Survey, or pass any Patents for Lands beyond the Bounds of their respective Governments, as described in their Commissions."

35. Lindley, *Backward Territories, supra* note 30 at 307.

36. *Commentaries on the Constitution of the United States with a Preliminary Review of the Constitutional History of the Colonies and States Before the Adoption of Constitution* Volume I (New York: Da Capo Press, 1833; repr. 1970) at 6.

37. Lindley, *Backward Territory, supra* note 30 at 26-27.

38. Lindley set out three classes used by the European sovereigns:
Class I - Those who regard backward races as possessing a title to the sovereignty over the territory they inhabit which is good as against more highly civilized peoples.
Class II - Those who admit such a title in the natives, but only with restrictions or under conditions.
Class III - Those who do not consider that the natives possess rights of such a nature as to be a bar to the assumption of sovereignty over them by more highly civilized peoples" (Lindley, *Backward Territory, supra* note 30 at 11 to 19).

39. Lindley, *Backward Territory, supra* note 30 at 20.

40. Williams, *Conquest, supra* at note 10 at 326.

41. D.J. Harris, *Cases and Materials on International Law* (London: Sweet & Maxwell, 1973): writes: "The law created to govern the diplomatic, commercial, military and other relations of the society of Christian states forming the Europe of that time that provides the basis for the present [international] law" at 12 [hereinafter Harris, *Materials*].

42. Christopher O. Quaye, *Liberation Struggles in International Law* (Philadelphia: Temple University Press, 1991) at 53. This author reviews the difficulties with the use of the term "international law."

43. George A. Finch, *The Sources of Modern International Law* (Washington: Carnegie Endowment for International Peace, 1937) at 3 [hereinafter Finch, *Sources*].

44. Marks, *Significance, supra* note 19 at 5.

45. Falk, *Peoples, supra* note 29 at 18.

46. The thesis upheld by Dr. Scott proclaims "an international community composed of all the nations, the vast majority being the small powers whose defense is righteousness, justice, and the moral standard" (Finch, *Sources, supra* note 43 at 13).

47. In addition, to the standard sources, the framers of the International Court of Justice have pointed to other areas as evidence of international law norms that would be considered by the Court. Within the rules of the court, the drafters had brought together the public international sources as set out in 38(1)(a), (b) and (c) of its founding statute. These provisions are discussed *infra* in this chapter [hereinafter ICJ].
Statute of the ICJ, Article 38 states:
1. The Court, whose function is to decide in accordance with international law such disputes as are submitted to it, shall apply:
(a) international conventions, whether general or particular, establishing rules expressly recognized by the contesting States;
(b) international custom, as evidence of a general practice accepted as law;
(c) the general principles of law recognized by civilized nations;
(d) subject to the provisions of Article 59, judicial decisions and the teachings of the most highly qualified publicists of the various nations, as subsidiary means for the determination of rules of law.
2. This provision shall not prejudice the power of the Court to decide a case ex aequo et bono, it the parties agree thereto.

48. Finch, *Sources, supra* note 43 at 45.

49. *North Sea Continental Shelf Cases, Federal Republic of Germany v. Denmark and v. Netherlands'* [1969] ICJ Reports 3 [hereinafter *North Sea*].

50. Isabelle R. Gunning, "Modernizing Customary International Law: The Challenge of Human Rights" [1991] 31 *Virginia Journal of International Law* at 214.

51. Ian Brownlie, *Principles of Public International Law 4th ed.* (Oxford: Oxford University Press, 1991) at 5 [hereinafter Brownlie, *Principles*].

52. *Access to Information Act*, Revised Statutes of Canada, 1985, c. A-1..

53. *North Sea, supra* note 49 at 44.

54. Mark E. Villiger, *Customary International Law and Treaties A Study of their Interactions and Interrelations with Special Consideration of the 1969 Vienna Convention on the Law of Treaties* ((Dordrecht: Martinus Nijhoff Publishers, 1985) at 26 [hereinafter Villiger, *Treaties*].

55. Ibid. at 27.

56. Brownlie defines a treaty as based on the Vienna Convention on the Law of Treaties which applies only to written treaties, but treaties can also be oral: "A 'treaty' as an international agreement in written form, whether embodied in a single instrument or in two more related instruments and whatever its particular designation (treaty, convention, protocol, covenant, charter, statute, act, declaration, concordat, exchange of notes, agreed minute, memorandum of agreement *modus vivendi* or any other appellation), concluded between two or more States or other subjects of international law and governed by international law" Brownlie, *Principles, supra* note 51 at 601.

57. "There is no substantive requirement of form, and thus, for example an agreement may be recorded in the minutes of a conference" Brownlie, *Principle, supra* note 51 at 603.

58. P.K. Menon, *The Law of Treaties between States and International Organizations* (Lewiston, N.Y.: The Edwin Mellen Press, 1992): "The classical form of treaty is a single formal instrument. In the increasingly growing modern practice, international agreements are often concluded not only by less formal instruments but also by means of two or more instruments. In recognition of this fact, the Vienna Convention states that a treaty is "an international agreement. . . . whether embodied in a single instrument or in two or more related instruments' " at 12 [hereinafter Menon, *Law of Treaties*].

59. Finch, *Sources, supra* note 43 at 61-62. See also, Villiger, *Treaties, supra* note 54 at 147.

60. Hugh M. Kindred et al. ed., *International Law Chiefly as Interpreted and Applied in Canada 4th ed.*, (Canada: Emond Publications Limited, 1993) at 89.

61. "Vienna Convention on the Law of Treaties" (1969) 1155 UNTS 331 [hereinafter Vienna Convention].

62. Ibid. at Article 1(a).

63. Ibid. at Article 9 (2). Adoption of the text. (2) The adoption of the text of a treaty at an international conference takes place by the vote of two-thirds of the states present and voting, unless by the same majority they shall decide to apply a different rule.

64. Menon, *Law of Treaties, supra* note 58 at 33. Also, see: *Vienna Convention, supra* note 61

Article 10.

65. Menon, *Law of Treaties, supra* note 58 at 32.

66. Statute of the International Court of Justice (1945) Article 2: "The Court shall be composed of a body of independent judges, elected regardless of their nationality from among person of high moral character, who possess the qualifications required in their respective countries for appointment to the highest judicial offices, or are jurisconsults of recognized competence in international law."

67. *North Sea, supra* note 49.

68. Sir Ian Sinclair, *The Vienna Convention on the Law of Treaties,* 2d. ed. (Manchester: University Press, 1984) at 25 [hereinafter Sinclair, *Law of Treaties*].

69. Ibid. Sinclair defines *jus cogens*: " It is not a concept which has been specially developed within the framework of public international law; on the contrary, it derives from, and is deeply embedded in, particular systems of private law" (at 203).

70. *Vienna Convention, supra* note 61 at Article 53.

71. Conference on International Law, *Papers and Proceedings: The Concept of Jus Cogens in International Law* (Geneva: Carnegie Endowment for International Peace, 1967) at 10.

72. Sinclair, *Law of Treaties, supra* note 68 writes: "the definition and identification of these rules of the 'higher law' is surrounded by immense difficulties. The Commission itself admitted that there is no simple criterion by which to identify a general rule of international law as having the character of *jus cogens*. The records of the Conference also reveal a wide variety of opinions as to the scope and content of *jus cogens*" (at 18).

73. ICJ, *supra* note 49 Article 38(1)(c).

74. "In committee of jurists which prepared the Statute there was no very definite consensus on the precise significance of the phrase. The Belgian jurist, Baron Descamps, had natural law concepts in mind, and his draft referred to the 'rules of international law recognized by the legal conscience of civilized peoples.' Root considered that governments would mistrust a court which relied on the subjective concept of principles of justice. However, the committee realized that the Court must be given a certain power to develop and refine the principles of international jurisprudence. In the result a joint proposal by Root and Phillmore was accepted and this is the test we now have" (Brownlie, *Principles, supra* note 51 at 16).

75. Harris, *Materials, supra* note 41 at 44.

76. [1950] ICJ Reports 3.

77. Ibid. at 148.

78. ICJ, *supra* note 49 Article 38(1)(d):"subject to the provisions of Article 59, judicial decisions and the teachings of the most highly qualified publicists of the various nations, as subsidiary means for the determination of the rules of law.

79. Finch, *Sources, supra* note 43 at 30.

80. Finch, *Sources, supra* note 43 at 20.

81. International Law Commission was established by a resolution of the General Assembly UN Doc. A/AC.10/SR. 15. For a detailed discussion of the history of the International Law Commission and its mandate from the General Assembly, see: R.P. Dhokalia, *The Codification of Public International Law* (Dobbs Ferry: Oceana Publications Inc.) at 147-321. "In 1966 the Commission's programme of study had the following eight topics on its agenda, of which the first three mentioned formed the main topics and the rest additions of more or less limited scope; the law of treaties, state responsibility; succession of states and governments; special mission; relations between states and intergovernmental organizations; principles and rules of international law relating to the right of asylum; juridical regime of historical waters, including historical bays; and most-favoured nation clauses in the law of treaties" (at 321).

82. Charles Henry Alexandrowicz, *The Law-Making Functions of the Specialised Agencies of the United Nations* (Sydney: Angus & Robertson 1973) at 2.

83. Ibid. at 11.

84. Dianne Otto, "A Question of Law or Politics? Indigenous Claims to Sovereignty in Australia"[1995] 21 *Syracuse Journal of International Law & Commerce* at 76.

2

Modern International Organizations

Introduction

The denial of the rights of Indigenous Peoples persists in the formation of two international organizations: the League of Nations and the United Nations (UN). The League and the UN members are all nation-states who have vested interests to protect their sovereignty and authority. The League of Nations fails to promote international cooperation and international peace and security. It does not take any action to protect the rights of Indigenous Peoples. The challenge for the United Nations and Indigenous Peoples is to fulfill the UN Charter commitments while maintaining the interests of nation-states members. There is an inherent legal contradiction which persists since the evolution of international law must overcome the doctrine of discovery prior to recognizing the rights of Indigenous Peoples.

Despite the large number of instruments and bodies established to handle violations, the United Nations' structure still lacks any procedures to deal with the rights of collectives.[1] All the UN declarations, covenants and resolutions that have been passed for the protection and recognition of rights of Peoples, have not been applied to the collective rights of Indigenous Peoples. With the exception of the treaty sponsored by a UN specialized agency—the International Labour Organization's (ILO) Convention 169 (discussed in section C)—there is no international legal instrument to protect the collective rights of Indigenous Peoples as Peoples. A review of the history of the ILO sheds light on how this particular specialized agency adopted conventions and recommendations related to Indigenous Peoples.

This chapter considers international initiatives related to Indigenous Peoples as defined by states acting through such international organizations as the League of Nations and, later, the United Nations and its specialized agencies. There will also be a review of the non-UN organizations like the Organization of African States and the Organization of American States. Each of these organizations have attempted to deal with the rights of Peoples. Despite the efforts by nation-states to limit the effectiveness of their actions, Indigenous Peoples have worked within international organizations to expand and gain greater support for recognition of their rights by expanding norms of international law. Finally, the World Bank has issued a "Citizens' Guide to the Multilateral Development Bank and Indigenous Peoples" in relation to lands, resources and development. This chapter reviews each of the developments on the rights of Indigenous Peoples and their struggle for recognition.

League of Nations

The first attempt to establish an international body to deal collectively with the problems associated with maintaining peace by developing an international system occurred at the end of the First World War.[2] The parties emerging victorious from the First World War formed the League of Nations. Through a multilateral treaty entitled the Covenant of the League of Nations,[3] the League of Nations was created. In addition to its provisions on peace and security, the Covenant contained articles related to the protection of rights of minorities in eastern Europe.[4] This intention to maintain peace was not successful. However, the seeds were laid for the later formation of the United Nations (UN). One of the significant developments of the League was the emphasis placed on the protection of minorities.[5]

Important initiatives were taken by the League in relation to the protection of the minorities in eastern Europe. "President Woodrow Wilson, US President and Chair of the drafting of the League of Nations Covenant, was active in pressing for international protection of 'racial and national minorities' and was conscious of the international repercussions which might arise from their ill-treatment."[6] The policies and treaties of the League related to the protection of minorities failed to prevent the outbreak of the Second World War. But a number of important initiatives arose during the course of the League's existence, *inter alia*, the establishment of the Permanent Court of Justice.[7] As a further protection of the rights of minorities and others, the League developed a system of mandated territory so that all the German and Ottoman colonies could be put under the protection of the League of Nations. "Under League of Nations Mandate, the well-being and development of native populations of former German and Ottoman dependent territories were considered sacred trusts and placed under control of Allied powers."[8] The same extension of a sacred trust did not extend to Indigenous Peoples in colonies of the French, British, Spanish, Dutch, Portuguese and Americans. President Wilson said that:

> The Covenant of the League is one of the greatest and most satisfactory advances that have been made. We are done with annexa-

tion of helpless people meant, in some instances by some powers, to be used merely for exploitation.[9]

The U.S. President, speaking from a land taken from American Indigenous Peoples and used by the colonizers for their own benefit, spoke with unintended irony.

The establishment of the League of Nations did not go unnoticed by the Indigenous Peoples of the Americas. One event of significance to Indigenous Peoples occurred in 1924 when a representative of the Haudenosaunee[10] petitioned the League of Nations to be admitted as a member. The Chief approached the Dutch government "because they had been allies of the Iroquois during the seventeenth century."[11] As a result of direct British intervention, the petition never reached the floor of the League of Nations.[12] When presented with a challenge from Indigenous Peoples, the member-states closed ranks to exclude the petition for admission. Indigenous Peoples were objects and not subjects of international law. Indigenous Peoples were a domestic 'problem' of the national government involved. Their voice was not heard within the League of Nations. It was all right to have a sacred trust obligation to the Indigenous Peoples of the colonies of defeated European nations but the same right was not extended to the Indigenous Peoples of the Americas.

International Labour Organization

The Articles of the League[13] contained a plan to help maintain peace. In order to promote world peace, there was a need to have a peaceful relationship with the labour force.[14] As a result, the members of the League established an international organization for labour matters. Under Article 23(a) of the Covenant,[15] the members of the League undertook to maintain fair and humane labour conditions for men, women and children "in their own countries and in all countries to which their commercial and industrial relations extend."

The League's Covenant obligated states to establish a specialized international organization devoted to commercial and industrial relations in the field of labour. When the constitution of the ILO came into force on 11 April 1919, the primary purpose of the ILO was to improve the working conditions of labour all over the world.[16] As may be inferred from the objectives of the ILO, there was a strong input from the labour movement.

The ILO continued to function after the League of Nations failed, adopting labour conventions and proceeding with the work of the organization. The ILO survived the Second World War and was prepared for the establishment of the new international organization that would replace the League of Nations. When the League was formally dissolved, the ILO needed only to amend its constitution to associate with the new international organization—the United Nations.

With the formation of the United Nations, the ILO changed its constitution to comply with the UN Charter. The original mandate of the ILO related directly to matters concerned with labour standards and the collection and distribution of information on labour and industrial conditions. The amendment to the aims and purposes of the ILO by the "Philadelphia Declaration"[17] provided the opportunity for the ILO to become more involved with matters related to the promotion and protection of workers' rights in relation to their human rights.

Contribution to International Law

Perhaps one reason the ILO could transfer its function from the League to the UN was its unique structure, which is extremely simple. The ILO has three main components: an International Labour Conference, a Governing Body and an International Labour Office.[18] The International Labour Conference is the policy-making and legislative organ of the ILO. The Governing Body is the executive organ while the International Labour Office is the secretariat.

Due to the tripartite arrangement, the ILO has some distinctive characteristics it has developed in relation to the adoption of Recommendations and Conventions. Generally, it is admitted that specialized agencies cannot make international rules and regulations binding on state parties to the constituent treaty unless that treaty permits such conduct.[19] Nonetheless, there are processes that permit the specialized agency to bind its members to certain courses of action. The ILO's adoption of Conventions and Recommendations are a good example of this process.

When a vote is taken at the annual Conference, every delegate has a vote. In order to pass a motion to adopt a convention or recommendation, the vote must have a two-thirds majority.

> Upon adoption these [Conventions or Recommendations] are signed by the President of the Conference and the Director-General[20] for purposes of authentication; they are not signed by delegates. In the case of a Convention, this is then communicated to all members for ratification, not merely those whose government delegates voted for the proposal. Thereupon, *all* members are bound to submit the Convention to the appropriate authorities within the State for enactment of the legislation or other action necessary to give the Convention application within the State. . . . This is not an obligation to ratify, but an obligation to submit to the

appropriate authorities who can give consent to ratification. Moreover each member must inform the Director-General of the measures taken in pursuance of this obligation, and of which authorities are competent and of the action taken by them.[21]

Thus, the state delegation must submit the Convention to their government. Having submitted the document to the relevant body, the member is further obligated under the terms of the ILO Constitution to inform the Director-General of having complied with the provisions. This process is completely different from the manner of ratification of other multilateral treaties or resolutions of the United Nations where, generally, the state having voted or absented itself is not obligated to follow up. If a state chooses not to support a particular covenant, declaration, recommendation or resolution, it is within its right to do so. However, the ILO requires that a state which decides not to ratify an ILO document must notify their government and then inform the Director-General of the ILO. This obligation is binding on all states when they become members of the ILO. This same obligation exists for the passage by the General Conference of recommendations: "Conventions are instruments designed to create international obligations for the States which ratify them, while Recommendations are not designed to create obligations but to provide guidelines for government action."[22] These processes are of paramount importance to documents related to the rights of Indigenous Peoples.

Action on Indigenous Peoples

The original function and mandate of the ILO had some involvement with Indigenous Peoples' issues, dating back to 1936. The ILO drafted Convention No. 50[23] on the Recruiting of Indigenous Workers, and supplemented it by Recommendation (No. 46) of 1936.[24] The Convention and Recommendation were further complemented by two conventions to prevent abuse in contracting Indigenous Peoples into a workforce. In 1939, the ILO drafted Convention (No. 64)[25] on contracts of employment together with Recommendation No. 58.[26] During the Second World War, there were no recommendations or conventions adopted by the ILO in relation to Indigenous workers in need of protection against exploitation and coercion. In 1947, the ILO passed Convention (No. 86) with further reference to contracts with Indigenous workers.[27] The ILO viewed Indigenous Peoples as being in a disadvantaged position vis-a-vis the rest of society and the organization's broad approach to eliminate discrimination in the workplace extended to groups perceived as disadvantaged. This conclusion was reached in a study commissioned by the ILO in 1930. The author, Alberta Thomas, concluded that:

> [T]he introduction of an industrial civilization was too sudden to allow natives the time to abandon their centuries-old existence of hunting and agriculture and become educated in the need and habit of regular and sustained work. . . . Education lay at the base of any improvement in the condition of the native, but this could only be achieved slowly. . . . In the meantime, the ILO should try to lift the chains that still bound the native so as to prepare him for the next educative stage.[28]

Indigenous Peoples were being abused by private businesses in colonial states and, in some cases, enslaved. Thomas's underlying assumption explaining why Indigenous Peoples were in these situations was that Indigenous Peoples were too uneducated to participate fully in the wage economy. To suggest that people were enslaved due to lack of education blames the victims for their oppression. Was the ILO's suggested redress to change the colonial system that oppressed Indigenous Peoples? No, the ILO decided that Indigenous Peoples should be treated as objects: they should be changed. The ILO proceeded on the assumption that it had an obligation to bring Indigenous Peoples to a sufficient level of education to participate in the wage economy.

The ILO expressed the view that the "ultimate aim of transforming the presently existing primitive society into a producer and consumer society like that of the white man presupposed the introduction in the colonies of the white man's methods and means of labour."[29] The ILO was supporting the model of colonization. Indigenous Peoples could not be allowed to exist in their territories. The intent was to change Indigenous Peoples and their rights rather than respecting their rights.

In 1944, following the Philadelphia mandate, the ILO took a more social and humane approach to labour issues with the passage of Recommendation (No.70).[30] The Recommendation was followed by two Conventions on penal sanctions against Indigenous workers.[31]

In 1946 and 1949,[32] the American Regional Conference of the ILO passed a resolution establishing a committee of experts to review the social problems of the Indigenous Peoples. The ILO established the Committee of Experts on Indigenous Labour in 1951 who:

> approached the various questions submitted to it, not as problems peculiar to particular racial groups, but rather as problems affecting sectors of the population which for historical reasons have not as yet been fully integrated into the social and economic life of the communities surrounding them. Among the factors which continued to prevent such integration the Committee considered that the economic inferiority of the indigenous groups and their deficient education play an important part.[33]

As a result of the study undertaken by the experts, the Governing Body of the ILO determined that a specific program was needed. One interesting note from the meeting relates to the conclusions reached by the experts that the problems of Indigenous workers were historical wrongs rather than racially motivated. As a result of the colonization of their lands, Indigenous Peoples did not participate in the wage economy. The experts concluded that Indigenous workers needed education and, as a result:

> at the first meeting of the ILO Committee of Experts on Indigenous Labour (La Paz, 1951) the idea was put forward . . . Action units and comprehensive demonstration projects were set up within the Indian communities with the aim of diversifying their economy, developing co-operation for both production (especially handicrafts) and consumption, providing public health and social welfare training, improving general education, and organizing a seasonal rotation of manpower.[34]

A highly intensive program[35] of education was undertaken in South America to bring the Indigenous Peoples to the "next level of civilization." It was determined that, with sufficient education, the Indigenous workers would be able to benefit from the economy of a state. It was a result of the Andean Programme[36] on the living and working conditions of Indigenous Peoples in South America that in 1957 the ILO undertook to adopt the Indigenous and Tribal Populations Convention (No. 107) and Recommendation 104.[37] The Convention initiated principles and standards for Indigenous Peoples for their assimilation into the life of ILO member states. Convention 107 and its revision in the 1980s are discussed in Chapter 3.

Non-UN Organizations

In addition to the international organizations with global scope, a number of regional organizations have drafted and implemented instruments relating to the rights of Peoples. There are such regional organizations for Africa (Organization of African Unity), Europe (Council of Europe) and the Americas (Organization of American States). The regional initiatives to deal with the rights of Peoples, such as the African Charter on Human and Peoples' Rights [39](African Charter) and, to a lesser extent, the draft of the Inter-American declaration on the Rights of Indigenous Peoples[40] of the Organization of American States (OAS), are discussed. Detailed descriptions of the regional human rights organizations are not required for the purposes of these discussions. Rather, the instruments of two regional organizations having a direct impact on the rights of Indigenous and Peoples' rights are presented here.

Organization of African Unity

Under the auspices of the Organization of African Unity, the African Charter was adopted in 1981 and entered into force in 1986.[41] Unlike similar American and European organizations, which opt for both a commission and a court[42] to enforce their Conventions, the African Charter provides only for an African Commission on Human and Peoples' Rights to enforce its provisions.[43] The Africans modelled their Commission on the provisions contained in the First Optional Protocol of the International Covenant of Civil and Political Rights (discussed in Chapter 3) and the Covenant itself.[44] The Commission has the power to write its own rules of procedure as set out in Article 42(2). However, the basic function of the Commission, as outlined in Article 45 (1)(a), is:

> to collect documents, to undertake studies, and researches on African problems in the field of human and peoples' rights, organize seminars, symposia and conferences, disseminate information and encourage national and local institutions concerned with human and peoples' rights, and should the case arise, give its views or make recommendations to Governments.

The African Commission has a two-fold mandate: (1) to receive communications by one state party that another state party has violated the terms of the Charter (Articles 47-54) and (2) to carry out extensive educational programs related to human and Peoples' rights.

The African Charter strives for the peaceful settlement of issues within the family, the community, the state and, finally, the Commission. A tremendous effort is placed within the African Charter for states to reach friendly settlements without formally involving the Commission's mechanisms (Article 52). Finally, the provisions for the individual to bring a complaint before the Commission have some limitations. For example, the complaint must not be "written in disparaging or insulting language directed against the State concerned and its institutions or to the Organization of African Unity" (Article 56(3)) or "based exclusively on news disseminated through the mass media" (Article 56(4)). These practical provisions allow individuals from the communities to bring their complaints but with limitations designed to avoid violations based on hearsay and false reports.

The African Charter reflects a strong propensity for mediation, conciliation and consensus building as opposed to confrontational or adversarial approaches common under Eurocentric jurisdictions. There is a provision to keep matters in confidence "until such a time as the Assembly of Heads of State and Government shall otherwise decide" (Article 59(1)). The African Charter puts a human face on the provisions, giving maximum security to the individual, the family, the community and the state. One legal observer remarks:

> In bringing individual, collective and peoples' rights as well as duties together in one concept, the Charter can be considered the most comprehensive human rights instrument in existence. It integrates the three so-called generations of human rights in one single document. . . . Therefore, it may be considered as the expression of an African basic consensus in the field of human rights. Imagining the possible contents and procedures of an all-European Charter one can better appreciate the African achievement.[45]

The African Charter is an expression of the needs of the African Peoples. As included in the preamble,[46] the African Charter is built upon the traditions of the Peoples of Africa coming from Africa for Africans. An international law scholar comments:

> The sixth clause of the preamble illustrates that the Charter embodies a concept of duty different from that contained in the European and American Conventions. It provided that "[the] enjoyment of rights and freedoms also implies the performance of duties on the part of everyone." In other regional human rights instruments the concept of "duties" refers only to the obligations of a state towards its citizens or towards citizens of another state coming within its jurisdiction. . . . The notion of individual responsibility to the community is firmly ingrained in African tradition and is therefore consistent with historical traditions and values of African civilization upon which the Charter relied.[47]

For a number of reasons, the African Charter is unique in its approach to the protection of human and Peoples' rights. There are provisions for the rights of individuals,[48] the rights of the family[49], land and resource rights [50] and the right to self-determination.[51] Under Article 20, the African Charter recognizes that all Peoples have a right to existence. The African Charter recognizes that all Peoples have an inalienable right to self-determination, which is a fundamental right of existence that cannot be taken away. The provisions also refer to colonized peoples having the right to be free and Article 20 sanctions the use of any means recognized by the international community to free themselves. The right to free themselves is not unfettered, as indicated by Article 23(2)(a) and (b).[52]

Under the provisions of the African Charter, Peoples have the right of self-determination and a right to free themselves, as long as in the process of exercising that right the Peoples do not violate other provisions of the African Charter. While the African Charter contains some unique provisions in relation to peoples, the rights of Peoples continue to be a central feature of the Charter which is unique among the world's human rights instruments. The African Charter is a statement of the political will of the African Peoples, reflecting their historical and legal paradigms.

Organization of American States

In 1948, the Charter of the Organization of American States (OAS) was signed to establish a regional organization for the Americas.[53] The OAS Charter established the international organization of states "to achieve an order of peace and justice, to promote their solidarity, to strengthen their collaborations and to defend their sovereignty, their territorial integrity and their independence."[54] The OAS is composed of the colonial states of Indigenous America. The only state which is not an active member is Cuba. Canada became a member of the OAS on 1 January 1990. A recent OAS development relates to the rights of Indigenous Peoples. A draft declaration on the rights of Indigenous Peoples was drafted by the members of the Inter-American Commission on Human Rights without consulting with, or receiving the consent of Indigenous Peoples. The OAS draft follows the line taken by the ILO Convention 169 (discussed in Chapter 3) for the assimilation of Indigenous Peoples into the Eurocentric model of the colonizer states in the Americas.

The Inter-American Commission on Human Rights[55] was reorganized in 1979[56] to take into account the entry into force of the American Convention on Human Rights:[57] "The new statute establishes separate petition procedures for complaints against the member states of the Organization of American States (OAS)."[58] Article 41 sets out the main functions of the Commission in the area of human rights for the Peoples of the Americas:

> The main function of the Commission shall be to promote respect for and defence of human rights. In the exercise of its mandate, it shall have the following functions and powers:
> a. to develop an awareness of human rights among the peoples of the Americas;
> b. to make recommendations to the governments of the member states, when it considers such action advisable, for the adoption of progressive measures in favor of human rights within the framework of their domestic law and constitutional provisions as well as appropriate measures to further the observance of those rights;
> c. to prepare such studies or reports as it considers advisable in the

performance of its measures adopted by them in matters of human rights;

d. to request the governments of the member states to supply it with information on the measures adopted by them in matters of human rights;

e. to respond, through the General Secretariat of the Organization of American States, to inquiries made by the member states on matters related to human rights and, within the limits of possibilities, to provide those states with the advisory services they request;

f. to take action on petitions and other communications pursuant to its authority under the provisions of Articles 44 through 51 of this Convention; and

g. to submit an annual report to the General Assembly of the Organization of American States.

Under this provision of the statute, the Commission has a broad mandate to undertake a number of initiatives to develop an awareness of human rights among Peoples of Americas. In this regard, the Commission on Human Rights has developed a draft declaration on the rights of Indigenous Peoples.[59] Approved by the seven members[60] of the Inter-American Commission on Human Rights, this draft has not been approved by the governing body of the OAS.

In the preamble of the draft, the authors recalled that the:

Declaration of Principles issued by the Summit of the Americas, in December 1994, the Heads of State and Governments declared that in observance of the International Decade of the World's indigenous people, they will focus their energies on improving the exercise of democratic rights and the access to social services by indigenous peoples and their communities.[61]

Further, the draft declaration recognized that "Indigenous Peoples have been deprived of their human rights and fundamental freedoms, resulting *inter alia* in their colonization and the dispossession of their lands, territories and resources."[62] With these two broad statements, the Commission drafted the declaration based on the "preeminence and applicability of the American Declaration of the Rights and Duties of Man, the American Convention on Human Rights and international human rights law, to the States and peoples of the Americas."[63] There was also special note taken of the "sphere of the United Nations and the International Labour Organization, and in this regard recalling the ILO Convention 169 (discussed in detail in Chapter 3) and the Draft UN Declaration on this subject."[64]

The drafters did more than take note of the ILO agreement, they adopted the language contained in Convention 169 in relation to the restrictions on the rights of peoples defined as Indigenous Peoples and "Peoples." In Article 1(a) of the OAS draft declaration, on the definition of Indigenous Peoples, language almost identical to that in the revised ILO Convention 169 is used:

> The use of the term "peoples" in this instrument shall not be construed as having any implications with respect to any other rights that might be attached to that term in international law.

The Inter-American draft goes one step further by avoiding the recognition of all rights rather than just the right to self-determination (ie. the ILO restriction) for "Peoples." It is clear in the OAS draft that the rights of Indigenous Peoples are those protecting only the individual rather than the collective rights of Indigenous Peoples.

Although there are draft provisions that purport to protect the rights of the collective, they are limited: Article 11(3) recognizes the collective right simply to culture, spiritual beliefs and language. Draft Article 11(3) arguably goes further than Article 27 of the International Covenant on Civil and Political Rights[65] (ICCPR) in that the OAS draft explicitly recognizes the collective rights of peoples while Article 27 refers to the rights of individuals. In addition, ICCPR Article 27 recognizes rights as belonging to individual members of minorities. As discussed in Chapter 3, Indigenous Peoples are not minorities under international law. The OAS draft declaration is an attempt to impose on Indigenous Peoples a standard of rights that is not acceptable to Indigenous Peoples. Global institutions outside of the human rights arena have recognized that the rights of Indigenous Peoples must be considered.

The OAS draft declaration represents all that is wrong with drafting. Seven individuals drafted the document without consulting Indigenous Peoples. A consultation process was arranged only after the drafting was completed. It must be generally accepted by both the states and Indigenous Peoples for the document to have any comprehensive application throughout the Americas.

World Bank

Another global institutional organization outside of the human rights arena becoming involved with the rights of Indigenous Peoples is the International Bank for Reconstruction and Development (also known as the World Bank). The World Bank was formed in the same time period as the United Nations:

In the aftermath of World War II, a series of meetings were held by the western powers to map out a new international economic framework. These meetings, known as the Bretton Woods Conference, established the World Bank in 1946 as a multilateral institution to help finance the reconstruction and development of war-ravaged Europe. . . . From its 45 founding member nations, it has grown to 178 member countries in 1994.[66]

As a specialized agency[67] of the UN, the World Bank has provided an operational Directive to its personnel with universal application to state members in which the Bank is doing business. Two objectives of the Directive are as follows:

6. The Bank's broad objective towards indigenous people, as for all peoples in its member countries, is to ensure that the development process fosters full respect for their dignity, human rights, and cultural uniqueness. More specifically, the objective at the center of this directive is to ensure that indigenous peoples do not suffer adverse effects during the development process, particularly from Bank-financed projects, and that they receive culturally compatible social and economic benefits.

. . .

8. The Bank's policy is that the strategy for addressing the issues pertaining to indigenous peoples must be based on the *informed participation* of the indigenous peoples themselves.[68] [emphasis added]

There are 178 member states who, indirectly through loan agreements, have to follow the Directive if they wish to receive funds from the World Bank because the Directive is specifically directed to World Bank employees who then incorporate its provisions into the loan preparation and agreements.

The World Bank Directive outlines a process for informed participation by Indigenous Peoples. Most significantly, the Directive does not attempt to define Indigenous Peoples. Rather, the Directive sets out some criteria which can be followed in the application of the guidelines:

Simply stated that: because of the varied and changing contexts in which indigenous peoples are found, no single definition can capture their diversity.

Indigenous peoples can be identified in particular geographical areas by the presence in varying degrees of the following characteristics:

(a) a close attachment to ancestral territories and to the natural resources in these areas;

(b) self-identification and identification by others as members of a distinct cultural group;

(c) an indigenous language, often different from the national language;

(d) presence of customary social and political institutions; and

(e) primarily subsistence-oriented production.[69]

Without defining Indigenous Peoples, the directive makes the following statement:

> The terms "indigenous peoples," indigenous ethnic minorities," "tribal groups," and "scheduled tribes," describe social groups with a social and cultural identity distinct from the dominant society that makes them vulnerable to being disadvantaged in the development process. For the purposes of this directive, "indigenous peoples" is the term that will be used to refer to these groups.[70]

There are two significant provisions in relation to the statement. First, the Directive recognizes the Indigenous Peoples' right to define themselves. Second, the World Bank's Directive recognizes that there is a link between Indigenous Peoples and their ancestral lands. While it is not expressly stated, the Directive implies that the "close attachment" refers to lands that have always belonged to Indigenous Peoples. It is these lands and their link which give Indigenous Peoples a right to be involved and participate in development projects as informed participants.

In order to enforce the application of the Directive, the Bank made the following provision:

> the borrower's commitments for implementing the indigenous peoples development plan should be reflected in the loan documents; legal provisions should provide the Bank staff with clear benchmarks that can be monitored during supervision.[71]

The effect of such a Directive is to give a universal standard for the workings of the World Bank and its membership. The member state making application for funds can ignore the Directive at its peril as the Bank may not make the funds available if the member state does not comply.

The World Bank Directive has significant law-making functions, although it does not make international law in the strict legal sense. Rather, it creates a framework through a loan agreement between a member state and the World Bank to import into the agreement and domestic legal systems principles that are set out in the Directive. The Directive becomes binding on state members through loan agreements, which certainly gives the Directive a potentially universal application. If a member wants to borrow funds for a project and Indigenous Peoples are going to be affected by the project, a process must be followed which the Bank has ensured will occur by including an implementation process in the Directive.

United Nations

The League of Nations was not formally dissolved until 1946,[72] when the United Nations was established.[73] The Charter establishing the new body enshrined a number of guiding purposes contained in Article 1.[74] One of the guiding principles was to develop friendly relations based on respect for the principle of equal rights and self-determination of Peoples. Self-determination as a concept was enshrined within the Charter without any mention of minorities; rather, the Charter refers to "Peoples." This Charter provision will be discussed in Chapter 3.

With the establishment of the United Nations came provisions specifically to deal with the promotion and encouragement of the respect for human rights and fundamental freedoms.[75] There are six principal organs of the United Nations:[76] the General Assembly,[77] the Security Council,[78] the Economic and Social Council,[79] the Trusteeship Council,[80] the International Court of Justice[81] and the Secretariat.[82] This analysis concentrates on the United Nations organs which have contributed to the evolution of international law in relation to Indigenous Peoples.

General Assembly

The General Assembly (GA) is composed of all member states. Under the provisions of the UN Charter, the GA "may discuss any questions or any matters within the scope of the present Charter or relating to the powers and functions of any organ provided for in the present Charter, and, except as provided in Article 12."[83] Additionally, the Charter specifically provides under Article 13 for the GA to "initiate studies (discussed in Chapter 3) and make recommendations [for the purpose of] promoting international co-operation in the economic, social, cultural, educational and health fields, and assisting in the realization of human rights and fundamental freedoms for all without distinction as to race, sex, language, or religion."[84]

The GA is not a law-making body. However, GA resolutions can be persuasive in the making of international adjudicative decisions and in state judicial decisions and legislative enactments. Two examples of General Assembly resolutions that have established international norms are the adoption in 1948 of the Universal Declaration of Human Rights,[85] and the resolution adopting the Convention on the Prevention and Punishment of the Crime of Genocide.[86] The Universal Declaration was an amplification of the provisions of the Charter contained in Article 1(3) related to the promotion of and respect for human rights. The Universal Declaration was adopted by a General Assembly resolution, which would not have been binding on the state governments.[87] However, over the years, the Universal Declaration has had significant impact:

> The Universal Declaration has been the principle conduit for bringing the idea of human rights into the life of many nations: it is expressly referred to in state constitutions; its provisions are adopted or adapted in others. It is the source of numerous international covenants and conventions. It ranks with the U.N. Charter as one of the most celebrated and most respected international instruments.[88]

The General Assembly is a representative body of the community of states which has some very limited similarities with a political body of a national legislature:

> The widespread use and reliance upon resolutions of the General Assembly and Security Council which are intended to have law-making effect provide convincing indication that the matters relied upon constitute, at the least, important evidence of the existence of particular rules or principles of international law.[89]

General Assembly resolutions can be evidence of international law principles but are not international laws themselves. The GA does not adopt international law. It is not a law-making body like a legislature of a state. Rather, GA resolutions have been viewed as "not binding on member states, but, when they are accepted by a majority vote constitute evidence of the opinions of governments in the widest forum for the expression of such opinions."[90] General Assembly resolutions can be viewed as evidence of customary practice of states changing the complexity and development of international law.[91] In relation to Indigenous Peoples, the GA has resolved that "the violations of economic and political rights of an indigenous population constituted crimes against humanity." The GA may have labelled the violations against Indigenous Peoples as crimes; however, the GA did not establish a mechanism to deal effectively with these crimes.

If the Draft Declaration on the Rights of Indigenous Peoples makes its way through the UN system, it will come before the General Assembly. Potentially, the Draft Declaration could become a General Assembly resolution at some point in the future.

International Court of Justice

The International Court of Justice (ICJ) was created with the establishment of the UN. The UN Charter under Chapter XIV, established the ICJ as the principal judicial organ of the United Nations: "It shall function in accordance with the annexed Statute, which is based upon the Statute of the Permanent Court of International Justice and forms an integral part of the present Charter."[93] The ICJ established in 1945 was preceded by the Permanent Court of International Justice[94] established under the auspices of the League of Nations. The Court can function in an advisory capacity to the General Assembly, Security Council and other international organizations[95] rendering opinions on issues of interest to those bodies. The ICJ can also function to help settle disputes between state parties. However, the state parties must consent to the jurisdiction of the ICJ and, once given, decisions in inter-states cases are binding on the two states involved.[96] Although advisory opinions are not binding on the requesting organ, they can form the basis for future action by the GA as was the case in the *Western Sahara:*

> It is convenient to quote in full the passage of the Opinion[97] in which the Court affirmed the fundamental difference, in this respect, between its advisory and its contentious jurisdiction:
>
> The consent of the States, parties to the dispute, is the basis of the Court's jurisdiction in contentious cases. The situation is different in regard to advisory proceedings even where the Request for an Opinion relates to a legal questions actually pending between States. The Court's reply is only of an advisory character: as such it has no binding force. It follows that no State, whether a member of the United Nations or not, can prevent the giving of an Advisory Opinion which the United Nations considers to be desirable in order to obtain enlightenment as to the course of action it should take. The Court's Opinion is given not to the States, but to the organ which is entitled to request it; the reply of the Court, itself an "organ of the United Nations," represents its participation in the activities of the Organizations, and, in principle, should not be refused.[98]

The Court has been hindered by the provisions of its statute wherein Article 59[99] limits the application of the Court's decisions in contentious cases between states. However, the Court has been able to use its own judgments as persuasive evidence: "In fact, the practise of referring to its previous decisions has become one of the most conspicuous features of the Judgments and Opinions of the Court."[100] The ICJ has made a number of significant judgments related to the rights of peoples and the application of customary international law norms. Such a case is the advisory opinion given by the ICJ on the *Western Sahara*.[101]

The advisory opinion on the *Western Sahara*[102] determined a number of critical issues related to the rule and competence of the Court to render advisory opinions.[103] In addition, the Court addressed issues related to the notions of *terra nullius*, discovery and conquest, stating that the latter two concepts were not legitimate doctrines to assert sovereignty over a territory. The ICJ stated that land occupied by a group of people having some political and social organization was not *terra nullius*. The ICJ pronounced that the only way for a foreign sovereign to acquire any right to enter into territory that is not *terra nullius* is with the freely informed consent of the original inhabitants through an agreement.[104] In coming to this decision, the ICJ reviewed the colonial history of the settlement of the Western Sahara and the ties that existed between Spain and the leaders of the land in question. The ICJ determined that the treaties entered into with the leaders were sufficient to form a legal tie, which excluded the states of Morocco and Mauritania from claiming the lands. The result of this finding indicated that the only possible means to effect decolonization from Spain was through a popular referendum of the peoples' concerned. Finally, the Court enunciated the right of Peoples of the Western Sahara to self-determination as explained by Professor Janis:

> [T]he Court's conclusion is that the materials and information presented to it do not establish any tie of territorial sovereignty between the territory of Western Sahara and the Kingdom of Morocco or the Mauritanian entity. Thus the Court has not found legal ties of such a nature as might affect the application of resolution 1514 (XV) in the decolonization of Western Sahara and, in particular, of the principle of self-determination through the free and genuine expression of the will of the peoples of the Territory.[105]

The advisory opinion on *Western Sahara* is important for its discussion concerning the international legal status of Indigenous Peoples and the nature of their governing structures. The Court determined that the absence of settled towns and villages did not preclude Indigenous Peoples from having the right to self-determination in their territory. The structural form of the society is a not a condition precedent for determining the style and form of government. Professor Janis notes that finding of the ICJ: "At the time of colonization Western Sahara was inhabited by peoples which, if nomadic, were socially and politically organized in tribes and under chiefs competent to represent them."[106]

The ICJ in *Western Sahara* went on to discuss whether their status as civilized or uncivilized according to European standards affected Indigenous Peoples' rights to their territory. The Court determined that the degree of civilization was no longer a valid criterion for determining if a territory inhabited by Indigenous Peoples is *terra nullius* but rather it is a question of whether such peoples have social and political organization. In other words, Indigenous governments do not have to emulate European governmental structures to have sovereignty over their territory. European colonizing states could gain access to lands only through an agreement with the full consent of the Indigenous Peoples.

In 1995, the ICJ turned its attention again to the issues related to the rights of Indigenous Peoples and the role of self-determination in the decolonization process in the *Case Concerning East Timor*.[107] The majority of the Court did not deal with the issues related to self-determination and the rights of peoples of Non-Self-Governing Territory. Instead, the Court determined that it did not have the judicial competence to make a decision that would affect another party which did not consent to the jurisdiction of the Court:

> The Court concludes that it cannot, in this case, exercise the jurisdiction it has by virtue of the declaration made by the Parties under Article 36, paragraph 2, of its Statute because, in order to decide the claims of Portugal, it would have to rule, as a prerequisite, on the lawfulness of Indonesia's conduct in the absence of that State's consent.[108]

The third party was Indonesia, the country that annexed East Timor in contravention of Security Council and GA Resolutions,[109] including one which stated that East Timor was listed as a Non-Self-Governing Territory scheduled for decolonization. The dissenting opinion of Judge Weeramantry did address the issues that he considered crucial:

> If East Timor is still a non-self-governing territory, every member of the community of nations, including Australia, is under a duty to recognize its right to self-determination and permanent sovereignty over its natural resources. If this is so, as is indubitably the case, the Court would be in possession of all the factual material necessary for the Court to pronounce upon the responsibility of the Respondent State, which is in fact before it.[110]

The Court decided not to adjudicate the issues. However, the ICJ did determine some aspects related to the right of self-determination albeit in the decolonization context:

> The Judgment of the Court (para. 29) has categorically reaffirmed the principle of self-determination, pointing out that it has evolved from the Charter and from the United Nations practice, and observing further that the normative status of the right of the peo-

ple of East Timor to self-determination is not in dispute. . . . In the first place, the principle receives confirmation from all the sources of international law, whether they be international conventions (as with the International Covenant on Civil and Political Rights and Economic, Social and Cultural Rights), customary international law, the general principles of law, judicial decisions, or the teachings of publicists. From each of these sources, cogent authority can be collected supportive of the right, details of which it is not necessary to recapitulate here. . . . The Charter spells out its concerns regarding self-determination with more particularity in Chapter XI. Dealing specifically with the economic aspect of self-determination, it stresses, in Article 55, that stability and well-being are necessary for peaceful and friendly relations, which are to their turn based on respect for the principle of equal rights and self-determination.[111]

The Court acknowledged that self-determination is an important principle of international law and of concern to the family of nations. Unfortunately, there was no application of the legal principles in this case, which was dismissed for technical reasons. The substantial issues were not dealt with, other than to reaffirm the rights of Non-Self-Governing Territories to self-determination. The occupation of the lands by another state without the consent of the East Timor people did not get resolved. This decision points out some of the difficulties in using the ICJ to explore international legal questions. Perhaps the case would have had a different effect if an Advisory Opinion was requested by the GA, as the ICJ had shown in the *Western Sahara* Advisory Opinion its willingness to explore issues related to international legal matters of interest to the General Assembly.

Commission on Human Rights

Pursuant to Article 61 of the UN Charter, the Economic and Social Council (ECOSOC), under the authority of the General Assembly, may initiate or conduct studies, make recommendations and submit reports "with respect to international economic, social, cultural, education, health and related matters . . . may make recommendations for the purpose of promoting respect for, and observance of, human rights and fundamental freedoms for all."[112] A number of Commissions established under ECOSOC[113] consider specific questions: "These Commissions may be composed of governmental representatives, of experts, or of persons serving in their individual capacity. ECOSOC has also been assisted, upon occasion, by rapporteurs serving in their capacity as individuals."[114] One specific Commission reviews and deals with issues related to human rights: the Commission on Human Rights (CHR) has undertaken a number of studies including issues of self-determination, the rights of Indigenous Peoples and minorities.

The Commission on Human Rights (CHR) meets yearly at the Palais de Nations in Geneva, Switzerland for a six-week session. There are fifty-three members of the CHR elected every three years by the GA. Each member of the CHR has one vote. Observer states can co-sponsor resolutions but cannot vote in accordance with rule 69, paragraph 3 of the Rules of Procedure of the functional commissions of ECOSOC.

> In addition to the representatives of each State member of the Commission, the following may attend the sessions of the Commission: representatives of any United Nations Members who are invited by the Commission to participate in its deliberations; representatives of the specialized agencies; representatives of the Office of the United Nations High Commissioner for Refugees; representatives of nongovernmental organizations in consultative status with the Economic and Social Council; and observers from the Council of Europe, the Inter-American Commission on Human Rights, the Organization of African Unity and the League of Arab States, and from other regional inter-governmental bodies particularly concerned with human rights.[115]

The CHR is a state-controlled body, which is open to limited participation by non-state parties including the numerous non-governmental organizations and specialized agencies of the UN. Within the structure of the UN, the CHR is the first governmental body that has had to deal with the Draft Declaration on the Rights of Indigenous Peoples.[116] Before the Draft Declaration reached this level, it was worked on or addressed by the Working Group on Indigenous Peoples[117] and the Sub-Commission on the Prevention of Discrimination and Protection of Minorities. These two bodies are comprised of "human rights experts" acting in their individual capacities and not as representatives of state governments.[118]

In 1996, at its fifty-second session, the CHR added a new agenda item on "Indigenous Issues."[119] This represents a small step forward in placing issues related to Indigenous Peoples directly before a state governmental body of the United Nations. Now, Indigenous Peoples have the opportunity to address the state governments directly on issues of concern to them.

UN High Commissioner for Human Rights

The Charter of the United Nations contains language for the protection of human rights[120] which has led to a number of instruments dedicated to the protection and promotion of human rights. In 1993, the World Conference on Human Rights renewed the UN's "commitment to the fulfilment of obligations to promote universal respect for, and observance and protection of, all human rights and fundamental freedoms for all in accordance with the Charter."[121] The Vienna Declaration and Programme of Action was adopted by the World Conference on Human Rights, which:

> recommend[ed] to the General Assembly that when examining the report of the Conference at its forty-eighth session, it begin, as a matter of priority, consideration of the question of the establishment of a High Commissioner for Human Rights for the promotion and protection of all human rights.[122]

As a result of the recommendation, the GA did appoint a High Commissioner for Human Rights,[123] who makes his reports to the CHR for transmission to ECOSOC and to the GA. In his 1996 report to the CHR, the High Commissioner outlined his job:

> The Office of the High Commissioner for Human Rights is a new institution which came into being at almost the same time as the United Nations programmes and agencies were celebrating their fiftieth anniversary. The first High Commissioner is now at the mid-point of his four-year mandate. During these two years he has sought to improve the promotion and protection of human rights by generating dynamism and innovation and more effective coordination throughout the various sectors of the United Nations human rights programme.[124]

The High Commissioner reported on the coordinating human rights programmes, but he failed to mention any work taking place in relation to Indigenous Peoples. Since the office is new, there is still an opportunity for Indigenous Peoples to have input in the work of the High Commissioner as the Programme of Action from the World Conference on Human Rights contained provisions related to Indigenous issues.[125]

Two of the five recommendations from the World Conference have been acted on by various UN bodies. First, the Working Group was urged to complete the drafting of the Declaration, and this was accomplished in 1994. There was a recommendation that a UN Decade for the world's Indigenous Peoples which began in January 1994. The Decade was proclaimed, but little activity has taken place. However, the Centre on Human Rights has contracted a person to work on Decade activities.[126] The Centre now operates under the authority of the High Commissioner for Human Rights.

Sub-Commission on the Prevention of Discrimination and the Protection of Minorities

Following the work undertaken by the League of Nations in relation to minorities in 1947, the CHR established the Sub-Commission on the Prevention of Discrimination and the Protection of Minorities (Sub-commission) to "make studies and recommendations on the subject."[127] The Sub-commission is comprised of twenty-six human rights experts nominated by their state government but elected by the CHR on a staggered schedule.[128] The work of the Sub-commission is done in a four-week period each year in Geneva, Switzerland. It often appoints Special Rapporteurs from among its members to make reports on specific topics.[129] The Sub-commission has moved into studies related to contemporary problems. For example, in 1989 the Sub-commission adopted a resolution without a vote to appoint a Special Rapporteur to prepare a study on human rights and the environment.[130] As a result of studies undertaken by Special Rapporteurs, the United Nations has taken further action, such as the preparation of declarations on the rights of minorities and children. Progress on Indigenous issues is a good example of the contribution that can be made by Special Rapporteurs.

Role of Special Rapporteurs

Special Rapporteurs make reports to the UN which contributes to the evolution of international law. In 1969, the Sub-commission was considering a Special Rapporteur's report on Racial Discrimination in the Political, Economic, Social and Cultural Spheres,[131] which contains a chapter on measures to be taken in connection with the protection of Indigenous Peoples:

> This [study] started a process of discussion in the Sub-Commission and in the Commission. In 1970 the Sub-Commission recommended that a comprehensive study be made of the problems of discrimination against Indigenous Populations.[132] The recommendation passed the Commission and was finally taken up by the Economic and Social Council. The Council adopted resolution 1589 (L) of 21 May 1971, in which it authorized the preparation of such a study. Later in 1971, Mr. Jose R. Martinez Cobo[133] was appointed Special Rapporteur for the Study on the Discrimination against Indigenous Populations.[134]

The Cobo Study, started in 1971 and officially ended in 1984, fills eight volumes.[135] In the resolution setting out the mandate of the study, the Special Rapporteur was to:

> make a complete and comprehensive study of the problems of discrimination against Indigenous populations and to suggest the necessary national and international measures for eliminating such discrimination, in co-operation with the other organs and bodies of the United Nations and with the competent international organizations.[136]

In order to complete the mandate, the final report contained over six hundred conclusions, proposals and recommendations.[137] The first half of the final chapter contains the conclusions of the Special Rapporteur in all spheres of his study. The second half deals with recommendations and proposals on the subjects covered in the study. The Rapporteur, aware of omissions in the study, recommended a number of additional studies on: (1) self-determination with particular reference to the right of Indigenous Nations and Peoples to self-determination; (2) Declaration of the Principles for the Defence of Indigenous Nations and Peoples of the Western Hemisphere; and (3) a Study on Treaties entered into by Indigenous Peoples. In reference to the latter, in 1989 ECOSOC authorized a Special Rapporteur to undertake a Study on the Significance of Treaties, Agreements and Other Constructive Arrangements between States and Indigenous Populations.[138]

In addition to the ability to appoint Special Rapporteurs to undertake specific studies, the Sub-commission can authorize the establishment of Working Groups to assist in its work. Since the establishment of the Sub-commission, a number of Working Groups have been established, including the Rights of Mental Patients and the Rights of the Child, Slavery, Minorities and Indigenous Peoples. It was by a 1982 resolution that the Subcommission established the Working Group on Indigenous Peoples.[139]

Working Group on Indigenous Peoples

The Working Group's two-fold mandate is set out in a resolution:

> 1. Authorizes the Sub-Commission on Prevention of Discrimination and Protection of Minorities to establish a working group on indigenous populations which shall meet for up to five working days before the annual sessions of the Sub-Commission in order to review developments pertaining to the promotion and protection of the human rights and fundamental freedoms of

indigenous populations, including information requested by the Secretary-General annually from Governments, specialized agencies, regional intergovernmental organizations and non-governmental organizations in consultative status, particularly those of indigenous peoples, to analyze such materials, and to submit its conclusions to the Sub-Commission bearing in mind the report of the Special Rapporteur of the Sub-Commission;

2. Decides that the Working Group shall give special attention to the evolution of standards concerning the rights of indigenous populations, taking into account both the similarities and aspirations of indigenous populations throughout the world [140]

In accordance with the five regions of the Sub-Commission, a representative of each region was chosen to sit on the Working Group; for the first meeting of the Working Group, "the outgoing Chairman of the Sub-Commission, Mr. Raul Ferrero, in consultation with the geographical groups, then appointed Mr. Asbjorn Eide, Ms. Nasser Kaddour, Mr. Mohammed Yousif Mudawil, Mr. Jorge Eduardo Ritter and Mr. Ivan Tosevski to serve."[141] With the exception of 1986,[142] the five members of the Working Group have met each year, in Geneva, Switzerland to carry out their two-fold mandate.

At the first meeting of the Working Group on Indigenous Peoples in 1982, the Group was "ready to receive information from Indigenous organizations and groups which did not have consultative status."[143] Usually, only those non-governmental organizations (NGOs) having consultative status with ECOSOC are permitted to participate actively in meetings of subsidiary bodies.[144] It was a significant development to allow Indigenous representatives to speak directly to the Working Group members in their capacity as Indigenous Peoples—the first time in the history of the UN. The Working Group is now a well-attended meeting with "more than 700 people attend[ing] the thirteenth session"[145] in contrast with the twenty-two participants at the 1982 session.[146] It also stands in contrast to the reception received by the Haudenosaunee at the League of Nations. Indigenous Peoples are recognized as having a voice in their own right without needing another organization to speak for them at the UN. Under the Working Group's mandate, the Draft Declaration on the Rights of Indigenous Peoples has been drafted over an eight-year period. The Draft Declaration was subsequently forwarded to the Sub-Commission, which approved it in 1994.[147]

Conclusion

The establishment of the League of Nations and its successor, the UN, have continued the process of denying the colonization of the Indigenous Peoples. Despite resolutions, declarations and covenants, Indigenous Peoples are still not recognized as having any rights within the international law regime.

The International Court of Justice was established *inter alia* to advise the General Assembly, the Security Council and other international organizations on issues of interest related to them. It has had a number of opportunities to review principles and norms of international law. In one particular case, *Western Sahara*, it had an opportunity to review the doctrines of discovery and conquest which were deemed unacceptable as international law norms and principles. In addition, it reviewed the position of colonized Indigenous Peoples in relation to their territories. The Court determined that the only legitimate means under international law for states to acquire access to their territories was by agreement with the Indigenous Peoples based on full consent. As reviewed in Chapter 1, even when treaties were entered into, the Indigenous Nations were not recognized as being part of the family of nations.

The ICJ determined that the right of self-determination in the decolonization context is an important principle of international law which was of concern to the family of nations. Peoples who have been colonized and who have not been able to exercise their free will in relation to their territory and its disposition have a right of self-determination. Further, the recognition of the right relates directly to the implementation of the Charter of the United Nations for peaceful and friendly relations which is based upon the respect for the principle of equal rights and self-determination of Peoples as set out in Article 1. Peoples have a right to self-determination. The question remains: do Indigenous Peoples enjoy such a right? This question is covered in Chapter 3.

It is possible to conclude that the law made by international organizations is a secondary source of international law alongside custom, treaty making and general principles of law. As reviewed, the ILO engages in adopting Conventions passed on the principles of international law through a ratification process. However, the multilateral treaty creating the organization imposed upon members obligations that go beyond the bounds of usual treaty obligations. For other governing bodies, resolutions passed are not binding upon members unless they are legally considered by the organization's treaty to be binding decisions.

In the case of the African Charter, the OAU adopted a Charter which was appropriate for their circumstances by attaching duties as well as rights to peoples. This Charter broke from the conventional Eurocentric

American and European styles of human rights documents which protect the rights of the individual. The African Charter placed the individual within the family, the community and the state by placing obligations upon the individual. The African Charter is unique for its consideration of historical and colonial history to develop an instrument particular to their Peoples' situation. This is an objective Indigenous Peoples are striving to accomplish with the UN Draft Declaration. The history of the wrongs suffered by Indigenous Peoples cannot be discounted or shaded when drafting an instrument to protect the future. The African Charter provides a clear beacon.

If an international document on the rights of Indigenous Peoples is going to be acceptable and authoritative, it must achieve universal acceptance not only by *states* but also by Indigenous Peoples. The OAS did not consult with *Indigenous Peoples* during its drafting process. Rather they have opted for a consultation process after the drafting was complete. It is unacceptable for Indigenous Peoples not to be directly involved in the drafting of international instruments with application to them. In the spirit of the World Bank Directive, informed participation is critical in the process. It has taken some years to learn the complicated procedures and formalities of international organizations and determine where Indigenous Peoples must expend their efforts to have member states live up to international law standards. The struggle for international recognition in various processes has been long, but Indigenous Peoples appear to be progressing effectively.

Footnotes

1. Hugh M. Kindred, et al. ed., *International Law Chiefly as Interpreted and Applied in Canada* 5th ed. (Toronto: Emond Montgomery Publications Limited, 1993) states the problem: "Collective Rights raise problems, particularly from a First World perspective. Their potential to clash with individual rights (eg. affirmative action to protect one group may interfere with individual rights to equality) and the possibility of their expansion to include a myriad of issues (eg. the right to development; the rights of people to a clean environment) make them hard to define with any precision and difficult to reconcile with other rights" (at 615).

2. "One of the major tasks of the peace-making at the end of the First World War was to devise a permanent form for the habit of using international conferences as a means of settling disputes between States and organizing inter-State cooperation. That habit had been steadily gaining ground since the end of the Napoleonic wars; but only one serious attempt had been made to create permanent machinery for peaceful solution of conflicts. Before the Hague Conferences of 1899 and 1907, the movement for judicial settlement of inter-State disputes had advanced by single instances and bilateral treaties. By settling up a Permanent Court of Arbitration, the Hague Conventions demonstrated both the feasibility and the desirability of standing institutions for the elimination of war": Norman Bentwich and Andrew Martin, *A Commentary on the Charter of the United Nations* (New York: Kraus Reprint Co., 1969) at ix [hereinafter Bentwich, *Commentary*].

3. The Covenant of the League of Nations including amendments in force, 16 December 1935, as published by the Secretariat of the League of Nations in: Dr. Min-Chuan Ku, *A Comprehensive Handbook of the United Nations: A Documentary Presentation in Two Volumes,* (New York: Monarch Press, 1978) vol. 1 at 33-41 [hereinafter Ku, *Covenant*].

4. "The minority questions brought about by the repartitioning of post-World War 1 (WWI) Europe were resolved by special and general treaties. The treaty approach under the League of Nations was *ad hoc,* region- specific, racially orientated, and unconcerned with a general concept of minorities": Philip Vuciri Ramaga, "The Bases of Minority Identity" (1992) 14 *Human Rights Quarterly* 409.

5. "The object of the protection of minorities which those treaties committed to the League of Nations was to avoid the many inter-state frictions and conflicts which had occurred in the past, as a result of frequent ill- treatment or oppression of national minorities": Carol Weisbrod, "Minorities and Diversities: The "Remarkable Experiment" of the League of Nations" [1993] 8 Connecticut Journal of International Law at 367-368. The rights of minorities will be discussed in detail in Chapter 3.

6. Patrick Thornberry, *International Law and the Rights of Minorities* (Oxford: Oxford University Press, 1991) at 38.

7. Ibid. at 46: "Article 14 of the Covenant set up the Permanent Court of International Justice to hear and determine disputes referred to it by the Assembly or the Council of the League. Thus the political competence of the League Council was supplemented by the jurisdictional and advisory competence of the Court." The Covenant relates only to minority cases before PCIJ whereas the PCIJ was set up under a separate statute to take contentious cases between states on all legal issues.

8. Louis B. Sohn, "The New International Law: Protection of the Rights of Individuals Rather than States" (1982) 32 *American University Law Review* at 6.

9. Itsejuwa Sagay, *TheLegal Aspects of the Namibian Dispute* (Ile Ife, Nigeria: University of Ife Press, 1975) at 3.

10. Faithkeeper of the Onodaga Nation Oren Lyons, Panel discussion at the American Society of International Law, *American Society of International Law--Annual Proceedings of the 87th Annual Meeting,* 31 March - 3 April 1993 at 194. Haudenosaunee means the People of the Longhouse. The Haudenosaunee travel to the United Nations under a Haudenosaunee passport and not under a passport issued by the Government of Canada or by the United States of America. In the same presentation, Oren Lyons recounts a story of the visit by Chief Diskahay to Geneva to petition the League of Nations. At the first Non-Governmental Meeting on the Rights of Indigenous Peoples in the Americas held in Geneva in 1977, the Mayor of Geneva in addressing the delegation remembered the visit with these words: "In 1924, I remember a meeting that was so crowded that people spilled out onto the streets, I remember a speaker, a very dignified gentleman who was an American Indian, and he talked to me. Amongst all the people that were there, he took the
time to talk to a ten-year old boy-me. I remember, and that is why you came through that frontier, that border. I made them let you in, and you can come here any time; you will be welcome with your passport" (at 196).

11. E. Brian Titley, *A Narrow Vision--Duncan Campbell Scott and the Administration of Indian Affairs in Canada* (Vancouver, University of British Columbia Press, 1986) at 120. Titley recounts the history of the Haudenosaunee representative's work in England and in Geneva. Canada did not have a seat at the League of Nations, having its ties to the British government which was concerned with the activity in Geneva. There were governments

who were prepared to place the case before the League of Nations. Titley, reviewing the history of the Canadian response and British reaction to the petition by the Haudenosaunee, writes: "The Estonians and the Irish, naturally tended to sympathize with the sovereign claims of small nations . . . However, when they attempted to pursue the issue once more in the spring of 1924, they were to find that it could prove an expensive exercise. At this stage, the British government decided to intervene. The Foreign Office informed the offending governments that their efforts to re-open the Iroquois case were resented as 'impertinent interference' in the internal affairs of the Empire by 'minor powers.' This sabre-rattling produced the desired effect, and by May London had been assured that the 'minor powers' had abandoned the case" (at 123).

12. "Their complaints were rejected on the grounds that such problems fell within the scope of the domestic jurisdiction of the national governments involved. Again in the 1940s and 1950s, similar appeals were made to, and rejected by, the officials of the United Nations" Franke Wilmer, *The Indigenous Voice in World Politics Since Time Immemorial* (Newbury Park: Sage Publications, 1993) at 3.

13. Ku, *Covenant, supra* note 3.

14. Ernst B. Haas, *Beyond the Nation-State-Functionalism and International Organization* (Stanford, Cal.: Stanford University Press, 1964) at 141.

15. "[The] members of the League: (a) will endeavour to secure and maintain fair and humane conditions of labour for men, women, and children, both in their own countries and in all countries to which their commercial and industrial relations extend, and for that purpose will establish and maintain the necessary international organizations." Alfred Zimmern, *The League of Nations and The Rule of Law 1918-1935* (New York: Russell & Russell, 1939; reissued 1969) at 524 [hereinafter Zimmern, *League of Nations*].

16. The ILO purpose was related to: "regulation of hours of work, including the establishment of a maximum working day and week; regulation of the labour supply; prevention of unemployment; provision of an adequate living wage; protection of workers against sickness, disease and injury arising out of his employment; protection of children, young persons and women; provision for old age and injury; protection of the interests of the workers when employed in countries other than their own; recognition of the principle of equal remuneration for work of equal value; recognition of the principle of freedom of association and the organization of vocational and technical education" (Bentwich, *Commentary, supra* note 2 at 121).

17. "Under the "Philadelphia Declaration" (April-May 1944), in which the aims and purposes of the ILO were redefined, the Organization took power to examine and consider, not only matters strictly concerned with conditions of labour, but also all international, economic and financial policies and measures which are relevant to the attainment of conditions in which human beings can pursue both their material well-being and their spiritual development, 'in conditions of freedom and dignity, of economic security and equal opportunity'": D.W. Bowett, *The Law of International Institutions* (London: Stevens & Sons, 1982) at 142 (hereinafter Bowett, International Institutions].

18. The Constitution of the International Labour Organization, Article 2. In addition, the ILO has a unique voting and participation structure. Every delegation has four members: 2 from government, 1 from labour and 1 from the employers. For more information on the tripartite arrangement see: Osieke *infra* note 19.

19. "Since its inception, the ILO has adopted a considerable number of instruments in the form of International Labour Conventions which are capable of creating binding legal obli-

ations for the member States, as well as International Labour Recommendations. This has led modern legal commentators to conclude without difficulty that the Organization exercises a legislative, or at least, a quasi-legislative function" E. Osieke, *Constitutional Law and Practice in the International Labour Organisation* (Dordrecht: Martinus Nijhoff Publishers, 1985) at 144 [hereinafter Osieke, *Constitutional Law and the ILO*].

20. Article 19(4) refers to the authentic text of the Convention or Recommendation and the authority of the Director-General to communicate the copy to members for ratification or for notification by the competent authority.

21. Bowett, *International Institutions, supra* note 17 at 141-142.

22. Nicolas Valticos, *International Labour Law* (The Netherlands: Kluwer, 1979) at 44 [hereinafter Valticos].

23. "The Recruiting of Indigenous Workers Convention, 1936 (No.50) which had been ratified by some 30 States and declared applicable to some 20 non-metropolitan territories and it laid down various standards aimed at avoiding the use of coercion, at protecting the communities against the repercussions of the withdrawal of too many adult males, at protecting non-adult persons against recruiting" (Ibid. at 202).

24. "This Convention advocated a number of measures aimed at hastening the progressive elimination of recruiting" (Ibid. at 202).

25. "Convention (No. 64) which has been ratified by 29 States and declared applicable to 20 non- metropolitan territories, provides that these contract [of employment] should be made in writing when they are made for a period of 6 months or more or when they stipulate conditions of employment which differ materially from or when they stipulate conditions of employment which differ materially from those customary in the district" (Ibid. at 203).

26. "Recommendation (No. 58) adopted in 1939 at the same time as the Convention (no. 64) deals with the maximum length of written contracts of employment of indigenous workers" (Ibid. at 203).

27. Convention (No. 86) dealt with the "matter of contracts of employment of indigenous workers laid down standards about the maximum period of service which may be stipulated or implied in these contracts, whether written or oral. Such period shall not exceed 12 months, or if the workers are accompanied by their families - - two years, when the contract does not involve a long and expensive journey. Otherwise, the contract shall not exceed 2 or 3 years, according to the case. This Convention has been ratified by some 20 States and declared applicable to some 20 non-metropolitan territories" (Ibid. at 203).

28. Anthony Alcock, *History of the International Labour Organisation* (New York: Octagon Books, 1971) at 82-84 [hereinafter Alcock, *History*].

29. Ibid. at 83.

30. "[S]ocial policy in dependent territories which was based on the principle according to which States should take steps to promote the well-being and development of the peoples of such territories through the effective application of the general principles and the minimum standards set forth in the Recommendation (No.74) included supplementary provisions on a series of other questions. . . . In 1947 the question of social policy in non- metropolitan territories was dealt with in a Convention (No. 82)" (ibid. at 204).

31. "Convention 1939 (No. 65), Penal Sanctions (Indigenous Workers) and Abolition of

Penal Sanctions (Indigenous Workers) Convention 1955 (No. 104)": International Labour Organization, *The Impact of the International Labour Conventions and Recommendations* (Geneva: International Labour Office, 1976).

32. G.A. Johnston, *The International Labour Organisation--Its Work for Social and Economic Progress* (London: Europa Publications, 1970) at 258 [hereinafter Johnson, *ILO*].

33. Ibid. at 258.

34. Alcock, *History, supra* note 28 at 251.

35. In 1953, the ILO published a book: *Indigenous Peoples: Living and Working Conditions of Aboriginal Populations in Independent Countries* (Geneva: International Labour Organization, 1953).

36. For an account of the Andean Indian Programme, see Jeff Rens: "The Andean Programme", in *International Labour Review,* December 1961, at 423-461; and "The Development of the Andean Programme and its future" in *International Labour Review,* December 1963, at 547-563.

37. Convention Concerning the Protection and Integration of Indigenous and Other Tribal and Semi-Tribal Populations in Independent Countries (ILO 40th Sess. (no. 107, 328 U.N.T.S. 247 (1959)).

38. The African Charter on Human and Peoples' Rights [hereinafter African Charter] was adopted on 27 June 1981 in Nairobi, Kenya at the Eighteenth Assembly of Heads of State and Governments of the Organization of African Unity: OAU-Doc. CAB/LEG/67/3/REV.5. It entered into force in October 1986. See: Chris Maina Peter, *Human Rights in Africa--A Comparative Study of the African Human and Peoples' Rights Charter and the New Tanzanian Bill of Rights* (New York: Greenwood Press, 1990) for a detailed history and analysis of the Charter. In addition to the African Charter, the Council of Europe adopted the Convention for the Protection of Human Rights and Fundamental Freedoms of 4 November 1950 entered into force 3 September 1953 (1950) 213 U.N.T.S. 221. The Organization of American States adopted the American Convention on Human Rights on 22 November 1969 entered into force on 18 July 1978 O.A.S. Doc. OEA/ser. L/V/II.23 doc. 21 rev. 6 [hereinafter American Convention] See: Cecilia Medina Quiroga, *The Battle of Human Rights - Gross, Systematic Violations and the Inter-American System* (Dordrecht: Martinus Nijhoff Publishers, 1988) at 1 [hereinafter Quiroga, *Battle of Human Rights*].

39. African Charter, *supra* note 38.

40. Draft of the Inter-American Declaration on the Rights of Indigenous Peoples, draft approved by the IACHR at the 1278 session held on 18 September 1995. Organization of American States, OEA/Ser./L/rev.1; 21 September 1995. At present the draft has been sent to governments, Indigenous Organizations, other interested institutions and experts. On the basis of their answers and comments, the IACHR will prepare its final proposal to be presented to the General Assembly of the OAS [hereinafter OAS draft declaration]. See: Appendix II for a copy.

41. African Charter, *supra* note 38.

42. The European Commission and Court of Human Rights will be merged into one court under Protocol 12. Also, see:, The Inter-American Court of Human Rights and Inter-American Commission on Human Rights in Quiroga, *Battle of Human Rights, supra* note 39.

43. African Charter, *supra* note 38: Article 30 states: "An African Commission on Human and People's Rights hereinafter called 'the Commission', "shall be established within the Organization of African Unity to promote human and people's rights and ensure their protection in Africa". Articles 31 to 61 relate to the workings and mandate of the Commission.

44. "The African Charter shied away from juridical implementation measures. Unlike the Latin American and the European instruments which established a court of human rights, (American Convention, 1969 Article 33; European Convention, 1953, Article 19(2)), the African Charter opted for the model of the International Covenant on Civil and Political Rights": Tunguru Huaraka ed., "Implementation Mechanism in the African Charter on Human and Peoples' Rights" in African Law Association, *The African Charter on Human and Peoples' Rights: Development, Context, Significance* (Marbury: S&W Druchkerei und Verlag GmbH, 1991) at 71.

45. Wolfgang Benedek, "The Significance of the African Charter on Human and Peoples' Rights for the Progressive Development of the International Concept and Protection of Human Rights" in ibid. at 16.

46. African Charter, *supra* note 38: Preamble states: "Conscious of their duty to achieve the total liberation of Africa, the peoples of which are still struggling for their dignity and genuine independence, and undertaking to eliminate colonialism, neo-colonialism, apartheid, zionism and to dismantle aggressive foreign military bases and all forms of discrimination particularly those based on race, ethnic group, colour, sex, language, religion or political opinion; Reaffirming their adherence to the principles of human and people's rights and freedoms contained in the Organization of African Unity, the Movement of Non-Aligned Countries and the United Nations; Firmly convinced of their duty to promote and protect human and people's rights and freedoms taking into account the importance traditionally attached to these rights and freedoms in Africa."

47. Richard Gittleman, "The African Charter on Human and Peoples' Rights: A Legal Analysis" (1982) 22 *Virginia Journal of International Law* at 657-676.

48. African Charter, *supra* note 38: Articles 2-15, 27, 28 and 29 outline the right of the individual to themselves, to the family, to the society and to the state.

49. African Charter, *supra* note 38: Articles 18 and 19 outline the rights of the family. Article 18 states: "The family shall be the natural unit and basis of society. It shall be protected by the State which shall take care of its physical and moral health."

50. African Charter, *supra* note 38: Articles 21 and 22 relate to the disposition of wealth and natural resources.

51. African Charter, *supra* note 38: Article 20 (1). "All peoples have the right to existence. They shall have the unquestionable and inalienable right to self-determination. They shall freely determine their political status and shall pursue their economic and social development according to the policy they have freely chosen; 2. Colonized or oppressed peoples shall have the right to free themselves from the bonds of domination by resorting to any means recognized by the international community; 3. All peoples shall have the right to the assistance of the State parties to the present Charter in their liberation struggle against foreign domination, be it political, economic or cultural."

52. African Charter, *supra* note 38: Article 23(2)(a) and (b): "For the purpose of strengthening peace, solidarity and friendly relations, State parties to the present Charter shall ensure that: (a) any individual enjoying the right of asylum under Article 12 of the present Charter

shall not engage in subversive activities against his country of origin or any other State party to the present charter; (b) their territories shall not be used as bases for subversive or terrorist activities against the people of any other State party to the present Charter."

53. Charter of the Organization of American States, Law and Treaty Series, No. 23 Pan American Union, Washington, D.C. 1948 [hereinafter OAS Charter] as amended.

54. OAS Charter, Article 1.

55. "Created in 1959 by a political organ of the OAS, and this Commission has developed from a study group into an action body actively performing the task of investigating human rights violations taking place in the continent" (Quiroga, *Battle of Human Rights, supra* note 38 at 60). A detailed account of the events relating to the approval of the Commission's first Statute can be found in: Anna P. Schreiber, *The Inter-American Commission on Human Rights* (Leyden: A.W. Sijthoff, 1970).

56. Robert E. Norris, "The Individual Petition Procedure of the Inter-American System for the Protection of Human Rights" in Hurst Hannum, ed., *Guide to International Human Rights Practice* (Philadelphia: University of Pennsylvania Press, 1984) at 108 [hereinafter Norris, *Inter-American System*].

57. American Convention, *supra* note 38.

58. Norris, *Inter-American System, supra* note 56 at 108. Also Quiroga remarks: "The American Convention on Human Rights entered into force on July 18, 1978, when the eleventh OAS member state, Grenada, deposited its ratification. There was, therefore, a two-month period of uncertainty for the Commission. Once Resolution 253 of the Permanent Council was approved, the Commission began to operate under its authority. This situation continued until the General Assembly of the OAS adopted the new Statute of the Commission, on October 31, 1979. The Commission itself adopted its Regulations on April 8, 1980" (Quiroga, *Battle of Human Rights, supra* note 38 at 116).

59. OAS Draft Declaration, *supra* note 40, See also: Appendix II.

60. "According to Article 34 of the Convention, the Commission shall be composed of seven member, who shall be persons of high moral character and recognized competence in the field of human rights. The Commission's members are elected in a personal capacity by the General Assembly of the OAS from a list of candidates proposed by the governments of all OAS member states. . . . No two nationals of the same state may be members of the Commission at the same time. The Commission's members are elected for a term of four years and may be reelected only once" (Quiroga, Battle of Human Rights, supra note 38 at 119 and 120).

61. OAS Draft Declaration, *supra* note 40.

62. OAS Draft Declaration, *supra* note 40.

63. OAS Draft Declaration, *supra* note 40.

64. OAS Draft Declaration, *supra* note 40.

65. (1966) 999 U.N.T.S. 171, in force 1976. Article 27: "In those States in which ethnic, religious or linguistic minorities exist, persons belonging to such minorities shall not be denied the right, in community with the other members of their group, to enjoy their own culture, to profess and practice their own religion, or to use their own language." See discussion in

Chapter 3.

66. Cindy M. Buhl, *A Citizen's Guide to the Multilateral Development Banks and Indigenous Peoples* (Washington: The Bank Information Center, November 1994) at 4 [hereinafter *World Bank's Citizen's Guide*]. The IMF was also established at the same meeting.

67. "There are also regional banks--The Inter-American Development Bank, the Asian Development Bank and the African Development Bank--which have been established under auspices of the regional economic commissions of the UN and which co-ordinates with the IBRD" (Bowett, *International Institutions, supra* note 17 at 109).

68. *World Bank Citizen's Guide, supra* note 66 at 91, at Appendix D at 1 of 6. *The World Bank Operational Manual Operational Directive,* September 1991. The directive was prepared for the guidance of the staff of the World Bank.

69. Ibid.

70. Ibid.

71. Ibid.

72."The utter failure of the League to avert a new world war has given rise to a notion that the legal organization of the international community collapsed altogether at the outbreak of the hostilities in September 1939. Constitutionally, that view is unfounded. The war did not destroy the legal existence of the League; the Covenant continued in force until the formal winding-up of the organization by a resolution passed at its last Assembly in April, 1946" (Bentwich, *Commentary, supra* note 2 at xi).

73. The United Nations was formed with the adoption of the Charter of the United Nations signed and entered into force in 1945, making the Charter its constitution (1946)1 *United Nations Treaty Series* xvi.

74. The purposes of the United Nations set out in Article 1 are: (1.) To maintain international peace and security, and to that end: to take effective collective measures for the prevention and removal of threats to the peace, and for the suppression of acts of aggression or other breaches of the peace, and to bring about by peaceful means, and in conformity with the principles of justice and international law, adjustments or settlement of international disputes or situations which lead to a breach of the peace; (2.) To develop friendly relations among nations based on respect for the principle of equal rights and self-determination of peoples, and to take other appropriate measures to strengthen universal peace; (3.) To achieve international co-operation in solving international problems of an economic, social, cultural, or humanitarian character, and in promoting and encouraging respect for human rights and for fundamental freedoms for all without distinction as to race, sex, language, or religion; and (4.) To be a centre for harmonizing the actions of nations in the attainment of these common ends.

75. UN Charter Article 1 (3), see Appendix III for a structural view of the UN Human Rights Bodies and their interaction.

76. UN Charter Article 7.

77. UN Charter Ch IV, Articles 9-22 sets out the composition, the functions and powers and rules of procedures of the GA.

78. UN Charter Ch V, Articles 23-32 sets out the provisions for the establishment of the

Security Council which is comprised of five permanent members (China, Federation of Russia, the United Kingdom of Great Britain and Northern Ireland, France and the United States of America) and ten other non-permanent members elected by the GA for a term of two years. Decisions of the Security Council are reported to the GA on an annual basis.

79. UN Charter Ch X, Articles 61-72 sets out the provisions for an Economic and Social Council (ECOSOC) which consists of fifty-four members elected from the GA for a term of three years.

80. UN Charter Ch XIII, Articles 86-91 established the Trusteeship Council to assist the GA to carry out its trust obligations to trust territories.

81. UN Charter Ch XIV, Articles 92-96 set out the provisions for the establishment of an International Court of Justice (ICJ) through a Statute annexed to the Charter.

82. UN Charter Ch XV, Articles 97-101 established the office of the Secretary-General--chief administrative officer of the organization--who is appointed by the GA on the recommendation of the Security Council.

83. UN Charter Article 10.

84. UN Charter Article 13.

85 General Assembly Resolution 217A (III) 10 December 1948.

86. UN General Assembly, Resolution 174 (A/180), 1948. Text in 45 *American Journal of International Law* (1951) Suppl., at 6.

87. UN Charter, Articles 10-14. The General Assembly can pass resolutions of recommendatory effect only.

88. Louis Henkin, "The International Bill of Rights: the Universal Declaration and the Covenants" in ibid. at 2.

89. Lauri Hannikainen, *Peremptory Norms* (Jus Cogens) *in International Law* (Helsinki, Finland: Lakimiesliiton Kustannus, 1988) at 233.

90. Ian Brownlie, *Principles of Public International Law 3rd. ed.* (Oxford: Oxford University Press, 1979) at 14.

91. Philip Alston wrote: "While some commentators are convinced that the Declaration in its entirety is binding on all states as part of international law, others would agree with Cassese that, 'in formal terms, it is not legally binding, but possesses only moral and political force'. . . In general terms, however, it is today widely, and possibly even unanimously, accepted that at least some international legal obligations flow from the Declaration, despite its original non-binding nature" in "Human Rights in a Pluralist World" in Jan Berting et al. ed. *Human Rights in a Pluralist World* (London: Meckler Ltd. 1990) at 3.

92. General Assembly Resolutions 2148 [XXI] of 12 December 1966 and 2202 [XXI] of 16 December 1966.

93. Statute of the International Court of Justice annexed to the Charter of the United Nations and forming an integral part thereof. UN Charter, Article 92.

94. *Supra*, note 7 for discussion on the Permanent Court of International Justice

95. Chapter IV of the Statute of the International Court of Justice sets out the court's authority to give advisory opinions. Article 65 (1): "The Court may give an advisory opinion on any legal question at the request of whatever body may be authorized by or in accordance with the Charter of the United Nations to make such a request."

96. ICJ Statute, Articles 36 and 59.

97. *Interpretation of the Peace Treaties with Bulgaria, Hungary and Romania*, I.C.J. Reports, 1950.

98. Sir Hersch Lauterpacht, *The Development of International Law by the International Court* (Cambridge: Grotius Publications Limited, 1982) at 354-355 [hereinafter Lauterpacht, *International Court*].

99. "The decision of the Court has no binding force except between the parties and in respect of that particular case."

100. Lauterpacht, *International Court, supra* note 98 at 11.

101. "The Western Sahara is a territory of some 105,448 square miles populated by about 75,000 people, most of whom are Moslem nomads. The issue before the ICJ arose from the international controversy surrounding the proposed Spanish decolonization of the phosphate rich territory. Both Morocco and Mauritania sought to incorporate the Western Sahara without a referendum of the territory's population": Mark W. Janis, "The International Court of Justice: Advisory Opinion on the Western Sahara", (1976) 17 *Harvard International Law Journal* 609 [hereinafter Janis, Western Sahara].

102. International Court of Justice, *Western Sahara: Advisory Opinion of 16 October 1975*, ([1975] The Hague: ICJ Reports) [hereinafter ICJ, *Western Sahara*].

103. "Since the questions put to the Court confined the period to be taken into consideration to the time of the territory's colonization by Spain, the view was expressed that in order to be a 'legal question' within the meaning of Article 65, paragraph 1 of the Statute, a question must not be of a historical character, but must concern or affect existing rights or obligations. The Court asserted that there was nothing in the Charter or the Statute to limit either the competence of the General Assembly to request an Advisory Opinion, or the competence of the Court to give one, to legal questions relating to existing rights or obligations" B.O. Okere, "The Western Sahara Case", [1979] 28 *International and Comparative Law Quarterly* at 302).

104. For more detailed discussion of the decision related to the doctrine of *terra nullius* and its application see: Janis, Western Sahara, *supra* note 101 at 61.

105. Janis, Western Sahara, *supra* note 101 at 68.

106. Janis, Western Sahara, *supra* note 101 at 39.

107. *Case Concerning East Timor (Portugal v. Australia)* [1995] ICJ Reports at 95, para.11: "The Territory of East Timor corresponding to the eastern part of the island of Timor lies opposite the north coast of Australia, the distance between them being approximately 430 kilometres. In the sixteenth century, East Timor became a colony of Portugal; Portugal remained there until 1975. The matter came before the Court due to a Treaty entered into between Indonesia and Australia concerning the continental shelf between Australia and the province of East Timor. The Portuguese Government raised the issue at the Court concerning the Treaty and the ability of Australia to enter into such a treaty considering that East

Timor is on the list of non-self-governing territories within the meaning of the Chapter XI of the Charter; and the Special Committee on the Situation with Regard to the Implementation of the Declaration on the Granting of Independence to Colonial Countries and Peoples remains seized of the question of East Timor. . . . Australia, in negotiating and concluding the Treaty . . . has acted unlawfully" (pages 11-12).

108. Ibid. at 105.

109. "The resolutions of the General Assembly are the following: 3485 (XXX), 31/53, 32/34, 33/39, 34/40, 35/37, 36/50 and 37/30. Some of these resolutions expressly recognized the status of Portugal as the administering Power (resolutions 3485 (XXX), 34/40, 35/27, 36/50 and 37/30) and not one of them recognizes the legal status of Indonesia. Rather, some of them (resolutions 31/53, 32/34, 33/39) reaffirm the Security Council resolutions and draw the attention of the Security Council to the critical situation of East Timor, and recommend that it take all effective steps for the implementation of its resolutions, with a view to securing the full exercise by the people of East Timor of their right to self-determination" ibid. at 182-183.

110. Ibid. at 154.

111. Ibid. at 193-195.

112. UN Charter, Article 61(1) and (2) see Appendix III Chart for the bodies under ECOSOC in the UN.

113. Under Article 68 of the UN Charter authorizes the establishment of six functioning Commissions: "Statistical Commission, Population Commission, Commission for Social Development, Commission on Human Rights, Commission on the Status of Women and Commission on Narcotic Drugs": Peter I. Hajnal, *Guide to United Nations Organization, Documentation & Publishing For Students, Researcher and Librarians* (Dobbs Ferry, New York: Oceana Publications, Inc. 1978) at 42.

114. United Nations, *The United Nations and Human Rights* (New York: United Nations, 1973), at 3 [hereinafter UN Human Rights].

115. Ibid. at 4.

116. For a complete discussion, see Chapters 4 and 5 of this thesis.

117. The formal name of the Working Group uses "Indigenous Populations" rather than "Indigenous Peoples." The use of the term "Populations" instead of "Peoples" was the choice made by governments for political reasons. State governments did not want to use the term "Peoples" as the term implies the right of self- determination for Indigenous Peoples. "Since the establishment of the Working Group, the Sub-Commission on Human Rights has agreed to refer to the agenda item using "peoples" rather than "populations" but the formal name of the Working Group has never been changed. As Indigenous Peoples are offended by being referred to as "mere" populations and use the term "peoples"' Catherine Iorns,"Indigenous Peoples and Self-Determination: Challenging State Sovereignty" (1992) 24 *Case Western Reserve Journal of International Law* at 203. In this thesis, I use the title Working Group on Indigenous Peoples as agreed upon by the Indigenous Peoples in numerous preparatory meetings. The official title of the documents on the Working Group uses "Populations" which will be referred to in its correct form for citation. However, in the body of the text, "Peoples" will be used.

118. For discussion on the role of the Sub-Commission and the Working Group on

Indigenous Peoples, see *infra*. Provisional Agenda, Commission on Human Rights, Fifty-Second Session, agenda item 23.

120. UN Charter Articles 1(3) and 13 contain specific language related to human rights as a purpose of the United Nations and a function of the General Assembly. See also: Articles 55-56.

121. World Conference on Human Rights Vienna, Vienna Declaration, 14-25 June 1993. A/CONF.157/23 [hereinafter Vienna Conference].

122. Ibid. para. 18.

123. Jose Ayala Lasso of Ecuador was appointed for a four-year term which expires in 1998. For specific responsibilities see: Janet E. Lord, "The United Nations High Commissioner for Human Rights: Challenges and Opportunities", (1995) 17 Loyola L.A. *International Law and Comparative Law Journal* 329.

124. Report of the United Nations High Commission for Human Rights E/CN.4/1996/103 at para. 6.

125. Vienna Conference, *supra* note 121 at paras. 28 to 32.

126. Jose Carlos Morales from Costa Rica has been contracted by the Human Rights Centre in Geneva to work exclusively on the programme of action for the decade.

127. United Nations, *Everyman's United Nations--The Structure, Functions and Work for the Organization and its Related Agencies during the years 1945-1962 and a United Nations Chronology for 1963, 7th ed.*, (New York: United Nations 1964) at 312 [hereinafter Everyman's]: "In 1951, the Economic and Social Council discontinued the Sub-Commission, but in 1952, at the request of the General Assembly, it was re- established."

128. "In accordance with Economic and Social Council resolutions 1334 (XLIV) of 31 May 1968 and 1986/35 of 23 May 1986, the decisions 1978/21 of 5 May 1978 and 1987/102 of 6 February 1987, the Commission on Human Rights at its forty-fourth session (39th meeting, 29 February 1988) elected by secret ballot twenty-six members of the Sub-Commission on Prevention of Discrimination and Protection of Minorities from nominations of experts made by States Members of the United Nations on the following basis: (a) seven members from African States; (b) five members from Asian States; (c) three members from Eastern European States; (d) five members from Latin American States; (e) six members from Western European and other States. Pursuant to Council resolution 1986/35, members of the Sub-Commission were to be elected for a term of four years and half of its membership and the corresponding alternatives, if any were to be elected every two years": Commission on Human Rights, Election of Member of the Sub-Commission on Prevention of Discrimination and Protection of Minorities, E/CN.4/1996/104.

129. "Studies have been made of discrimination in education, discrimination in religion rights and practices; discrimination in political rights; discrimination in respect of right of everyone to leave any country, including his own, and to return to his country; discrimination against persons born out of wedlock; equality in administration of justice; and racial discrimination in the political, economic, social and cultural spheres" UN *Human Rights, supra* note 114 at 4.

130. For a complete history of the study and its objectives, see the final report submitted by Ms. Fatma Zohra Ksentinit, Special Rapporteur of the Sub-Commission (E/CN.4/Sub.2/1994/9), which was adopted by the Commission on Human Rights on 24

February 1995 by Resolution 14.

131. UN Doc. E/CN.4/Sub.2/1969/301.

132. Resolution 48 (XXIII) of 26 August 1970.

133. Resolution 8 (XXIV) of 18 August 1971.

134. Erica-Irene Daes, Chairperson/Rapporteur of the Working Group on Indigenous Populations, "The Struggle to Become Visible--United Nations and Indigenous Peoples from 1969 to 1993" (unpublished paper on file with the writer) at 1 and 2.

135. The Study on the Problems of Discrimination against Indigenous Populations undertaken by Martinez Cobo is widely known as the "Cobo Study." For the purposes of this thesis, the familiar term of Cobo Study will be used rather than the official cumbersome title. The conclusions, proposals and recommendations are contained in Volume V of the Study, UN Doc. E/CN.4/Sub.2/1986/7/Add.4.

136. See Resolution 1589(L) of 21 May 1971 of the Economic and Social Council. The idea of conducting such a study was initiated by resolution 4B (XXII) on 26 August 1970 of the Sub-Commission on the Prevention of Discrimination and Protection of Minorities.

137. Study on the Problem of Discrimination Against Indigenous Populations, Chapter XXI "Conclusions, Proposals and Recommendations" (E/CN.4/sub.2/1983/21/Add.8), 30 September 1984.

138. Economic and Social Council Resolution 1989/77 of 24 May 1989 on the basis of Commission on Human Rights resolutions 1988/56 of 9 March 1988 and 1989/41 of 6 March 1989. In this regard, the Special Rapporteur Miguel Alfonso-Martinez, expert of the Sub-commission, has submitted an outline, a preliminary report, a first progress report, a second progress report and a third progress report. It is anticipated that the final report will be tabled in 1997.

139. See Resolution 1982/34 of 7 May 1982 of the Economic and Social Council. The idea was first proposed by resolution 2(XXXIV) of 8 September 1981 of the Sub-Commission and endorsed by resolution 1982/19 of 10 March 1982 of the Commission on Human Rights [hereinafter *Working Group*].

140. Ibid.

141. *Report of the Working Group on Indigenous Populations on its first session*. E/CN.4/Sub.2/ AC.4/1982/2 [hereinafter 1982 *Working Group*].

142. In 1986, owing to budgetary difficulties of the United Nations, the Sub-Commission and all the working groups were cancelled. There was an informal meeting held at the Palais des Nations reported to the 1987 Working Group, E/CN.4/Sub.2/ AC.4/1987/22.

143. *1982 Working Group, supra* note 141 at 10.

144. Article 71 of the UN Charter allows for: "Non-governmental organizations may be consulted by the Economic and Social Council on questions with which they are concerned. Organizations are divided thus: those with a basic interest in most of the activities of the Council (Category A); those with a special competence but concerned with only a few of the Council's activities (Category B); those placed on a register for ad hoc consultations. All these organization may send observers to the public meetings of the Council and its comis-

sions" *Everyman's, supra* note 127 at 17.

145. *Report of the Working Group on Indigenous Populations on its thirteenth session.* E/CN.4/ Sub.2/1995/24.

146. *1982 Working Group, supra* note 141 at 2 and 3.

147. Sub-Commission on Prevention of Discrimination and Protection of Minorities resolution 1994/45 of 26 August 1994. The resolution was drafted based on a recommendation of the Working Group. Working Groups cannot pass resolutions for action, but they can make recommendations to the Sub-commission which can pass a resolution for transmission to the Commission on Human Rights. Further discussion of this process is in Chapter 5. Another Working Group committed to issues similar to those of the Indigenous Working Group was created in March 1995. The Commission on Human Rights created an Open-ended Inter-sessional Working Group with the sole purpose of elaborating a draft declaration (Commission on Human Rights resolution 1995/32 of 3 March 1995). The CHR decision was endorsed by the Economic and Social Council in resolution 1995/32 of 25 July 1995. The first meeting of the Inter-sessional Working Group was held 20 November to 1 December 1995 in Geneva. (*Report of the Working Group established in accordance with Commission on Human Rights resolution* 1995/32: E/CN.4/1996/84.) A more detailed discussion of the work of the Inter-sessional Working Group is in Chapter 5.

3

Indigenous Peoples and Minorities in International Law

Introduction

With the establishment of the United Nations, worldwide acceptance that self-determination must be subject to international concern has been growing. The UN has promoted self-determination and protection of human rights toward maintaining peace and friendly relations among member states in over sixty international treaties and declarations. Despite this apparent progress in international legal instruments, there remain two problematic areas: Indigenous Peoples and minorities within the member states of the United Nations. Are Indigenous Peoples "peoples"[1] or "minorities?" Are minorities considered peoples within the scope of the UN Charter? If Indigenous Peoples are not minorities, what rights should be accorded them? Attempts to resolve the dilemma of these identifications pose challenges for the UN as it moves to respond to the needs of Indigenous Peoples and minorities within states while upholding its Charter.

Rights of Peoples

The first instance of an international organization attempting to protect the rights of a group was the UN's precursor, the League of Nations. The groups of concern then were minorities. While there was no specific reference in the Covenant of the League on the rights of minorities, the treaties that signalled the end of the First World War contained provisions for their protection:

> [The] treaties imposed on a number of nations after the First World War . . . [were] understood to be the protection of certain minorities, particularly ethnic, linguistic, and religious. These treaties were between governments, in the conventional sense. These treaties, broadly speaking, assured the rights of internal minorities in countries whose majority populations were understood to be

different ethnically, nationally, or religiously. These Treaties were signed between 1919 and 1920 by the Allies with five states: Poland, Czechoslovakia, Romania, Yugoslavia and Greece. Minorities' clauses were incorporated in treaties with four defeated states: Turkey, Austria, Bulgaria and Hungary. [2]

While the League's goal was to protect minorities, it was selective in its application. The victors imposed on the defeated nations provisions intended to protect minorities within defeated states, while no similar provisions were extended to minorities in the victorious nations. The 1919-1920 treaties were politically "suspect insofar as they were imposed by the victors on others, but not on themselves."[3] The ethnic, linguistic and religious characters of the minorities were protected in the treaties without any mention of territorial rights. The imposed treaties did not accomplish their stated goal of protecting minorities as the League did not have the legal capability to enforce its decisions on states that were violating the treaties.[4] Customary international law norms prohibited states from being imposed upon by other states without their consent. The League could not impose solutions without the consent of the state in which the minority group was found. The application of these international law norms hindered the League's ability to maintain peace leading to the eventual breakdown and war.

ILO Convention 107

Only one specialized agency of the UN, the International Labour Organization (ILO), has passed any international standards that affect the rights of Indigenous Peoples. In 1957, the ILO passed the Indigenous and Tribal Population Convention (No. 107).[5] Convention 107 was an international instrument—a multilateral treaty—directed toward the assimilation and integration of Indigenous Peoples into a state as suggested in Article 2 (1):

> Governments shall have the primary responsibility for developing coordinated and systematic action for the protection of the populations concerned and their progressive integration into the life of their respective countries.[6]

As promoted in the Andean Programme (discussed in Chapter 2), Indigenous Peoples would be integrated into the society of their respective countries through an education programme set out in Article 6.[7]

Convention 107 promoted the assimilation of the Indigenous Peoples into the general population of the state,[8] a goal rejected by Indigenous Peoples. In addition, the ILO also attempted to define Indigenous

Peoples so that they could be assimilated. The fact that Article 1 of Convention 107 includes a definition of Indigenous Peoples implies Indigenous Peoples had maintained a separate identity despite the colonization process. Article 1 also contained application provisions.[9] Rather than refer to Peoples, the Convention applies to "populations" who are descended "from the population which inhabited the country, or a geographic region to which the country belongs, at the time of conquest or colonization" and who tend to live "more in conformity with the social, economic and cultural institutions." Under this definition, Indigenous Peoples come from areas conquered or colonized. This is a small admission, but a significant one for the application of international standards established outside the ILO process.

The Convention did not envisage Indigenous Peoples continuing to exist on their lands. The language of the Convention projects gradual integration. Some Articles do refer to the protection of the Indigenous Peoples, but the conditions proposed are short term and transitory. For example, in Article 3(2)(b), the ILO recommends that: "Care shall be taken to ensure that such special measures of protection will be continued only so long as there is need for special protection and only to the extent that such protection is necessary." The whole Convention was designed for the integration and disappearance of Indigenous Peoples, which was promoted as the inevitable result of the integration and education of the Peoples. The Convention was strongly criticized by Indigenous Peoples for having:

> ethnocentric conceptions and programmes of directed integration. Rather than providing a source of rights for indigenous peoples seeking to retain their territorial, political, social, and cultural integrity, the instrument mandates the gradual integration of indigenous individuals into national societies and economies, thus legitimizing the gradual extinction of indigenous peoples as such.[10]

Convention 107 contained no special recognition that Indigenous Peoples have rights under any international law regime to their own identity or their own territories. Convention 107 framed some recognition of the rights to land under Part II. Article 11 recognized that: "The right of ownership, collective or individual, of the members of the populations concerned over the lands which these populations traditionally occupy shall be recognized." However, Article 12 allowed a state to take Indigenous traditional lands "under national laws and regulations for reasons related to national security and in the interests of national economic development." The positive aspects of the Convention were quickly overshadowed by the interests of the states in Indigenous lands and resources.

Although Convention 107 makes some move to protect Indigenous rights in a limited way, apparently this was not the main focus. The ILO Convention 107 provided for the recruitment, employment, training and education of Indigenous Peoples. All the measures were to last as long as it took to integrate Indigenous Peoples into a state, as set out in Article 22(1).[11] Through Convention 107, the ILO considered it was addressing problems by fitting Indigenous Peoples into their states. The Convention did not protect the right of Indigenous Peoples to remain Indigenous and to determine their way of life.

In the thirty years since Convention 107, there is little evidence that it was accepted by Indigenous Peoples.[12] Convention 107 was originally ratified by only twenty-six countries: "14 are in Latin America, four in Asia, six in Africa, and the Middle East, and two in Europe."[13] The limited number of state members of the ILO who ratified Convention 107, along with the strong Indigenous criticism of the Convention, led to a revision process. As acknowledged by the ILO, the instrument had become "repugnant."[14] The ILO wanted to retain its credibility on the international stage as a promoter of human rights and Convention 107 was creating difficulties for the image of the organization:

> International standards are likely to prove effective only if they are adapted to the needs of the people they protect and to the various national situations in which they are to be applied; and if the people concerned have the resources, knowledge and access to legal and administrative machinery necessary to secure their implementation.[15]

The original wording of this Convention did not meet standards of protection required by Indigenous Peoples. The instrument proved ineffective for the assimilation of Indigenous Peoples into national structures, so the ILO was obligated to revise Convention 107. The revision process is discussed later in this chapter.

UN Charter

The League of Nations wanted to protect minorities, but failed.[16] When the United Nations was established, rights of minorities were not mentioned in either the Charter or the Universal Declaration of Human Rights.[17] In the following years, there were several efforts to bring the organization back to the issue of minorities: "Three times—at its third, fourth and fifth session—the Sub-Commission has recommended that the Commission on Human Rights adopt a draft resolution defining minorities."[18]

When the League was formally dissolved by its membership in 1946 and replaced by the United Nations, the UN Charter set out a process for universal peace that was to be achieved and maintained through recognition of the right of self-determination of Peoples. The issue of its general application to minorities was not raised—it was assumed that minorities were protected under the general principles outlined in the Charter. The question as to whether minorities constituted Peoples as envisioned by the Charter was not addressed. It is unclear whether the Charter specifically rejects the protection of minorities as a viable aim of the United Nations. Further, difficulty is encountered with implementation since the interpretation of the language contained in the Charter and the purposes as set out in Article 1 is controversial. The interpretation that should be given to "nation," "self-determination" and "Peoples" has yet to be fully clarified. One of the main complications in extending rights to minorities and Indigenous Peoples is the position that international law is based on rights of states and not on rights of the people within the states. The lack of clear definitions was addressed often by the UN, as the organization has struggled to determine the scope of its Charter and the means to implement its provisions:

> In the discussion in the United Nations concerning the definition of the terms "people" and "nation" there was a tendency to equate the two. When a distinction was made, it was to indicate that "people" was broader in scope. The significance of the use of this term centered on the desire to be certain that a narrow application of the term "nation" would not prevent the extension of self-determination to dependent peoples who might not yet qualify as nations. . . . a nation was composed of the people belonging to the same ethnic group; that the land on which the nation was settled should be delimited; that the individuals concerned should show a collective will to live together; that a nation was the product of a common consciousness of common ideals which were reinforced often but not necessarily always by racial, linguistic, and cultural ties; that a nation was the community to which one belonged by one's own choice; and that in the last analysis the only valid standard was a subjective one, in the sense that any group of people living in a determinate territory constituted a nation if it were conscious of itself as a national entity and asserted itself as such.[19]

While no accepted definition for "Peoples" was inserted in Article 1(2) of the Charter, there are strong indicators that the Peoples must be collectively organized into a political authority with a territory within a state (discussed by Espiell *infra*). In the end, the Peoples as subjects in law themselves determine and assert their right of self-determination.

While no definition for "Peoples" has been ratified yet, some guidelines have been developed for detecting who are Peoples with a right to self-determination in need of protection. The UN has established that:

> The right does not apply to peoples already organized in the form of a State which are not under colonial and alien domination, since resolution 1514 (XV)20 and other United Nations instruments condemn any attempt aimed at the partial or total disruption of the national unity and the territorial integrity of a country. If, however, beneath the guise of ostensible national unity, colonial and alien domination does in fact exist, whatever legal formula may be used in an attempt to conceal it, the right of the subject people concerned cannot be disregarded without international law being violated.[21]

The UN has limited the exercise of the right of self-determination to those Peoples under colonial or alien domination through General Assembly resolution 1514 entitled Declaration on the Granting of Independence to Colonial Countries and Peoples, yet has circumscribed the right, as follows:

> Any attempt aimed at the partial or total disruption of national unity and the territorial integrity of a country is incompatible with the purposes and principles of the Charter of the United Nations.[22]

Thus, if a Peoples are under colonial or alien domination, they have a right to self-determination and to free themselves, but they cannot exercise the right if it results in disruption of the state. In the latter case, the right can be exercised only with the consent of the concerned state. It appears unlikely that a colonizing state will voluntarily allow its territorial integrity to be disrupted in order for the Peoples to exercise their right to self-determination. Indeed, given the resolutions passed by the GA, states have protected themselves against such an event. The limitation placed on the exercise of the right of self-determination by resolution 1514 in 1960 was further limited by GA resolution 2625 passed one decade later by the General Assembly. The 1970 Declaration on Friendly Relations states in part:

> Nothing in the foregoing paragraph shall be construed as authorizing or encouraging any action which would dismember or impair, totally or in part, the territorial integrity or political unity of sovereign and independent States conducting themselves in compliance with the principle of equal rights and self-determination of peoples as described above and thus possessed of a government representing the whole people belonging to the territory

without distinction as to race, creed or colour.

Every state shall refrain from any action aimed at the partial or total disruption of the national unity and territorial integrity of any other State or country.[23]

The application of the Declaration on Friendly Relations further qualifies the exercise of the right of self-determination by peoples within a state. There is also a restriction placed on a state from interfering with the internal unity of another state. This is the retrenchment of the customary international law norms whereby the domestic concerns of a state are strictly internal matters and are not subject to international review or concern.[24]

In Chapters XI, XII and XIII,[25] the UN Charter further stipulates responsibilities of members for Non-Self-Governing Territories and the role of the International Trusteeship system in relation to peoples who have not yet attained a full measure of self-government in their territory. These chapters of the Charter recognize that the problems of Non-Self-Governing Territories were of a concern to the UN if peace was to be maintained. There was a general recognition by the member states that certain territories should be decolonized to keep the peace.[26] It is a sacred trust of the members to promote the utmost right of peoples for the well-being of the inhabitants. The sacred trust when discharged would allow peoples to join the family of nations. The question remains: what meaning can be given to peoples? The Charter does not contain a definition of "peoples" who have a right to self-determination. However, there is some guidance in the Charter related to peoples and the right of self-determination in the provisions to the implementation of the right for Non-Self-Governing Territories:

> Chapter XI is a declaration on "Non-Self-Governing Territories." The territorial aspects is vital: the Chapter refers to "territories whose peoples have not attained a full measure of self-government;" the sacred trust is to promote "the well-being of inhabitants of these territories." A territorial concept of self-determination appears to rule out minorities without a specific territorial base.[27]

The Charter presented the members with established goals. The difficulty for the organization has been to achieve those goals.

Peoples living under a colonial or alien state imposed on them who sought to use the provisions of the UN Charter to free themselves, were limited by these two resolutions of the General Assembly. A state can use its national legal system to conceal or deny the right of the Peoples by claiming potential disruption of its territorial integrity. Violations of the Peoples rights ought to justify interference in the internal affairs of a state; however, the right of interference has been qualified by the right of the state to its territorial integrity. Following this analysis, the application of GA resolutions 1514 and 2625 allows for limitations on the state to promote the equal rights and self-determination of peoples as set out in the Charter. The member states of the UN may have constructed the limitations on the right of self-determination, but the principle of self-determination still needs to be addressed:

> The principle of self-determination is acceptable as a legal principle only in application to the liberation of colonial territories. . . . In international law, the principle of self-determination is applied to people who have been deprived of it–deprived of the right to determine their own political, social and economic status. . . . [Self-determination] is in reality a restoration of the status of which they were deprived by the colonial power.[28]

If the principle of self-determination relates to the liberation of a territory, then decolonization is a right that is applicable to all peoples except Indigenous Peoples who were originally colonized by the European sovereigns. The resolution applies to certain peoples, but peoples preceded by the word "Indigenous" are not accorded the same consideration by the General Assembly or the Special Committee established to oversee the decolonization process. The resolutions have been inconsistently applied. The reluctance of the UN to apply the Declaration to assist Indigenous Peoples to achieve self-government is a glaring example of a double standard and an unequal application of the principles as set down the General Assembly.

The UN General Assembly has continued to pass resolutions and declarations[29] and treaties[30] upholding the right to self-determination as a principal goal[31] in conventional and customary international law without deciding the legal nature of the principle. To remedy this omission, the Economic and Social Council commissioned a Special Rapporteur to conduct a study on the history of the right of self-determination within the United Nations.

Cristescu Study

Special Rapporteur Aureliu Cristescu undertook to review the principle of self-determination of peoples as a contribution to international law, taking special care to review the conventional law, custom, general principles of law and *jus cogens*. He reported: "As far as conventional law is concerned, the principle is stated in the Charter of the United Nations and the two International Covenants on Human Rights."[32] Following the review of the resolutions and other actions taken by the GA, Cristescu concluded that the principle is:

no longer just a moral or political postulate. Owing to the very close link which exists between self-determination and the maintenance of international peace and security, it is no longer regarded as a purely domestic problem.[33]

The Special Rapporteur spent some time in his report to address the issue of decolonization. He acknowledged that the right of self-determination of peoples is a critical element in the history of the UN and "has been invoked more often than any other Charter principle of international law, for it profoundly affects the lives of Peoples."[34] He found that there is no distinction between Peoples and Indigenous Peoples, stating that:

> the struggle against colonialism is the most important field of application of the principle of equal rights and self-determination of peoples. . . . In our era of decolonization and elimination of colonialism, the principle of equal rights and self-determination of peoples is of vital importance, for it represents the essential objective of peoples and countries struggling against colonial domination and exploitation, an objective for which those subject peoples have made enormous sacrifices.[35]

The report of the Special Rapporteur did not lead to the UN extending the provisions contained in the GA Declaration on Decolonization to Indigenous Peoples. The principle of self-determination is applicable to Peoples who meet the UN's criteria of "Peoples" and of colonized people. Cristescu acknowledged that Indigenous Peoples, such as those in the Americas, are appropriate peoples to whom the right of self-determination as a legal principle should be applied. The right of self-determination of Indigenous Peoples in the Americas is to determine their political, social and economic status denied by their colonizers. A recognition of the right of self-determination would restore the status of such Peoples to their pre-contact position.

Studying Minorities and Peoples

Following the formation of the United Nations, no immediate action was taken by either the Commission of Human Rights or its Sub-Commission on the Prevention of Discrimination and Protection of Minorities (Subcommission)[36] in relation to minorities or peoples. For the next thirty years, many studies were undertaken by the Sub-commission to review different aspects of the issues related to minorities. Three significant studies—by Espiell, Capotorti and Deschenes—were undertaken by the UN to review language for the implementation of the Charter and related resolutions, declarations and covenants. They are briefly reviewed herein to highlight some difficulties encountered with definitions. One recurring theme in the studies relates to the right of self-determination.

Espiell's Study

In 1974, Special Rapporteur Hector Gros Espiell undertook a review for the Sub-commission of the right to self-determination and its relationship to implementation of UN resolutions.[37] In determining the scope of the study, the Special Rapporteur needed to define the legal status of Peoples with a right to self-determination. Early in the report, Espiell concluded:

> Self-determination of peoples is a right of peoples, in other words of a specific type of human community sharing a common desire to establish an entity capable of functioning to ensure a common future. It is peoples as such which are entitled to the right to self-determination. Under contemporary international law minorities do not have this right. [38]

Under Espiell's study, Peoples were to be considered as different from minorities under contemporary international law. His analysis was based on international instruments that contained language related to the right of self-determination and to the process of decolonization, including the UN Charter and the two declarations on Decolonization and Friendly Relations. In this regard, the Special Rapporteur concluded:

> It is necessary, in the Special Rapporteur's view, to specify that if the national unity claimed and the territorial integrity invoked are merely legal fictions which cloak the real colonial and alien domination, resulting from actual disregard of the principle of self-determination, the subject people or peoples are entitled to exercise, with all the consequences thereof, their right of self-determination.[39]

If a state intends the argument of territorial integrity to deny the rights of peoples to self-determination, Espiell recommended that the international community view this misapplication of the principle of self-determination as contrary to the purposes of the UN Charter.

During Espiell's review, the International Covenant on Civil and Political Rights (ICCPR) and the International Covenant on Economic, Social and Cultural Rights (ICESCR) entered into force in 1976.[40] Both Covenants contain a provision on self-determination in their first Article.[41] Espiell reviewed Article 1 but omitted reference to ICCPR Article 27[42] on minority rights and its application, for the Rapporteur had concluded that minorities do not have a right to self-determination:

> The critical attitude shown by a considerable body of legal opinion in the 1950s towards the inclusion of the self-determination of peoples in the two International Covenants on Human Rights, an attitude based on a denial of the legal character of the principle of self-determination of peoples or on the essential difference in nature between this "right of peoples" and human rights has been already been overcome. For contemporary international law, the self-determination of peoples, in addition to being a principle of international law, is a right of peoples under colonial and alien domination and a condition or prerequisite for the existence and enjoyment of all the other rights and freedoms of the individual.[43]

Once the Special Rapporteur had decided that self-determination is a fundamental right of peoples under colonial and alien domination, he observed that, to enjoy their rights as peoples, they must be free from alien domination:

> Decolonization is the best guarantee that what remains to be done in this area can be done. . . . the last stage in the history of decolonization needs to be properly planned . . . to be completed should be as rapid, effective and radical as it ought to be and should remain consistent with respect for human rights and for the principles of international law laid down in the Charter of the United Nations.[44]

Espiell concluded that self-determination is a legal principle for the liberation of colonized peoples. He believed that the UN has a positive duty to states to support this goal.

As noted, the two 1976 Covenants contain identical language in Article 1 of each treaty: "All peoples have a right to self-determination."[45] It is a significant inclusion because both of the Covenants relate to the protection of individuals rather than "Peoples":

> The provision in Art. 1 of both Covenants is however important because for the first time this right has been formulated within a universal document concerning human rights, ie. a universal instrument which recognizes the legal beginning of both Covenants (and not within the list of other human rights) and is an indication that this right was considered as a prerequisite for the realization of all other human rights.[46]

Espiell's conclusion that minorities are not "Peoples" was further emphasized in the International Covenant on Civil and Political Rights (ICCPR), which contains a separate article for the rights of members of minorities, Article 27.[47] The final wording of Article 27 was thought to be a substantially weaker in two regards. "First, the right was vested in individuals, not groups, and second, it imposed a purely passive obligation on States."[48] The attempts by the United Nations to protect minorities in this Covenant was at best:

> the minimalist version of minority rights. Minority rights are not promoted by such a provision (Article 27). Minorities are not given special economic, social or political advantages, nor its their position made secure against majority culture, language, or religion.[49]

The difficulty presented by Article 27 for its implementation was the lack of a definition of a minority. This omission led to another study, this one on the scope of Article 27.

Capotorti Study

Special Rapporteur Francesco Capotorti commenced a study for the Sub-commission on Article 27 of the ICCPR, as "the first internationally accepted rule for the protection of minorities."[50] Capotorti's study points out the confusion of principles relating to protecting minorities. He was unable to come to any final resolution of the issues. In the end, he chose to recommend that the Sub-commission consider drafting a Declaration on the rights of minorities. In spite of his recommendation, there was very little activity until 1992. Then, the General Assembly adopted a resolution setting out the rights of minorities–forty-six years after the founding of the United Nations. The resolution was adopted without the inclusion of a definition of a minority group.[51] Capotorti did propose a definition of minority,[52] but it was never adopted by the Sub-commission. There was no mention of a right of self-determination in his definition, agreeing implicitly with the conclusion reached by Espiell's study. In spite of the very general nature of the proposed definition, no action was taken to adopt it. Rather than act on Capotorti's proposed definition, the Sub-commission wanted to be more certain and so undertook another study of the issue.

Deschenes Study

In 1985, a Canadian expert, Mr. Justice Jules Deschenes was asked by the Sub-commission to submit a report on the definition of minorities.[53] In his report submitted on 14 May 1985, Mr. Justice Deschenes attempted his own definition of "minority" as follows:

> A group of citizens of a State, constituting a numerical minority and in a non-dominant position in that State, endowed with ethnic, religious or linguistic characteristics which differ from those of the majority of the population, having a sense of solidarity with one another, motivated, if only implicitly, by a collective will to survive and whose aim is to achieve equality with the majority in fact and in law.[54]

There are similarities between the working definitions of Capotorti and Deschenes. Both Special Rapporteurs refer to minorities in relation to the majority population within a state. A numerical consideration is integral to the definition. In addition, both refer to the ethnic, religious and linguistic discreteness of the groups within the state. Both also infer that members of minority groups desire to maintain their sense of solidarity with one another.

In his report, Mr. Justice Deschenes examined the work of another Special Rapporteur, Martinez Cobo (discussed in Chapter 2). The Cobo and Deschenes studies for the Sub-commission were conducted in the same period. Cobo's working definition of Indigenous Peoples was:

> Indigenous communities, peoples and nations are those which, having a historical continuity with pre-invasion and pre-colonial societies that developed on their territories, consider themselves distinct from other sectors of the societies now prevailing on those territories, or part of them. They form at present non-dominant sectors of society and are determined to preserve, develop and transmit to future generations their ancestral territories, and their ethnic identity, as the basis of their continued existence as peoples, in accordance with their own cultural patterns, social institutions and legal system.[55]

Differences between Cobo's definition of Indigenous Peoples and the Capotortis' and the Deschenes' definitions of minorities are interesting. In the proposed definitions of minorities, the points of distinction separating the group from the surrounding society include ethnic, religious or linguistic characteristics. They do not include minority political rights nor their historical continuity to a territory and there is an unspoken assumption that minorities can exist without a tie to the territory. Mr. Justice Deschenes concludes:

> This text [Cobo's] contains elements which are characteristic, if not of all minorities, at least of some of them, such as historical conti-

nuity, distinction from other sectors of society, non-dominant situation, and determination to preserve distinctive characteristics. Firstly, however, these do not apply to all minorities. Secondly, a number of other typical characteristics are lacking, such as the numerical situation and reference to citizenship, to name only two. . . . It does not appear that the description of Indigenous populations proposed by Mr. Martinez Cobo can be used as a basis for a general definition of minorities.[56]

Mr. Justice Deschenes rejected including Peoples and minorities within the same definition. The fact that the Rapporteur felt the need to address the issue implies that there had been discussions on merging the two groups under one definition that could reflect a single reality.

Finally, Mr. Justice Deschenes refers to the state practice on the issue. He looks to the Norwegian government's Foreign Affairs Minister who in 1978 said of the proposed Declaration on the rights of minorities, which was before the Sub-commission:

It would seem appropriate to widen the scope of the declaration to include indigenous peoples as a separate category and pay attention to their specific needs and rights. Indigenous peoples do not necessarily constitute minorities and their situation is in many respects different from that of national, ethnic, religious and linguistic minorities.[57]

Then, Mr. Justice Deschenes refers to the Canadian situation for guidance and concluded that Canada recognizes the differences between Indigenous Peoples and minorities as evident from the treatment of the two groups in the Constitution Act of Canada:[58]

Moreover, the soundness of this conclusion is borne out by recent Canadian history. Under the major constitutional amendments of 1982, minorities and indigenous populations, far from being amalgamated, were treated separately, and the text makes it quite clear that they should not be considered jointly. Articles 15, 16, 23 and 29, for example, of the 1982 Act concern minorities, whereas articles 25, 35 and 37 relate to indigenous populations. The same is true of the first amendments of the new constitution proclaimed on 31 May 1984, which relate only to indigenous populations. . . . The unavoidable conclusion is that the definition which we seek should not attempt to deal with the question of indigenous populations.[59]

Deschenes concluded that the United Nations should avoid putting

Indigenous Peoples and minorities into the same definition.

The 1985 Deschenes report was supported further by subsequent events within[60] and outside the United Nations. On United Nations Day in 1991, the Home Rule Parliament of Greenland adopted a resolution making the distinction between Indigenous Peoples and minorities, stating how important it is:

> that the world's indigenous peoples have fundamental human rights of a collective and individual nature. Indigenous peoples are not, and do not consider themselves, minorities. The rights of indigenous peoples are derived from their own history, culture, traditions, laws, and special relationship to their lands, resources and environment. Their basic rights must be addressed within their values and perspectives.[61]

Mr. Justice Deschenes' study concurs, stating that the rights of Indigenous Peoples are rooted in their history, culture, traditions, laws and special relationship they have with their lands, resources and environment. These attributes are not ascribed to minorities in any of the studies undertaken by the UN.

In 1992, a General Assembly resolution did recognize rights extending to ethnic, religious and linguistic minorities, but as rights given to individuals not to collectives.[62] Under Article 9,[63] the Declaration on Minorities made room for the UN system to contribute to the full realization of rights for minorities. The Centre on Human Rights in Geneva hired staff to implement the Declaration, but they ran into difficulties. Because there was no definition for minorities within the Declaration, the staff could not identify the groups covered by the Declaration. A need arose to clarify the application of the Declaration. To this end, the Sub-commission, through Resolution 1994/115 of 26 August 1994, called for the establishment of a Working Group "to examine, *inter alia*, peaceful and constructive solutions to situation involving minorities."[64] This new Working Group will exist side-by-side with the Working Group on Indigenous Peoples ensuring clearer distinctions between their mandates and participants.

The UN is implementing Espiell's and Mr. Justice Deschenes's conclusions that minorities and Indigenous Peoples are dissimilar, with different rights under international law.

The studies undertaken by the Special Rapporteurs have clarified the issues of "Peoples," "self-determination" and "minorities." Because of the studies, the UN has been able undertake specific action towards carrying out the goals outlined in the Charter.

Indigenous Peoples at the UN

Article 1 of each of the UN Human Rights Covenants recognizes that all peoples have the right of self-determination. A fundamental difficulty, however, relates to the conflict between the state and peoples:

> First of all, it should be recalled that international law is essentially framed by States. They are still the main authors of international legislation. . . . [States] are reluctant to give their approval to new rules which might threaten their existence.
>
> A second consideration . . . . In spite of all their possible shortcomings, States generally protect law and order and ensure peaceful coexistence among the human beings subject to their jurisdiction.[65]

The International Covenant on Civil and Political Rights recognized that some human rights contain limitations on the rights of individuals within the state's jurisdiction, in order "to protect national security, public order (*ordre public*), public health or morals, or the rights and freedoms of others."[66] But, in acceptance and ratification of this Covenant, there are many obligations of states, for example, to respect human rights at the domestic level under Article 2(1), and to submit periodic reports on the Covenant's implementation as part of a process established to monitor state compliance. Part IV of the Covenant established a Human Rights Committee[67] (the Committee) with a twofold mandate.[68] The reports placed before the Committee are subject to review with representatives of the state present to answer questions. The Committee also oversees private communications made under the First Optional Protocol[69] (considered below). Under the preamble of the First Optional Protocol, the Committee has the competence to consider communications from "individuals claiming to be victims of violations of the rights set forth in the Covenant."[70] In order for the Committee to consider communications, the relevant state must have signed the First Optional Protocol to the Covenant, a voluntary move by that state.

First Optional Protocol

When a state ratifies the International Covenant Civil and Political Rights, it can also become a contracting party to the separate First Optional Protocol. In 1976, Canada ratified the First Optional Protocol which entered into force that year. Indigenous Peoples in Canada at once began to use it to take actions against Canada by sending communications to the Committee. The Committee has authority to receive complaints only from individuals and not from a collective group.[71] The question of who is covered by communications alleging breaches by the state of Article 1 or Article 27 has been raised before the Committee. In addition, the Committee's communication on the merits of a case is not legally binding on the state but has persuasive value only.

In three cases[72] taken by Indigenous Peoples from Canada, the Committee has refused to consider them under Article 1; instead, the Committee has used Article 27 to review the merits of each communication, implying that the Peoples are minorities.[73]

One of these cases, brought by Chief Bernard Ominayak on behalf of the Lubicon Cree, is a good example of the inability of the Committee, the ICCPR and the First Optional Protocol to address issues on the collective rights of Indigenous Peoples. In the *Lubicon* case,[74] the Chief used the procedure set out under the First Optional Protocol to communicate to the Committee that Canada was violating Lubicon rights under Article 1 of the ICCPR. The Committee held that collectives could not petition the Committee since only individual rights complaints were acceptable to the Committee. In response to the communication brought by Chief Ominayak, the Committee wrote:

> With regard to the States party's contention that the author's communication pertaining to self-determination should be declared inadmissible because the Committee's jurisdiction, as defined by the Optional Protocol, cannot be invoked by an individual when the alleged violation concerns a 'collective right', the Committee reaffirms that the Covenant recognizes and protects in most resolute terms a people's right of self-determination and its right to dispose of its natural resources, as an essential condition for the effective guarantee and observance of individual human rights and for the promotion and strengthening of those rights. However, the Committee observes (as it has already done with regard to communication no. 197/1985) that the author, as an individual, cannot claim under the Optional Protocol to be a victim of a violation of the right of self-determination enshrined in Article 1 of the covenant, which deals with rights conferred upon peoples, as such.[75]

The Chief, as an individual, could not make a claim that Article 1 of ICCPR was being violated. In spite of the wording of the First Optional Protocol and Article 1, the Committee reviewed the case under Article 27.

In another communication from Indigenous Peoples from Canada, *A.D. v. Canada*[76] claimed that their right to self-determination was denied by the state of Canada. The Committee decided that the communication was inadmissible as the author could not prove "that he was authorized to act as a representative on behalf of the Mikmaq tribal society and had failed to support his claim that he personally was a victim of a violation of any rights contained in the Covenant."[77] These two Canadian cases demonstrate that the Committee is only prepared to consider cases related to individual rights rather than to the collective rights of Peoples set out in the Covenant's Article 1.[78]

While the Covenant recognizes and protects a peoples' right of self-determination and its right to dispose of its natural resources, as an essential condition for the effective guarantee and observance of human rights and for the promotion and strengthening of those rights, it has not been extended to cover the rights of Indigenous Peoples. In the *Lubicon* case, the Committee observed that the author, as an individual, could not claim under the Optional Protocol that the collective right Lubicon to self-determination was being violated. Rather, the Committee used Article 27 that deals with the rights of individuals members of minorities to determine the scope and extent of the alleged violation of the Lubicon Peoples' rights under the ICCPR:

> The Committee has not attempted to define or establish criteria for a 'people' under the article 40 reporting procedure or in its general comment on article 40. Moreover, in its final view in *Lubicon Lake Band v. Canada* the HRC [sic] stated that "the question whether the Lubicon Lake Band constitutes a 'people' is not an issue for the Committee to address under the OP [sic] to the 'Covenant'." The decisions in the Lubicon Lake Case effectively take the right of self-determination out of the OP [sic] system.[79]

While the Committee was unable to provide a remedy for the Lubicon's collective rights, the remedy would only be a non-legally binding communication or statement. The *Lubicon* case continues to be examined by the Committee. The Committee appointed a Special Rapporteur[80] to provide periodic reports on the Lubicon situation and Canada's behaviour to the Committee for their review. This is not an adequate solution to the situation but at least the case remains an active complaint before the Committee:

> The very concept of self-determination remains a controversial one. The central difficulties of reconciling the right of self-determination with the preservation of the 'territorial integrity' of the State, of identifying the beneficiaries and content of the right, and the consequences of the international recognition of the right of self-determination in terms of international support remain. The practice of the HRC [sic] to date has done little or nothing to shed

light on these fundamental problems and appears unlikely to do so.[81]

The Committee cannot act when the alleged violation is of a "collective right." So far, the Committee has not found a way for Peoples alleging a violation of the right of self-determination to obtain a remedy under the First Optional Protocol.[82]

International Court Cases

The International Court of Justice (ICJ) in two significant cases in the early 1970s opened the issue of colonized peoples and their rights under international law. The first case before the International Court of Justice was the *Namibia* Advisory Opinion.[83] The second case to come before the ICJ related directly to the right of self-determination and the rights of peoples. In the *Western Sahara* Advisory Opinion,[84] the General Assembly had requested an advisory opinion concerning the status of the Peoples and territory known as the *Western Sahara*. Many key elements related to peoples and their rights under international law were addressed within the opinion, including the position of peoples in relation to their territories. The principle that colonial and other formerly dependent peoples have a right to self-determination is sufficiently well established so that the ICJ could accept it as part of international law. The ICJ defined the right of self-determination as a need to require "a free and genuine expression of the will of the peoples concerned."[85] Thus, the Court has issued opinions that recognize the rights of peoples to freely determine their own political future and, clearly, the judgments have implications for Indigenous Peoples beyond those in *Namibia* and the *Western Sahara*.[86] While the ICJ is not recognized as a source of international law, the judgments are capable of acquiring moral suasion throughout the international community by their own intrinsic authority. (See Chapter 2 for further discussion of these ICJ decisions). As the ICJ was making its way through the complex histories of Southwest Africa and the Western Sahara, the UN was moving on the rights of Indigenous Peoples worldwide.

Defining Indigenous Peoples and Rights

Since the inception of the United Nations, there have been some attempts to identify who Indigenous Peoples are. The Human Rights Committee has not provided a definition for "Peoples," although the Sub-commission attempted to deal with the issue early in the history of the UN only to be met by resistance by the state governments, particularly the United

States of America. In 1970, Special Rapporteur, Martinez Cobo of Ecuador studied the problems of discrimination against Indigenous Peoples. Over the next twelve years, periodic reports were made to the members of the Sub-commission.

Cobo's Study

Cobo prepared a working model of identification of the subject area, the key provisions of which bear recall: Cobo identified Indigenous communities, Peoples and nations as having political organization and a historical continuity with pre-invasion and pre-colonial societies on their territories. In the final report, Cobo put forward some key aspects in the description of Indigenous Peoples:

(a) Indigenous peoples must be recognized according to their own perception and conception of themselves in relation to other groups coexisting with them in the fabric of the same society;

(b) There must be no attempt to define them according to the perception of others through the values of foreign societies or of the dominant sections in such societies;

(c) The right of indigenous peoples to define what and who is indigenous, and the correlative, the right to determine what and who is not, must be recognized;

(d) The power of indigenous peoples to determine who are their members must not be interfered with by the State concerned, through legislation, regulations or any other means;

(e) Artificial, arbitrary or manipulatory definitions must be rejected;

(f) The special position of indigenous peoples within the society of nation-States existing today derives from their historical rights to their lands and from their rights to be different and to be considered as different.[87]

The key points of this framework relate to the ability of Indigenous Peoples to identify themselves according to their own perceptions, including the right to remain free of imposed definitions. If a state is going to recognize the rights of Indigenous Peoples, then having the state define who are Indigenous Peoples, and thus who is entitled to corresponding rights, would be a fundamental violation of their rights as Peoples. Finally, Cobo included the recognition of the Peoples' historical rights to their lands and territories in the definition, and their right to be different and to be considered different:

This historical continuity may consist of the continuation, for an extended period reaching into the present, of one or more of the following factors:

(a) Occupation of ancestral lands, or at least of part of them;
(b) Common ancestry with the original occupants of these lands;
(c) Culture, in general, or in specific manifestations (such as religion, living under a tribal system, membership of an indigenous community, dress, means of livelihood, lifestyle, etc.);
(d) Language (whether used as the only language, as mother-tongue, as the habitual means of communication at home or in the family, or as the main, preferred, habitual, general or normal language);
(e) Residence in certain parts of the country, or in certain regions of the world;
(f) Other relevant factors.

On an individual basis, an indigenous person is one who belongs to these indigenous populations through self-identification as indigenous (group consciousness) and is recognized and accepted by these populations as one of its members (acceptance by the group).

This preserves for these communities the sovereign right and power to decide who belongs to the group, without external interference.[88]

Who are Indigenous Peoples? The answer to this question has been obscured by centuries of definitions imposed on Indigenous Peoples by their colonizer states. They are the descendants of peoples occupying a territory when the colonizers arrived. Since the colonizers occupied Indigenous territory without their consent Indigenous Peoples are free to exercise their right of self-determination including the right to decolonize themselves.

ILO Convention 169

Between 1985 and 1988, the ILO undertook a process for revising Convention 107, resulting in Convention 169.[89] In 1985, the Governing Body of the ILO decided to hold a meeting of experts to advise it on the revision of Convention No. 107.[90] This meeting, held in 1986, and its report recommended:[91] "The Director-General is of the view that, in the light of the report of the meeting, the technical item proposed for the Conference agenda should henceforth be entitled `Partial Revision of the Indigenous and Tribal Populations Convention, 1957 (No. 107)'."[92] Two technical reviews of Convention 107 were held in 1988 and 1989. Due to the structure of the technical review, only NGO's accredited by the ILO were allowed to be observers at the meetings. Article 12 of the Constitution of the ILO allows for limited accreditation of NGO's to "international organizations, including international organizations of employers, workers, agriculturists and cooperators". The ILO arrangement meant that participation by Indigenous Peoples would differ from their participation at the UN Working Group on Indigenous Peoples. This participation was not accepted within the ILO as a UN specialized agency even for its revision process of a Convention about Indigenous Peoples:

> As a result of negotiations between the Office and the Committee chairperson and vice-chairpersons, each Indigenous organization with ILO accreditation was permitted to address the committee for 10 minutes following the close of business on the second day of actual deliberations. In addition, the organizations collectively were granted one 10 minute presentation for each category of articles placed before the committee. Aside from these few brief speeches, Indigenous representatives had no direct input into the process. The Indigenous NGO's had no involvement at all in the debates and deliberations of the committee during its article by article consideration of the Office text.[93]

The result was that Indigenous observers[94] could only watch as the rights of their Peoples were discussed. Indigenous Peoples were again being viewed as objects rather than as subjects of international law norms.

Indigenous Peoples argued that their rights are based on a principle of collective rights: the rights to land, government, laws and self-determination have collective application to a people. These collective rights function contrary to Eurocentric notions of individual rights that protect the rights of the individual over those of the collective. However, this is not always the case, as there are collective rights that states have promoted to protect themselves, for instance: enacting legislation for the "public good" protects a collective right of the state. Nevertheless, it has been a consistent challenge for Indigenous Peoples to promote their collective rights within the international community.

For Indigenous Peoples, the revision of Convention ILO 107 was frustrating. The ILO is set up on a tripartite basis, (discussed in Chapter 2) allowing representation by state, employer and employee delegates, but it does not allow for extensive participation by Indigenous delegates. Within the Working Group on Indigenous Peoples, Indigenous representatives can speak in their own right without being part of an NGO. However, the ILO was not structured similarly. As a result, the ILO revision took place without direct Indigenous involvement, and the definition of Indigenous Peoples was altered to limit the scope and application of the Convention. Indigenous Peoples had no way to change the minds of the state representatives in the ILO tripartite process. By contrast, Indigenous Peoples have been directly involved in the drafting of the Declaration on the Rights of Indigenous Peoples, as addressed in Chapters 4 and 5.

The ILO revision process was an important learning strategy for Indigenous representatives. The process showed how critical it was to maintain full participation of Indigenous representation in the procedures when their rights were being discussed. The lessons learned by Indigenous representatives in the ILO revision process proved useful during the debate on the Draft Declaration within the Working Group at the Sub-commission and at the Commission on Human Rights Open-ended Inter-sessional Working Group.[95] It is indeed ironic that a cornerstone of the revision process was "Consultation and Participation."

Despite the lack of Indigenous participation in the revision process, the ILO included measures that state governments must take in consulting with Indigenous Peoples in Article 6 of Convention 169.[96] This Article mandates and requires state governments who ratify the revised Convention to consult the Indigenous Peoples concerned whenever legislative or administrative measures may affect them. Thus, in a major revision to a Convention affecting Indigenous Peoples, the ILO continue to treat Indigenous Peoples as objects rather than subjects of international law.

Despite the considerable work elsewhere in the UN to meet the Charter commitments regarding self-determination, the ILO resisted. In the 1988 VI(2) Report of the Experts on the revision, the ILO noted:

> The majority of indigenous organizations from which information is available feel that the terms "consultation" and "participation" are inadequate; these terms were largely rejected by the indigenous and tribal representatives at the 1986 Meeting of Experts. They state that they should be more emphasis on the right of these peoples to "determine" and "control" their own affairs, and that economic and social self-determination should be the basic orientation of the revision.[97]

Four sections of the revised Convention caused difficulties for the Indigenous delegates: the use of the term "Peoples," land rights, resource rights and the right of self-determination. The issues of identification of peoples and self-determination are tied together, affecting land and resource rights. In Convention 107, there was no reference to "Peoples"; rather the original Convention applied to "populations." Under international law, "populations" are not defined in any instrument. "Populations" do not have rights under the Human Rights Covenants nor under the Charter of the United Nations; only "Peoples" have rights. In fact, the only international legal instrument in which "populations" have a legal definition or rights is the 1957 ILO Convention 107—the same instrument that promoted the assimilation and integration of Indigenous populations into the mainstream society of colonial states. During the discussion of the revision, the Inuit Circumpolar Conference representative made the following submission during the discussion on "population" *versus* "Peoples":

> (i) Indigenous and tribal peoples are distinct societies that must be referred to in a precise and acceptable manner. ICC (Canada) and other Indigenous NGOs find the term "populations" to be both demeaning and inaccurate in the present context. It is not how we as Indigenous Peoples describe ourselves.
>
> (ii) continued use of the term "populations" would unfairly deny us our true status and identity as indigenous peoples. Whether intentional or not, such action is contrary to the basic objectives of the ILO revision process;
>
> (iii) unless indigenous peoples are rightfully described as "peoples", the revised Convention 107 will lack credibility with the very peoples it is intended to benefit. The revised Convention will be unacceptable; and
>
> (iv) in light of the above reasons, use of the term "populations" would not promote social justice for indigenous peoples. In this way, it would fail to advance the fundamental aims and purposes of the ILO as set in the Declaration of Philadelphia (1944).
>
> Finally, we note that the League of Nations described all non-self-governing groups as "indigenous peoples," but in 1948 the United Nations began, under Latin American pressure, to distinguish between colonized "peoples" of Africa and Asia, and "indigenous (or Aboriginal) populations" in the Americas. This terminology reflected a policy distinction of liberating peoples and assimilating populations, which should no longer be applicable. "Peoples"should therefore be adopted in the revised Convention. [98]

Indigenous Peoples were promoting the use of "Peoples" rather than populations. The Report of the Experts[99] who reviewed Convention 107 noted that "the continued use of the term 'population' would unfairly deny them their true status and identity as indigenous peoples."[100] Indigenous Peoples, the UN Centre for Human Rights[101] and the Committee of Experts of the ILO wanted the language changed to reflect the reality of Indigenous Peoples. A last-minute amendment was made to limit the application of the term "peoples" in Convention 169 in Article 1(3):

> The use of the term "peoples" in this Convention shall not be construed as having any implications as regards the rights which may attach to the term under international law.[102]

Government delegates were opposed to the use of the term "Peoples":

> State governments resist the term "peoples" because of its association with the term "self-determination" (ie. all Peoples have the right to self-determination) which in turn is associated with a right of independent statehood for overseas colonial territories. Indigenous peoples invoke a right of "self-determination" as an expression of their desire to continue as distinct communities free from oppression but in virtually all instances deny aspiration to independent statehood.[103]

In the end there was a compromise among the delegates on the drafting of the revision. "Peoples" replaced "population" in Convention 169 but with a limitation placed on its use. It seems doubtful that in light of other international instruments—such as the Human Rights Covenants—and decisions taken by the ICJ on the term "Peoples," the ILO can include a binding clause limiting the right attaching to the term in a fundamental manner by defining an international law principle.[104]

By July 1996, Convention 169 has been ratified by only ten countries.[105] Canada is not one of the ten. ILO Convention 169 requires the ratification of only two states for it to enter into force. State governments pushed the revision of Convention 107 when Indigenous Peoples wanted the Convention to be struck from the books. In the revision process, Indigenous Peoples were excluded from direct participation in the process. The entry into force of Convention 169 in only ten countries has been a result of lobbying by Indigenous Peoples against the Convention. The ILO has tried to promote the Convention as a leader in setting international legal standards but has failed to convince Indigenous Peoples and other academic writers of the merits of Convention 169.[106]

Working Group's Draft Declaration

Cobo's study was overtaken by events outside the Sub-commission. Two significant conferences on the rights of Indigenous Peoples in the Americas were held in Geneva, Switzerland in 1977[107] and 1981.[108] The conferences were convened by non-governmental organizations to put pressure on the UN to take action to protect the rights of Indigenous Peoples. Because of these conferences, the Sub-commission decided in 1981—without waiting for Cobo's final report—to recommend the establishment of a Working Group on Indigenous Peoples.[109]

The resolution establishing the Working Group in 1982 contained no definition of Indigenous Peoples. But the resolution did direct the Working Group to consider Cobo's recommendations. Cobo's final report was accepted and endorsed by the Sub-commission, the Commission on Human Rights and the Economic and Social Council. It could be argued that a working definition of Indigenous Peoples—Cobo's—has been accepted by the UN system.

The members of the Working Group represent states that are UN members. At the outset of the Working Group process some countries tried to adopt a definition without success:

> Countries that sought to undermine the drafting of the declaration on indigenous peoples' rights insisted on adopting a definition of indigenous peoples first. When this proved to be extremely difficult, these countries suggested an indefinite postponement of any work on the substance of the declaration. Yet the United Nations in its forty-five year-old history has not defined "minorities" nor "peoples" and this lack of definition was not crucial for its failures or successes in those domains.[110]

The major piece of work issued by this Working Group, the Draft Declaration on the Rights of Indigenous Peoples,[111] does not contain a definition of Indigenous Peoples. Article 8 of the Draft Declaration specifically recognizes that: "Indigenous Peoples have the collective and individual right to maintain and develop their distinct identities and characteristics, including the right to identify themselves as indigenous and to be recognized as such."[112] Draft Article 9 further clarifies the collective and individual rights of Indigenous Peoples:

> Indigenous peoples and individuals have the right to belong to an indigenous community or nation, in accordance with the traditions and customs of the community or nation concerned. No disadvantage of any kind may arise from the exercise of such a right.[113]

Clearly, the idea that Indigenous Peoples can decide their own identity as individuals and within the community or their group has strong acceptance. The Draft Declaration Articles, taken with draft Article 3 that sets out that Indigenous Peoples have the right to self-determination, are a strong indication that the definition must come, not from the UN member states, but from the Indigenous Peoples themselves. If a definition is imposed by state governments, then the rights of Indigenous Peoples will not be fully recognized. The debate on definition is far from over. When the Draft Declaration came before the Commission on Human Rights in the winter of 1995, the Commission tried to avoid accepting the Draft as presented. Instead, it decided to establish an Open-ended Inter-sessional Working Group to elaborate the Draft further.[114]

Indigenous Peoples have a unique historical circumstance that brings them to international forums to regain their status in international law. Indigenous Peoples are denied their international legal personality because colonizing states have suppressed it.[115] Indigenous Peoples are pushing for recognition as peoples to correct the historical and legal records:

> It will be very difficult for them [states] to contend that indigenous peoples are not peoples and as a result they would not be entitled to self-determination. The criticism of arbitrariness and double standards would definitely undermine such an argument. . . . It seems in any case that the debate over self-determination can hardly be based on whether indigenous peoples are peoples, because they clearly fulfil the generally accepted preconditions of peoples.[116]

Conclusion

The United Nations was formed to promote the principle of equal rights and self-determination of peoples. While the UN Charter did not mention the rights of minorities, there have been UN initiatives to identify and protect them. Considerable effort has contributed to clarifying the meaning of the Charter, especially concerning the rights of peoples. Early attempts to include Indigenous Peoples within the Charter principles were met with direct opposition by UN members that are colonizer states.

Why are "Peoples" recognized as having rights, but by placing "Indigenous" before "Peoples" any recognized rights are negated? It is the same argument by which Indigenous Nations were recognized as having an international capacity to enter into treaties to allow for settlement of their lands. Once settlement was achieved, the international capacity was discounted. The principle laid down with the Papal Bulls continues to dominate the international law agenda despite the ICJ's decisions in the *Western Sahara* and the *East Timor* cases. In the *Western Sahara* Advisory Opinion, the ICJ decided that no lands of Indigenous Peoples could be claimed by European sovereigns under any theories of *terra nullius*, discovery or conquest. The ICJ reviewed the application of the principle of self-determination of Non-Self-Governing Peoples who have a right of self-determination under international law. Peoples have the right of self-determination.

The studies by Cristescu, Espiell, Capotorti and Deschenes were authorized by the Sub-commission on Prevention of Discrimination and Protection of Minorities on issues related to self-determination and peoples. Through all the studies a link was recognized between peoples and the exercise of self-determination. Peoples who are living under colonial or alien domination have a right to self-determination; this is the conclusion of the UN's Special Rapporteur, Espiell. Indigenous Peoples live under colonial and alien domination with a discrete historical link with their territory, their history and their governmental structures. Thus, Indigenous Peoples ought to have the right to decolonize themselves and enjoy self-determination.

While the UN has been unable to determine definite definitions for "self-determination," "Peoples" and "nations," the member states have developed guidelines for their application. The scope of "friendly relations" in Article 1(2) of the Charter has been deemed to mean non-interference in the internal affairs of the state. Indigenous Peoples continue to address the UN to work with the Charter and the obligations of the member states in an attempt to implement the principles of self-determination.

The ILO is a specialized agency of the United Nations with obligations to implement the provisions of the Charter. However, the ILO adopted Convention 169 with a disclaimer clause relating to the rights of Indigenous Peoples in international law. The UN Charter provides in Articles 2 and 55 the right of "self-determination of peoples" without any limitation. There is no international precedent which permits a specialized agency to have a disclaimer clause which would amend and/or limit the application of the UN Charter. Is such a disclaimer clause binding on member states of the ILO? With ratification by only ten states, it does not appear to have universal acceptance or application.

In 1992, the General Assembly passed resolution 47/135, accepting the Draft Declaration on Minorities. As the UN struggled to put in place the working mechanisms for implementation of this Declaration, there was still no working definition of "minority". The definition proposed by Mr. Justice Jules Deschenes was rejected by his fellow experts on the Sub-commission and was not received warmly by the parent body that had requested his work. Deschenes' definition really pointed the way for the minorities who have and exercise the rights accessible to most of the population within a state.

The aim of Indigenous Peoples is not to be assimilated into the state that has colonized and dispossessed them, but to persist as Indigenous Peoples within their territories. It is generally held that the main difference between peoples and minorities is that the former has the right of self-determination and the latter do not. The difficulty for Indigenous Peoples has been to obtain the rights which have been applied and accepted as rights of Peoples, that is, to add "Indigenous" to "Peoples." The long and difficult debate on peoples and minorities has clarified that Indigenous Peoples are not minorities under international law. The evolving Draft Declaration is striving to incorporate the right of self-determination for Indigenous Peoples into an international instrument. It is the right under which the historical wrongs committed through the colonization process may be redressed. The struggle is far from over.

Footnotes:

1. Dalee Sambo, an Inuit scholar from Alaska recently wrote: "Indigenous peoples feel that an individual rights orientation would be assimilationist and contrary to the basic objectives of standard-setting processes, namely to promote the integrity of indigenous communities and societies through the full exercise and enjoyment of their fundamental human rights. Without explicit and clear recognition of collective rights, indigenous societies and cultures would remain unnecessarily exposed to deterioration, if not possible, destruction, by outside forces" "Indigenous Peoples and International Standard-Setting Processes: Are States Governments Listening?" (1993) 3 *Transnational Law & Comparative Problems* at 22-23.

2. Carol Weisbrod, "Minorities and Diversities: The 'Remarkable Experiment' of the League of Nations," [1993] 8 *Connecticut Journal of International Law* at 366-367.

3. Ibid. at 370.

4. "From the constitutional standpoint the League had several defects. . . . [including] the unanimity rule, inherited from the traditional diplomatic conference, proved a severe hinderance and the Assembly's move towards simple majority was a clear recognition of this." D.W. Bowett, *The Law of International Institutions* (London: Stevens & Sons, 1982) at 20 [hereinafter Bowett, *International Institutions*].

5. "Indigenous and Other Tribal and Semi-Tribal Populations in Independent Countries", ILO, 40th Sess. No. 107, 328 U.N.T.S. 247 (1959) [hereinafter ILO Convention No. 107] 6. Ibid. Article 2(1).

7. Ibid. Article 6: The improvement of the conditions of life and work and level of education of the population concerned shall be given high priority in plans for the over-all economic development of areas inhabited by these populations. Special projects for economic development of areas in question shall be so designed as to promote such improvement.

8. "This Convention explicitly provided the aim to assimilate indigenous populations into states on an equal basis with other inhabitants": Catherine J. Iorns, "Indigenous Peoples and Self-Determination: Challenging State Sovereignty," (1992) 24 *Case Western Journal of International Law* at 201 [hereinafter Iorns].

9. ILO Convention 107, *supra* note 5 Article 1: "(a) members of tribal or semi-tribal popula-

tions in independent countries whose social and economic conditions are at a less advanced stage than the stage reached by other sectors of the national community, and whose status is regulated wholly and partially by their own customs or traditions or by special laws or regulations; (b) members of tribal or semi-tribal populations in independent countries which are regarded as indigenous on account of their descent from the populations belongs, at the time of conquest or colonisation and which, irrespective of their legal status, live more in conformity with the social, economic and cultural institutions of that time than with the institutions of the nation to which they belong. 2. For the purposes of this Convention, the term "semi-tribal" includes groups and persons who, although they are in the process of losing their tribal characteristics, are not yet integrated into the national community. 3. The indigenous and other tribal or semi-tribal populations mentioned in paragraphs 1 and 2 of this article are referred to hereinafter as 'the populations concerned.'"

10. Howard Berman, "The International Labour Organisation and Indigenous Peoples: Revision of ILO Convention No. 107 at the 75th Session of the International Labour Conference, 1988", (1988) 41 International Commission of Jurists—The Review at 48 [hereinafter Berman, ILO *Revision*].

11. ILO Convention 107, *supra* note 5 Article 22(1): "Education programmes for the populations concerned shall be adapted, as regards methods and techniques, to the stage these populations have reached in the process of social, economic and cultural integration into the national community."

12. "Although directed integration of the kind contemplated by Convention 107, was viewed as progressive in the 1940s and 50s, in the context of indigenous peoples it is readily apparent that state programmes of this nature have been a dead letter for many years. Indigenous peoples and human rights NGO's have avoided attempting to utilize the restricted through excellent review of procedures of the ILO for fear of giving any credibility to the substantive provisions and general orientation of the instrument" (Berman, ILO *Revision, supra* note 10 at 49).

13. Lee Swepston and Roger Plant, "International Standards and the Protection of the Land Rights of Indigenous and Tribal Populations", (1985) 124 *International Labour Review* at 93 [hereinafter Swepston and Plant, *Standards*].

14. "Indeed, Convention 107 has been an embarrassment to the ILO. At the opening session of the revision committee . . . Mr. Aamir Ali, representing the Director General, described the philosophy of the Convention as 'repugnant' " (Berman, ILO *Revision, supra* note 10 at 49).

15. Swepston and Plant, *Standards, supra* note 13 at 92.

16. "For quite a long time (at least 20 years) after the end of the Second World War, it was thought—and stated in writing—that the question of international protection of minorities was no longer topical. The system of protection built up under the League of Nations had collapsed with the demise of that organization, and the Universal Declaration of Human Rights adopted in 1948 by the General Assembly of the United Nations did not mention the question of the treatment of persons belonging to ethnic, religious or linguistic minorities. Moreover, the emphasis placed in the international order on the imperative need to ensure respect for basic human rights seemed to imply that it was no longer necessary to protect in any special way the interests of minority groups, or, more specifically, of individuals belonging to each groups": Francesco Capotorti, Study on the Rights of Persons Belonging to Ethnic, Religious and Linguistic Minorities (New York: United Nations 1979) E/CN.4/ Sub.2/ 384/Rev. iii [hereinafter *Capotorti Study*].

17. UNGA Resolution 217A (III), U.N. Doc. A/810, 3rd Sess. The Universal Declaration is not a treaty but a resolution adopted by the GA which has no force of law. "Some lawyers have argued that the Universal Declaration of Human Rights has, over the time, become part of customary international law, or at least strong evidence of custom. Even if this is true, the Universal Declaration per se does not establish international legal obligations": Jack Donnelly, *International Human Rights* (Boulder, Col: Westview Press, 1993) at 11. The Declaration was not binding on the member states. It was not an instrument to be signed. "The Declaration was designed as its preamble indicates, to provide 'a common understanding' of all human rights and fundamental freedoms referred to in the United Nations Charter, and to serve as a common standard of achievement of all peoples and nations": Thomas Buergenthal, "International Human Rights Law and Institutions: Accomplishments and Prospects" (1988) 63 *Washington Law Review* at 8.

18. *Capotorti Study, supra* note 16 at 5 at para. 22.

19. The author went on to link the right of self-determination to peoples and nations and the limitations of the use of the terms set out in the UN Charter. He wrote: "Article 1(2) of the Charter mentioned the right of self- determination of peoples in connection with a statement that one of the purposes of the United Nations was to develop friendly relations among nations. In this regard the word 'peoples' was synonymous with 'nations' and signified a group forming a political unit within a state under the authority of a government. It would therefore not apply to dependent people": Harold S. Johnson, *Self-Determination within the Community of Nations* (Leyden: A.W. Sijthoff, 1967) at 55-56.

20. Declaration on the Granting of Independence to Colonial Countries and Peoples Resolution 1514 (XV) 14 December 1960, GA Official Records, 15th Session, Suppl. no. 16 (A/4884) at 66 [hereinafter Declaration on Decolonization].

21. Michla Pomerance, *Self-Determination in Law and Practice: The New Doctrine in the United Nations* (The Hague: Martinus Nijhoff Publishers 1982) at 15 [hereinafter Pomerance, *Self-Determination*].

22. Declaration on Decolonization, *supra* note 20.

23. Declaration on Principles of International Law concerning Friendly Relations and Co-operation among States in accordance with the Charter of the United Nations, General Assembly Resolution 2625 (XXV) of 24 October 1970 [hereinafter Declaration on Friendly Relations].

24. "Under international law any government, whatever its nature, dictatorial, democratic (western style) or military, so long as it is in effect control, is admitted in the international community. The question of determination of its nature is not raised. This is because the international community presumes (fiction) that an effective established, sovereign, independent government is a self-determined government. It is, therefore, fit to participate in international obligations. If the criterion of self-determination, in the sense of a free expression of popular choice, were applied to a dictatorial government, such a government would not be allowed to participate in international obligations and would thus be treated as unfit to take a place in the international community": R.S. Bhalla, "The Right of Self-Determination in International Law" in William Twining, ed., *Issues of Self-Determination* (Aberdeen: Aberdeen University Press, 1991) at 92.

25. UN Charter, Chapter XI is the "Declaration Regarding Non-Self-Governing Territories," while XII and XIII relate to trusteeship.

26. The drafting of these provisions in the Charter were not without controversy. Charmian

Edwards Toussaint reviewed the drafting of the Chapter as a disagreement between the colonized and the colonizer. Toussaint writes that "in reality, however, had Chapter XI not been loosely drafted it would probably have been impossible to obtain the agreement of all the participants in the San Francisco Conference to its incorporation in the Charter, leaving it with no word of concern for non-self-governing peoples. A loose and vaguely worded legal instrument tends to be an asset rather than a liability inasmuch as it is capable of development without formal amendment" in "The Colonial Controversy in the United Nations" [1956] 10 *Yearbook of World Affairs* at 171.

27. Patrick Thornberry, Self-Determination, Minorities, Human Rights: A Review of International Instruments [1989] 38 *International and Comparative Law Quarterly* 867 at 872.

28. Ibid. at 91-92.

29. "In United Nations practice, for General Assembly resolutions a 'declaration' is a formal and solemn instrument, suitable for rare occasions when principles of great and lasting importance are being enunciated such as the Declaration on Human Rights. A recommendation is less formal. Apparent from the distinction just indicated, there is probably no difference between 'recommendation' and a 'declaration' in the United Nations practice as far as strict legal principle is concerned" Hanna Bokor-Szego, *The Role of the United Nations in International Legislation* (Amsterdam: North-Holland Publishing Company, 1978) at 71.

30. International Covenant on Economic, Social and Cultural Rights (1966) 993 U.N.T.S. 3 (adopted on 16 December 1966 and entered into force on 3 January 1976) [hereinafter ICESCR] and International Covenant on Civil and Political Rights (1966) 999 U.N.T.S. 171 (adopted on 16 December 1966, entered into force 23 March 1976) [hereinafter ICCPR].

31. United Nations General Assembly resolutions 1654(XVI), 1810 (XVII), 1956 (XVII), 2105 (XX), 2189 (XXI), 2311 (XXII), 2326 (XXII), 2426 (XXIII), 2465 (XXIII), 2540 (XXIV), 2555 (XXIV), 2621 (XXV), 2704 (XXV), 2706 (XXV), 2870 (XXVI), 2908 (XXVII), 3118 (XXVII), 3163 (XXVIII), 3328 (XXIX), 3300 (XXIX), 3481 (XXX), 3482 (XXX) and 381 (XXX). Cited in: *The historical and current development of the right of self-determination on the basis of the Charter of the United Nations and other instruments adopted by United Nations organs, with particular reference to the promotion and protection of human rights and fundamental freedoms*, Aureliu Cristescu, Special Rapporteur E/CN.4/Sub.2/L.641 at 4, 8 July 1976 [hereinafter *Cristescu Study*].

32. Ibid. at 9 para 30.

33. Ibid. at 11 para 44.

34. Ibid. at 31 para 139.

35. Ibid. at 32 paras. 140 and 141.

36. See, Appendix III for a chart of the UN human right bodies and the Sub-commission's position in the hierarchy.

37. *The Right to Self-Determination Implementation of United Nations Resolutions* (New York: United Nations, 1980) E/CN.4/Sub.2/405/Rev.1 [hereinafter *Espiell Study*]. A resolution adopted by the Commission on Human Rights on 20 February 1974 set out the mandate of the study which took six years to complete: "The General Assembly considering resolution VIII of the International Conference on Human Rights (Teheran, 1968), emphasized the importance of the universal realization of the rights of peoples to self-determination and of the speedy granting of independence to colonial countries and peoples for the effective guarantee and observance of human rights. . . . [The] General Assembly deemed it neces-

sary to continue the study of ways and means of ensuring international respect for the rights of peoples to self-determination" (at 1 at para. 2).

38. Ibid. at 9 at para. 56.

39. Ibid. at 14 at paras. 90-91.

40. ICCPR and ICESCR, *supra* at note 30.

41. ICCPR, *supra* at note 30, Article 1.

42. ICCPR , *supra* at note 30, Article 27: 'In those States which ethnic, religious or linguistic minorities exist, persons belonging to such minorities shall not be denied the right, in community with the other members of their group, to enjoy their own culture, to profess and practice their own religion, or to use their own language."

43. *Espiell Study, supra* note 37 at 9 at para. 52.

44. *Espiell Study, supra* note 37 at 66 at para. 285.

45. ICESCR and ICCPR, *supra* note 30 .

46. Anna Michalska, "Rights of Peoples to Self-determination in International Law" in William Twining, ed., *Issues of Self-Determination* (Aberdeen: Aberdeen University Press, 1991) at 81.

47. ICCPR *supra* note 30. Philip Vuciri Ramaga has written a complete analysis of article 27 and its long drafting history in: "The Bases of Minority Identity" (1992) 14 *Human Rights Quarterly* at 409. He writes: "The history of the drafting of Article 27 illustrates that the identities specified in it were meant to be exhaustive, so that 'race' is excluded. While the article specifies ethnicity, religion and language, these terms need to be interpreted separately from their common meaning in sociology and linguistics. The difference between the League and the UN criteria underlines the requirement of interpretation in light of the particular circumstance of the situations addressed" (at 428).

48. Asbjorn Eide, "The Sub-Commission on Prevention of Discrimination and Protection of Minorities", in Philip Alston ed., *The United Nations and Human Rights A Critical Appraisal* (Oxford: Clarendon Press, 1992) at 220.

49. Ibid.

50. *Capotorti Study, supra* note 16 at 1 para. 1.

51. UNGA Resolution 47/135 which proclaimed the Declaration on the Rights of Persons Belonging to National or Ethnic, Religious and Linguistic Minorities, 18 December 1992 [hereinafter Declaration on Minorities].

52. Capotorti proposed the following definition for minority "is a group numerically inferior to the rest of the population of a State, in a non-dominant position, whose members— being nationals of the State—possess ethnic, religious or linguistic characteristics differing from those of the rest of the population and show, if only implicitly, a sense of solidarity, directed towards preserving their culture, traditions, religion or language" Patrick Thornberry, *International law and the Rights of Minorities* (Oxford: Oxford Press, 1991) at 6.

53. *Promotion, Protection and Restoration of Human Rights at the National, Regional and International Level Prevention of Discrimination and Protection of Minorities, Proposal concerning*

a definition of the term "minority": UN Doc. E/CN.4/Sub.2/1985/31 and Corr. 1 [hereinafter *Deschenes Study*].

54. Ibid. at para. 181.

55. This working definition forms part of Chapter XXII (Proposals and Recommendations para. 379) in the third (and last) part of the 1986 final report entitled: "Conclusions, proposals and recommendations", UN Doc. E/CN.4/Sub.2/1986/7 and Add. 1-4, Section F, para. 362 and 382.

56. *Deschenes Study, supra* note 53 at paras. 26, 27 and 28.

57. *Deschenes Study, supra* note 53 at para. 29.

58. *Constitution Act*, 1982, being Schedule B to the *Canada Act 1982* (U.K.), 1982, c. 11.

59. *Deschenes Study, supra* note 53 at paras. 37 and 38.

60. The Commission on Human Rights established a Working Group on Minorities, which drafted the text of the Declaration on the Rights of Persons Belonging to National or Ethnic, Religious and Linguistic Minorities. Also, it established a Working Group on Indigenous Peoples which drafted the Declaration on the Rights of Indigenous Peoples.

61. Elsa Stamatopoulou, "Indigenous Peoples and the United Nations: Human Rights as a Developing Dynamic" (1994) 16 *Human Rights Quarterly* at 73 [hereinafter Stamatopoulou].

62. Declaration on Minorities, *supra* note 51.

63. "The specialized agencies and other organizations of the United Nations system shall contribute to the full realization of the rights and principles set forth in this Declaration, within their respective fields of competence" Declaration on Minorities, *supra* note 51 article 9.

64. G.A. Resolution 1994/115.

65. Christian Tomuschat, "Self-Determination in a Post-Colonial World" in Christian Tomuschat, ed., *Modern Law of Self-Determination* (Dordrecht: Martinus Nijhoff Publishers, 1993) at 10-11.

66. United Nations, *The United Nations and Human Rights* (New York: United Nations, 1978) at 29.

67. The Human Rights Committee, a special organ established by the state parties who signed the ICCPR which provides for the election of eighteen experts nominated and elected by the state parties who serve in their personal capacity. ICCPR, supra note 30. (Article 28): "The Committee is the principle organ involved in implementing the Covenant. The members of the Committee are elected by the parties who are State parties to the Covenant. . . . In the end, it is State parties who nominate and elect the members. These members sit in their capacity and serve a four year term": Jay A. Sigler, *Minority Rights—A Comparative Analysis* (Westport Conn.: Greenwood Press, 1983) at 81 [hereinafter Sigler, *Minority*]. See also: Appendix III to see the position of the Committee within the UN structure. Their reports go directly to ECOSOC.

68. "To study reports on the measures States Parties to the Covenant have adopted which give effect to the rights recognized therein, and on the progress made in the enjoyment of those rights; to transmit its reports, and such general comments as it may consider appro-

priate, to the State Parties. . . . [and] to consider communications received from individuals, subject to the jurisdiction of the State Party which has recognized the competence of the Committee to this effect, who claim to be victims of a violation by that State Party of any of the rights set forth in the Covenant" Sigler, *Minority, supra* note 67. ICCPR. supra note 30 Article 28.

69. For copies of the First and Second Optional Protocols to the I CCPR, see: Dominic McGoldrick, *The Human Rights Committee Its Role in the Development of the International Covenant on Civil and Political Rights* (Oxford: Clarendon Press, 1991) at 525 and 531 [hereinafter McGoldrick]. The First Optional Protocol allows for communications from individuals claiming to be victims of any of the rights set forth in the Covenant. The Second Optional Protocol relates to the abolition of the death penalty.

70. Ibid. at 525.

71. First Optional Protocol, Article 1 sets outs that competence of the Committee to receive commun- ications from individuals: A State party to the Covenant that becomes a party to the present Protocol recognizes the competence of the Committee to receive and consider communications from individuals subject to its jurisdiction who claim to be victims of a violation by that State Party to any of the rights set forth in the Covenant. No communication shall be received by the Committee if it concerns a State Party to the Covenant which is not a party to the present Protocol.

72. Three cases concerning Indigenous Peoples arose from Canada: Sandra Lovelace, UN GAOR, 36th Sess. Supp. No. 40 at 134, *Bernard Ominayak*, U.N. Doc. CCPR/C/30/D/167/1984 and *Mi'kmaq* Case, UN Doc. CCPR/C/43/D/205/1986. Other Indigenous Peoples have cases before the committee, including the Sami from Finland and the Maori of New Zealand concerning their fishing rights.

73. Under the ICCPR, a Human Rights Committee has been established with the power to scrutinize alleged human rights violations. For the Committee's view on minorities see: Sigler, *Minority, supra* note 67 at 81.

74. The Lubicon Cree are a band located in northern Alberta. They never signed a Treaty with the British or Canadian Crown. As a result, they claim that their territory and resources continue to remain under their jurisdiction for their own use and disposal. The Lubicon's rights were recognized indirectly when the International Court of Justice in *Western Sahara* determined that Indigenous Peoples could not have their lands taken without their consent. A complete history of the Lubicon People's conflict with Canada is well documented in: John Goddard, *Last Stand of the Lubicon Cree* (Vancouver: Douglas & McIntyre Ltd., 1991). See also: Boyce Richardson, "The Lubicon of Northern Alberta—Wrestling with the Canadian System: A Decade of Lubicon Frustration" in Boyce Richardson ed., *Drumbeat: Anger and Renewal in Indian Country* (Toronto: Summerhill Press Ltd., 1989) at 265.

75. Human Rights Committee, CCPR/C/30/D167/1984, 27 July 1987, para. 14.3.

76. Human Rights Committee, CCPRA/Doc. A/39.

77. McGoldrick, *supra* at note 69 at 254.

78. "The view of the HRC [sic] then appeared to be appeared to be that an individual can only bring a self- determination claim in a representative capacity and only for violation of the peoples' right to self-determination though no indication is given of what that right includes" McGoldrick, *supra* at note 69 at 255.

79. McGoldrick, *supra* at note 69 at 255-256.

80. Janos Fodor, Special Rapporteur for Follow-up on Views of the Human Rights Committee.

81. McGoldrick, *supra* at note 69 at 257.

82. "The debate over self-determination of indigenous peoples has one major advantage over the debate of minorities. Minority issues have often involved conflict between neighbouring states, have been exploited in the form of hostile propaganda by one state against another, and have threatened international peace": Stamatopoulou, *supra* note 61 at 80.

83. Advisory Opinion of the International Court of Justice [1971] ICJ Reports 16 [hereinafter *Namibia*].

84. Advisory Opinion of the International Court of Justice Concerning the Western Sahara, [1975] ICJ Reports 12. The questions before the Court had been asked "were laid before the Court by a letter dated 17 December 1974, filed in the Registry on 21 December 1974, addressed by the Secretary-General of the United Nations to the President of the Court. In his letter, the Secretary-General informed the Court that, by resolution 3292 (XXIX) adopted on 13 December 1974, the General Assembly of the United Nations had decided to request the Court to give an advisory opinion at an early date on the questions set out in the resolution" at 2 of Advisory Opinion.

85. Ibid. at 33.

86. *Case Concerning East Timor* (Portugal v. Australia) [1995] ICJ Reports 90.

87. Cobo Report, E/CN.4/ Sub.2/1986/7/Add. 4 (Vol. V of the final report) at para. 368-377.

88. Ibid.

89. Convention 169 Concerning Indigenous and Tribal Peoples of Independent Countries (1989) [hereinafter ILO Convention 169]. Under Article 36 (2) of ILO Convention 107, the revision does not affect the countries that have ratified it: "This Convention shall in any case remain in force in its actual form and content for those Members which have ratified it but have not ratified the revising Convention."

90. Report of the Governing Body, International Labour Office GB. 234/2/1 234th Session, Geneva 17-21 November, 1986 wherein the Governing Body determined the date, place and agenda of the 75th (1988) session of the Conference [hereinafter Governing Body 234th Session].

91. See, Extracts From the Report of the Meeting of Experts on the Revising of the Indigenous and Tribal Populations Convention, 1957 (No. 107) in: International Labour Conference, *Partial Revision of Indigenous and Tribal Populations Convention, 1957 (No. 107)*, Report VI (1), 75th Session, 1988, at 100-118 [hereinafter ILO *Partial Revision*]. See also: International Work Group on Indigenous Affairs Yearbook, *IWGIA Report on the ILO Meeting of Experts on Convention 107*, 1988 IWGIA Yearbook 73-92.

92. *ILO Partial Revision, supra* note 91 at 38.

93. Berman, *ILO Revision,* supra note 10 at 51-52.

94. The author of this thesis was present during the month long discussions in 1989 at the

ILO headquarters in Geneva. Each day, there would be a caucus of Indigenous delegates to determine who would speak for the 10 allocated minutes. The frustration level amongst the Indigenous delegates was very high as the final wording of the Convention was being debated in the room. It was strange to sit and listen to people talk about Indigenous Peoples as if we were not present. It was a demeaning and humiliating process. See: Sharon Venne, "The New Language of Assimilation: A Brief Analysis of ILO Convention 169," (1990) *Without Prejudice* 53 for an analysis of the provisions of the Revised Convention especially relating to the provisions on Peoples, lands and resource rights. The International Labour Organization representative Lee Swepston, who is the Assistant to the Director of the International Labour Standards Department of the International Labour Office, described the ILO's perspective on the revision process: Lee Swepston, "A New Step in the International Law on Indigenous and Tribal Peoples: ILO Convention No. 169 of 1989," (1990) 15 *Oklahoma City University Law Review* at 677.

95. Participation by Indigenous Organizations in the drafting process is discussed in Chapters 4 and 5.

96. 1. In applying the provisions of this Convention, governments shall: (a) consult the peoples concerned, through appropriate procedures and in particular through their representative institutions, whenever consideration is being given to legislative or administrative measures which may affect them directly; (b) establish means by which these peoples can freely participate to at least the same extent as other sectors of the population, at all levels of decision-making in elective institutions and administrative and other bodies responsible for policies and pro- grammes which concern them; (c) establish means for the full development of these peoples' own institutions and initiatives, and in appropriate cases provide the resources necessary for this purpose. 2. The consultations carried out in application of this Convention shall be undertaken, in good faith and in a form appropriate to the circumstances, with the objective of achieving agreement or consent to the proposed measures.

97. Provisional Record, International Labour Organisation, 75th Session, Geneva, 1988 #32.

98. Inuit Circumpolar Conference statement on "Peoples" *versus* "Populations." The document is on file with the author.

99. "The experts' conclusions, set out at the end of their report, covered the various points forming the background against which the priority attaching to a review of the 1957 Convention should be considered, namely the emphasis to be placed on self-determination —defined by the experts as control by indigenous populations over their own economic, social and cultural development—rather than on integration; the right of indigenous populations groups to interact with the national society on a footing of equality through their own institutions; the land rights issue, which the experts had recognized but concerning which they made no specific recommendation, although they had noted that the representatives of indigenous populations at the meeting unanimously considered such rights to be inalienable; the point that removal of indigenous people from their land should be limited to exceptional cases and should take place only with their informed consent and subject to appropriate compensation; and the need for full involvement of the indigenous and tribal populations themselves in all future action affecting them, whether by the ILO or by ratifying States" (Governing Body 234th Session, supra note 90, at I/5).

100. Partial Revision of the Indigenous and Tribal Populations Convention 1957 (No. 107) 1989, 5. Report IV (2A), *International Labour Conference*, 76th Session.

101. Mr. Mompoint (representing the UN Centre for Human Rights) speaking at the meeting of the Governing Body of the ILO said: "It was striking to promote and protect the basic

rights of indigenous populations, particularly by including the question in the agenda of the International Labour Conference in 1988, a step which the United Nations fully endorsed. The UN would go on consistently supporting the ILO's efforts in this field, and it firmly hoped that the revision process would be carried out successfully. . . . First, an exhaustive report on discrimination against these population groups had been prepared by Mr. Martinez Cobo, Special Rapporteur of the Subcommission on Prevention of Discrimination and Protection of Minorities. That report, completed in 1984, had highlighted the ILO's activities and called for a revision of Convention No. 107 aimed at taking fuller account of the desires of the peoples concerned, with stress on ethno-development and self-determination rather than on integration and protection" (Governing Body 234th Session, *supra* note 90 at I/6-I/7).

102. See: Sharon Venne, "The New Language of Assimilation: A Brief Review of ILO 169" (1990) *Without Prejudice* 53, which is an analysis of the failure of the revision to address the issues pursued by Indigenous Peoples including the rights to lands, resources, self-determination and recognition of the legal system of the Indigenous nations. See also: Lisa Strelein, "The Price of Compromise: Should Australia Ratify ILO Convention 169?" in Greta Bird et al. eds., *Majah Indigenous Peoples and the Law* (Annandale, NSW: Federation Press, 1996) concludes: "The ideology of individual freedoms is the greatest threat to the rights of communities, and in accepting the instrument [ILO 169], one must accept the ideology upon which it is based. For this reason, I cannot recommend support for the ILO Convention Concerning Indigenous and Tribal Peoples in Independent Countries (No. 169)" at 86 [hereinafter Strelein].

103. S. James Anaya, "The Rights of Indigenous Peoples and International Law in Historical and Contemporary Perspective" (1988) *Harvard Indian Law Symposium* at 216-217.

104. "The Government member of Portugal supported the proposed amendment to paragraph 3. She expressed her Government's reservations over the explanatory text and stated that it was not for the ILO to address the question of self-determination. This was a basic human right that could not be taken away and she considered that it should not be referred to in the Convention. Her Government interpreted the text as having no implications for the universal right of self-determination. She would, however, respect the consensus which had been achieved": Provisional Record, International Labour Organisation, 76th Session, Geneva, 1989, #25 Fourth item on the agenda: revision of the Indigenous and Tribal Populations Convention, 1957 (No. 107).

105. Report of the International Labour Organization at the Working Group on Indigenous Peoples, Geneva, July 1996. The document is on file with the author.

106. See, Strelein, *supra* note 102 at 85-86.

107. "International Conference on Discrimination against Indigenous Peoples of the Americas—1977 Special NGO Committee on Human Rights Sub-Committee on Racism, Racial Discrimination, Apartheid and Decolonization 20-23 September 1977", (Nov. 1977) 3 *American Indian Journal* contains the summary of the Geneva conference, the final resolution and a Declaration of Principles for the Defence of the Indigenous nations and Peoples of the Western Hemisphere. This conference is discussed in detail in Chapter 4.

108. The second NGO conference on Indigenous Peoples and their land was held at Geneva in September 1981. *World Federation of Democratic Youth* (1981) contains a report of the conference. The delegates called for the United Nations to convene a forum for: "Indigenous nations and peoples to submit their complaints and make their demands known." The author of this thesis was a delegate at this conference along with a number of Chiefs from Canada.

109. See Resolution 1982/34 of 7 May 1982 of the Economic and Social Council. See also, footnote 117 in Chapter 2 on formal/informal name of Working Group [hereinafter Working Group].

110. Stamatopoulou, *supra* note 61 at 72.

111. *Report of the Working Group on Indigenous Populations on its eleventh session,* E/CN.4/Sub.2/ 1993/29, annex I.

112. Draft Declaration on the Rights of Indigenous Peoples, Article 8 [See: Appendix I for a copy].

113. Draft Declaration, Article 9.

114. By resolution 1995/32, the Commission decided to establish "an open-ended inter-sessional working group with the sole purpose of elaborating a draft declaration." Report of the Working Group established in accordance with Commission on Human Rights resolution 1995/32 of 3 March 1995, E/CN.4/1996/84. The effect of this resolution will be discussed in detail in Chapter 5 of this thesis.

115. Blaut writes: "The Purpose of this book is to undermine one of the most powerful beliefs of our time concerning world history and world geography. This belief is the notion that European civilization—'The West'—has had some unique historical advantage, some special quality of race or culture or environment or mind or spirit, which gives the human community a permanent superiority over all other communities, at all times in history and down to the present. . . . Europe eternally advances, progresses, modernizes. The rest of the world advances more sluggishly, or stagnates, it is 'traditional society.'" J. M. Blaut, *Colonizer's Model of the World Geographical Diffusionism and Eurocentric History,* (New York: Guilford Press 1992) at 1.

116. Stamatopoulou, *supra* note 61 at 80.

4

Key Provisions of
The Draft Declaration
On Indigenous Peoples' Rights

Introduction

The Working Group on Indigenous Peoples has been developing standards concerning the rights of Indigenous Peoples over a period of years. The development of a Draft Declaration is an example of one such standard. The unique aspect of the Declaration by the Working Group was due to the direct participation by Indigenous Peoples in the drafting process. From 1985 until 1993,[1] a Draft Declaration on the rights of Indigenous Peoples was discussed and drafted in the Working Group.

Indigenous Peoples had been treated as "objects" of international law development that excluded them from active participation. The direct and open participation by Indigenous Peoples in the Working Group has promoted them from reacting to standards, to developing standards that will affect their lives. Indigenous Peoples are attempting, through the United Nations to begin to establish international legal principles to protect themselves against further exploitation. They are fully aware that the United Nations is an international organization established by nation-states. However, under the Charter, member states who made commitments to recognize Self-determination of peoples have yet to fulfill the provision when it relates to Indigenous Peoples.

Chapter 4 focuses on the Draft Declaration on the Rights of Indigenous Peoples. The context in which international rights standards are being developed is presented, as well as the role and scope of the participation by Indigenous Peoples. Attention is given to the major rights for which there was consistent consensus among participating Indigenous Peoples: self–identification and Self-determination, collective land rights and collective resource rights.

Background to The Declaration

As described in Chapter 3, UN human rights agencies have been examining issues related to the UN Charter rights, particularly those of Indigenous Peoples. Various studies have been undertaken by the human rights experts of the Sub-commission to clarify legal points and develop international standards. The Special Study on Racial Discrimination in the Political, Economic, Social and Cultural Spheres (Hernan Santa Cruz, Special Rapporteur), prepared for the Sub-commission in 1971 recommended a broader study of: "Measures taken in connection with the protection of indigenous peoples."[2] The Cobo Study, discussed in Chapter 3, was completed from 1972 to 1984 with a final report containing twenty-four documents, covering a large range of issues from political and land rights to health, housing, education, culture and religious rights.[3] In the conclusions and recommendations, Cobo suggested that an international instrument be drafted to protect the rights of Indigenous Peoples.[4]

Continuing UN Charter Activities

Before the final report from Cobo was submitted, the United Nations Economic and Social Council established the Working Group on Indigenous Peoples with a mandate to deal exclusively with issues concerning Indigenous Peoples. The state-based UN organ did not decide independently that this action was needed; rather pressure was applied from within and outside the UN. Work by the ILO and other Sub-commission Rapporteurs was provoking widespread interest on rights issues. In 1977 and 1981, two conferences of non-governmental organizations (NGOs)[5] sponsored and held in Geneva, Switzerland drew world attention to the plight of Indigenous Peoples.

The 1977 Conference was "the fourth such conference organized by the Geneva NGO Sub-committee on Racism, Racial Discrimination, Apartheid and Decolonization of the Special NGO Committee on Human Rights."[6] The series of conferences were organized within the framework of the UN Decade for Action to Combat Racism and Racial Discrimination. The 1977 Conference, which focused on discrimination against Indigenous Peoples of the Americas, called for the UN Special Committee on Decolonization to hold hearings on all issues affecting Indigenous Peoples of the Americas to establish an appropriate forum of the UN Trusteeship Council[7] for the decolonization of Indigenous Peoples in the Americas.[8] In addition, the conference recommended the establishment "of a working group under the Sub-commission on the Prevention of Discrimination and Protection of Minorities."[9]

In the following year, at the World Conference to Combat Racism and Racial Discrimination, the final communique endorsed the right of Indigenous Peoples:

> to maintain their traditional structure of economy and culture, including their own language, and also recogniz[ing] the special relationship of indigenous peoples to their land and stress[ing]

that their land, land rights, and natural resources should not be taken away from them.[10]

The impact Indigenous Peoples were making on the international standard setting agenda merited special treatment in the Declaration from the World Conference. The World Conference had set goals for the UN to work toward during the Decade to Combat Racism. One of the key areas needing immediate and special attention related to the rights of Indigenous Peoples. Despite the strong language contained in the communique from the World Conference, no action was taken by the UN. The lack of action led to a second NGO sponsored conference in 1981 on Indigenous Peoples and the Land. The UN may have been inactive on the rights of Indigenous Peoples, but Indigenous Peoples were extremely busy organizing themselves:

> [In 1977] the World Council of Indigenous Peoples met in Sweden. The following year, the World Conference to Combat Racism and Racial Discrimination endorsed some of the rights claimed by Indigenous groups. The VIIIth Inter–American Indian Congress took place in Merida, Mexico, in 1980. In 1984, the World Council of Indigenous Peoples met in Panama, and adopted a Declaration of Principles on Indigenous Rights.[11]

The work which was done in Panama was submitted to the members of the Working Group in 1985 as part of the Draft Declaration of Principles (discussed *infra*).

Participation by Indigenous Peoples

Indigenous Peoples throughout the world were invited to take part in the 1981 NGO Conference. The ability to invite Indigenous Peoples from other parts of the world was accomplished by three Indigenous-based NGO's which actively participated in the organization and planning of this international conference. Article 71 of the UN Charter sets out procedures within ECOSOC for the participation of NGO's. An NGO must be accredited through the process established by the NGO committee. Once accredited, an NGO is allowed to participate in matters within their competence. In the past twenty years, a dozen Indigenous based NGO's have received accreditation by ECOSOC, allowing them to fully participate in all meetings held within the competence of ECOSOC.

    The first Indigenous-based NGO accredited in 1977, was the International Indian Treaty Council (IITC) which "arose out of the frustration experienced by the North American based American Indian Movement in its attempts to have the Indian Treaties with the United

States and Canada recognized and the violations redressed."[12] In 1979, the World Council of Indigenous Peoples (WCIP) and the Indian Law Resource Centre were given ECOSOC status. By 1987, eight more Indigenous–based NGO's became accredited: South American Indian Council (CISA), the National Aboriginal and Islander Services (NAILS), Inuit Circumpolar Conference (ICC), National Indian Youth Council, Indigenous World Association, Four Directions Council, Grand Council of the Cree and the National Indian Youth Council. Recently, the Aboriginal Torres Straits and Islander Commission (ATSIC) received ECOSOC status. With the exception of the CISA, NAILS and ATSIC, all other Indigenous based NGO's are from North America.

The 1981 NGO conference recommended that the UN act immediately to establish a forum for Indigenous Peoples. Theo van Boven, Director of the United Nations Division of Human Rights, told the Sub-commission:

> Indigenous peoples existing in various parts of the world present themselves in varying numbers and situations. They may range from a considerable part of the population or they may be a scattered few submerged in the hinterlands of their respective countries. Some have been chased from their ancestral lands and driven to areas where survival is harsh while others have been forced to co-exist in an often undignified manner with their conquerors. . . . The question may be asked, what is the responsibility of the international community for those whose very rights of survival are in jeopardy? This question is particularly acute when the States concerned do not exercise their duty to guarantee protection to such vulnerable groups. Is there not a special responsibility upon the international community and upon the United Nations to take measures to protect the human rights of these people and to save them from dangers of extinction? . . . **It has become clear, first of all, that there is need for further standard-setting regarding the human rights of indigenous peoples**. It has also become clear that indigenous peoples need an appropriate forum within the United Nations to which they can address themselves on a regular basis and which may give regular consideration to their problems. Thirdly, it has also become clear that there is a need within the United Nations for an on-going system of fact-finding into problems affecting the enjoyment of human rights by indigenous peoples. It may be asked whether the time is not ripe for the Sub-commission to request permission to establish, as it has done for the problem of slavery, a regular working group on the human rights of indigenous peoples[13] [emphasis added].

Based on the timely intervention by Mr. van Boven, along with the minutes of the NGO conferences and the Declaration to Combat Racism, the Sub–commission recommended to the CHR and then to ECOSOC that the Working Group be established. ECOSOC acted within the year. Since 1982, the Working Group has attempted to address the issues initially outlined by van Boven. Now there is a forum within the UN whereby Indigenous Peoples can address their issues. It meets annually; even in 1986 when a UN financial crisis forced cancellation of the Sub-commission and its Working Groups, Indigenous organizations and their supporters were able to convene an informal meeting in Geneva with two members of the Working Group in attendance.[14] The establishment of the Working Group has helped promote an international understanding of the rights of Indigenous Peoples:

> The establishment of this new international forum [Working Group] for debate under the wings of the United Nations created the conditions for the emergence of new interlocutors. Until that time, indigenous movements had been confined to dialogue with and bargaining over the decisions of each of the states where indigenous peoples happen to be located.[15]

As a UN forum, the Working Group follows certain rules and procedures. An initial challenge for Indigenous Peoples was to amend the rules relating to participation.

The Working Group also provides a forum for Indigenous Peoples to bring factual materials directly to the attention of the UN system for future action. An important result of the work by the Working Group is the number of initiatives undertaken by the Human Rights Centre, including an experts meeting to review the experiences of countries in the operation of schemes of internal self-government for Indigenous Peoples,[16] the UN technical conference on practical experience in realization of sustainable and environmentally sound self–development of Indigenous Peoples and the environment held in Santiago, Chile,[17] and, most recently, the meeting of experts on land rights of Indigenous Peoples held in Whitehorse, Canada in March 1996.[18] The Working Group also pressed for organization of United Nations seminars such as the one in 1989 on the effects of racism and racial discrimination on the social and economic relations between Indigenous Peoples and states.[19] The findings of the seminar concluded:

> Indigenous Peoples have been, and still are, the victims of racism and racial discrimination; that relations between states and Indigenous Peoples should be based upon free and informed consent and cooperation, not merely consultation and participation, and that Indigenous Peoples should be recognized as proper sub-

jects of international law with their own collective rights.[20]

Another unique aspect of this seminar related to the selection of the rapporteur: "Ted Moses of the Grand Council of the Cree (Quebec) was acknowledged as an indigenous expert . . . [which] has been considered as a seminal development in the field of international law."[21] Indigenous delegates have been direct participants in the review and development at these international meetings, relating direct information on the daily existence of Indigenous Peoples. The need for the UN to have an on–going process for fact finding into the problems of Indigenous Peoples was stressed in 1981 by Theo van Boven. International seminars and meetings have helped Indigenous Peoples to participate actively in these processes involved in the evolution of standards related to their rights.

The UN system had to make structural adjustments to accommodate Indigenous Peoples. Within the UN, only states, specialized agencies and NGOs have the right to participate in UN meetings.[22] At the first meeting of the Working Group held in the fall of 1982, the expert members decided to suspend the UN rules on participation:[23]

> At its first session, the Working Group took the almost unprecedented step of allowing oral and written interventions from all indigenous organization which wished to participate in its work, not limiting such participation to those with formal consultative status.[24]

As a result of this decision—which has not been overturned or changed by any subsequent Working Group meetings, the Sub-commission or the CHR—Indigenous Peoples from the communities, territories and organizations have the right to participate fully and directly in the meetings of the Working Group. It was a significant first step in the process.

The Draft Declaration

Ultimately, the Draft Declaration could become a General Assembly resolution in Declaration form like the Universal Declaration of Human Rights (discussed in Chapter 5). The draft United Nations Declaration on the Rights of Indigenous Peoples[25] is divided into preambular paragraphs and operative paragraphs. The nineteen preambular paragraphs affirm that Indigenous Peoples are equal in dignity and rights to all other peoples (paragraph 1). It is recognized that there are violations of Indigenous Peoples' rights and loss of freedom which has been caused by colonization and dispossession of their land, territories and resources, preventing Indigenous Peoples from freely determining their future (paragraph 5). The Draft recognizes that Indigenous Peoples urgently need to have their inherent rights respected and protected (paragraph 6). The preambular paragraphs also acknowledge the right of Indigenous Peoples to self-determination (paragraph 15), as such recognition will contribute to the peace, economic and social progress of Indigenous Peoples, and on promotion of friendly relations among nations and peoples of the world (paragraph 10). The Draft uses the language of the UN Charter but extends it to recognize that Indigenous Peoples are unique. Points raised by the Indigenous delegates in 1985, which are incorporated are: rights to land, resources, Self-determination and recognition of "peoples." Finally, the preambular paragraph acknowledges that Indigenous Peoples have been colonized and deprived of their rights. The title of the draft is a reflection of the progress made in the UN. It is the Draft Declaration on the Rights of Indigenous Peoples and does not use the word "populations." The original drafts presented to the Working Group referred to the Draft Declaration on Indigenous Rights, but over the years of drafting, the Declaration took on a more precise and descriptive form.

In the forty-five operational paragraphs of the draft articles, there are seven parts. The first part refers to the universal rights of Indigenous Peoples who are equal and free to enjoy all of other peoples rights (Article 2). The right to self-determination is also included (Article 3). There is an affirmation of the collective rights of Indigenous Peoples. As stated: "This provision also suggests that Indigenous Peoples have the right to exercise as collective rights those individual rights which are proclaimed in the international instruments."[26]

The second part refers to the collective rights of Indigenous Peoples to live in freedom and peace and to be free of genocide (Article 6), to belong to their own community (Article 9), not to be forcibly removed from their lands or territories (Article 10) and to have special protection and security in time of war (Article 11).

The third part refers to Indigenous Peoples' right to practise and revitalize their cultural traditions and customs (Article 12), to have the right to manifest, practice, develop and teach their spiritual and religious traditions (Article 13), to revitalize, use, develop and transmit to future generations their histories, languages, oral traditions, philosophies, writing systems and literatures (Article 14).

The fourth part is concerned with education, media and labour rights of Indigenous Peoples.

The fifth part concerns the rights of Indigenous Peoples to participate in decisions which will affect their lives and rights (Article 19), to have their fully informed consent prior to adopting and implementing state measures (Article 20), to have the right to maintain and develop their own political, economic and social systems (Article 21), and to use their traditional medicines and to have access if desired to medical institutions of the state (Article 24).

The sixth part refers to land, territories, waters and coastal seas, and other resources (Article 25), to the ability of Indigenous Peoples to use, own, develop and control those areas (Article 26), to have the rights to restitution of the lands, territories and resources of Indigenous Peoples (Article 27), to have the right to conserve, restore and protect total environments of Indigenous Peoples (Article 28), to have their full ownership of cultural and intellectual property recognized (Article 29), and to have the right to determine and develop their own priorities and strategies for the development and use of lands, territories and other resources (Article 30).

The seventh part refers to the exercise of the right of Self-determination (Article 31), to have a collective right to their own citizenship (Article 32), to promote, develop and maintain their institutional structures (Article 33), to have the collective right to maintain contact with their relations despite state boundaries (Article 35) and to have treaties, agreements and other constructive arrangements honoured by state governments (Article 36).

In the eighth part, the duty of States in relation to the implementation of this draft are outlined (Article 37). States have the duty to allow Indigenous Peoples to have access to adequate funding and technical assistance to pursue their political, economic, social, cultural and spiritual development (Article 38), and provide access to and prompt decisions in conflicts and disputes with States (Article 39). Furthermore, the organs and specialized agencies of the UN system must promote the Declaration (Article 40) and the UN is to take the necessary steps to implement the Declaration (Article 41).

In the last part, it is stated that the rights which are recognized in the draft are the minimum standards (Article 42) and the Declaration is not to be interpreted as diminishing or extinguishing existing or future rights of Indigenous Peoples (Article 44).

The Draft has many articles which refer to the collective rights of Indigenous Peoples: to freely pursue their right to self-determination (Article 3), to live in freedom, peace and security as distinct Peoples (Article 6), to maintain and develop their distinct identities and characteristics (Article 8), to belong to indigenous communities or nations (Article 9), to retain their shared responsibility for the upbringing, training, education and well-being of their children (Article 11), to practice their cultural traditions and customs (Article 12), to uphold their responsibilities to future generations (Article 25), to use and own their traditional land in accordance with their traditions and customs (Article 26), to select the membership of their institutions in accordance with their own procedures (Article 32), to promote, develop and maintain their institutional structures to their distinctive juridical customs, traditions, procedures and practices (Article 33) and to the collective right to determine the responsibility of individuals to the communities (Article 34).

The Draft Declaration is the first UN document which extensively addresses the collective rights. Human rights instruments[27] have referred only to the rights of individuals within states and state responsibility to those individuals. Brownlie comments:

> inherent in the concepts of equality and of human rights is the idea that groups as such may have rights. The classical human rights instruments say little or nothing about the rights of groups as such, apart from the right of Self-determination. . . . [However] the assumption lying behind the classical formulations of standards of human rights . . . has been that group rights would be taken care of automatically as a the result of the protection of the rights of the individual.[28]

The UN has not been able to deal with the rights of the collective under the present system; hence the Human Rights Committee does not hear complaints from groups.

A complete analysis of the contents of the Draft Declaration is not possible within the context of this thesis. Detailed attention is given to four areas that Indigenous Peoples agreed are of paramount significance and which were put before the Working Group in 1985, in the form of a joint resolution: recognition of peoples with no imposed definition, self-determination, and land and resource rights. While the drafting process underwent revision upon revision, Indigenous Peoples never varied from their original position. Gradually, the Working Group came to understand and accept the principles outlined by the Indigenous delegates, as Madame Daes has written:

> My colleagues, members of the Working Group, and I, as the principal drafter of the draft declaration made every effort to incorporate primarily, Indigenous Peoples' aspirations fully in the final text, although naturally the language has been condensed and the language used is that of the United Nations. I doubt that any other United Nations human rights instrument was prepared with so much direct involvement of its intended beneficiaries.[29]

Indigenous participants needed to review the norms of international law on which Indigenous Peoples were relying and to education experts on the Working Group to understand Indigenous positions. The world view of Indigenous Peoples needed to be reflected in any Draft Declaration before it could be presented for adoption. As expressed, the Working

Group felt: "The approaches used to protect Indigenous Peoples and promote their rights and interests [were] unique and radical."[30] The resulting Draft Declaration, as indicated in Article 42, is a minimum international standard that Indigenous Peoples can accept (Article 42).

Right to Self-Identification

The issue of the legal nature of Indigenous Peoples in law has received considerable study by the UN, as noted in Chapter 3. There is no definition of "Indigenous Peoples" in the Draft Declaration. State governments have raised the question of the definition of Indigenous Peoples since the Cobo study was undertaken. Cobo's working model (quoted in Chapter 3) appears to be based on the 1930 Permanent Court of International Justice Greco-Bulgarian case which, in the context of a minorities rights case, defined "people" as:

> A group of persons living in a given country or locality, having a race, religion, language and traditions of their own and united by the identity of race, religion, language and traditions in a sentiment of solidarity, with a view to preserving their traditions, maintaining their own form of worship, insuring the instruction and upbringing of their children in accordance with the spirit and traditions of their race and rendering mutual assistance to each other.[31]

Indigenous Peoples are not minorities–as acknowledged by Cobo, Deschenes and Espiell. Cobo added Indigenous Peoples' relationship to their lands and the colonized nature of their existence to make his working definition unique. Cobo's work was accepted by the Sub-commission, CHR and ECOSOC without diminishing or amending his working model. As discussed earlier, it was not always the case with other attempts which have tried to include definitions in studies submitted to the Sub-commission. Mr. Justice Deschenes working definition on minorities, also discussed in Chapter 3, was not accepted by the Sub-commission nor by the CHR. The uniqueness of Indigenous Peoples and their connection to the land and territories, acknowledged by the UN, is essential to the Draft Declaration on the Rights of Indigenous Peoples.

There is no officially recognized UN definition for Indigenous Peoples. There is also still no accepted definition in international law for "peoples."

> There is not even an accepted sociological or political definition of a people. The United Nations carefully avoided to define "people," even as it has conceded all peoples have the right of Self-determination.[32]

When the UN established the Working Group, the ECOSOC resolution directed its members to "bear in mind the report" by Special Rapporteur Cobo. The Working Group used Cobo's model as the basis for its work for the next fourteen years. Definition continues to be an issue because state governments keep raising it. "Governments often have sought to narrow the definition of 'peoples' in order to limit the number of groups entitled to exercise a self-determination claim."[33]

At its fourteenth session, the Working Group had an extensive debate on the definition of Indigenous Peoples. Madame Daes, Chairperson/Rapporteur, prepared a working paper[34] for discussion in response to the raising of this issue by governments at the thirteenth session:[35]

> The observers governments of Bangladesh and India emphasized the need for a clear definition of "indigenous people" in the interest of an effective focus on the true Indigenous people of the world. The observer of Bangladesh said that a procedure based on self-identification could be self-defeating and that it would be a great disservice to the true indigenous people if the agenda for indigenous people were allowed to be confused with the agenda of other subnational and tribal groups that constituted minorities within their respective countries.[36]

Other governments and Indigenous organizations had supported the need to recognize self-definition, as drafted in Article 8. Some governments were particularly outspoken:

> Australia strongly opposed the idea of a formal definition of Indigenous Peoples. . . .They stated that the qualification and definition of "Indigenous" could only be based on the inherent right to self-determination. Essential elements of this approach were said to be descent, self-identification, group identity or group acceptance and a historical connection with the land.[37]

As a result of those discussions, the Working Group recommended to the Sub-commission that the Chairperson/Rapporteur prepare a note on criteria for a definition of Indigenous Peoples based on "information which might be submitted by Governments, intergovernmental organizations and indigenous peoples' organizations." The CHR approved the Sub-commission resolution. It also recommended that the Working Group make its final report of the discussions to the Inter-sessional Working Group.[39] When the Inter-sessional Working Group meets in October 1996, Madame Daes's final report based on the discussions at the fourteenth session of the Working Group will be tabled. Debate on the report is expected to be extensive.

The issue of definition intensified in 1994. When the Afrikaner of South Africa and the Rehoboth of Naimbia—both descendants of colonial settlers—appeared at the Working Group claiming to be Indigenous, Indigenous Peoples refused to accept them as "Indigenous." The incident led to a note being prepared to classify the legal point, based on previous Working Group work on criteria for Indigenous Peoples to attend the Working Group. Indigenous Peoples refused to accept them as "Indigenous."

The Working Group accepted certain basic criteria including: historical continuity, distinctive cultural characteristics, traditional lands, non–dominance, self–identification and group consciousness, which were essentially the points used by Cobo in his study. As a result of the note, the whole question of the need for a definition in the Draft Declaration was raised in the Working Group by state governments.

The consistent position of Indigenous Peoples has been that including a definition limits the rights contained in the Draft Declaration. Consequently, there is a specific provision in the Draft Declaration which recognizes the right of Indigenous Peoples to identify themselves (Article 8).[40] Also, in Article 9, the Draft Declaration recognizes the right of Indigenous Peoples "to belong to an indigenous community or nation, in accordance with the traditions and customs of the community or nation concerned." In Article 32, which states that Indigenous Peoples have the collective right to determine their own citizenship in accordance with their customs and traditions, self-identification is recognized as an inherent collective right:

> Indigenous representatives on several occasions have expressed the view, before the Working Group that a definition of the concept of "Indigenous People" is not necessary or desirable. They have stressed the importance of self-identification as an essential component of any definition which might be elaborated by the United Nations. . . . Indigenous groups insist on their right to define themselves both in terms of an individual's "self–identification" as an Indigenous person and with respect to the community's right to define its members. This subjective approach–that Indigenous Peoples are those who feel themselves to be Indigenous and are accepted as such by members of the group has been widely supported.[41]

For Indigenous Peoples, it is important that a person can identify with the cultural group but, equally important, that the group accept that person as Indigenous. Madame Daes has recently written:

> The Draft Declaration not only acknowledges Indigenous Peoples

as "Peoples" in the international sense, but recognizes that they continue to possess a distinct legal character and standing even in cases where they have agreed to be incorporated into existing states. This is of cardinal importance because indigenous peoples generally do not aspire to separate statehood; while at the same time, they do not see that they can ever accept complete integration into the states which comprise the United Nations.[42]

After eight years of discussions, the Working Group members have accepted that Indigenous Peoples are "peoples" in the international sense as subjects and not objects of international law. It is now a matter for the UN system to accept, reject or amend the findings of its human rights experts.

In developments outside the Working Group, the 1991 meeting of experts in Nuuk, Greenland affirmed that Indigenous Peoples constitute "distinct peoples and societies, with the right to self-determination, self-government and self-identification." Furthermore, the UN Committee on the Elimination of Racial Discrimination has determined that self-identification should be the basis for identification as a member of a racial or ethnic group. The Draft Declaration recognizes that Indigenous Peoples have a collective and individual right to maintain and develop their distinct identities and characteristics. It follows the lead shown by the Committee on the Elimination of Racial Discrimination and other UN sponsored seminars and meetings.

Self-Determination

The issue of recognition of Indigenous Peoples as "Peoples" and subjects in law is tied to the recognition of the right of self-determination. UN Charter Article 1(2) recognizes the right of Self-determination of all peoples: "Despite its collective overtones, Self-determination has increasingly been spoken of as a human right, and included in the international human rights instruments."[45] If Indigenous Peoples are recognized as Peoples, then the right of self-determination should apply to them:

If one considers the political implications of classification of indigenous societies as "peoples" in the juridical sense and the rights it has granted to them to determine their own political status. . . . If there are specific indigenous communities who deserve to be categorized as "peoples" in this juridical sense, this is not because of the mere fact that they are "indigenous" in the territories concerned, but because they have the political features which peoples under colonial or alien domination or occupation possess.[46]

But state governments continue to resist such recognition because they fear that, if the right of self-determination is recognized for Indigenous Peoples, their states would be dismembered. There are two General Assembly resolutions[47] on this issue: the 1960 Declaration on the Granting of Independence to Colonial Countries[48] (operative paragraph 6) and the Declaration on Principles of International Law Concerning Friendly Relations[49] (operative paragraph 8). The latter Declaration protects the territorial integrity and national unity of countries with peoples residing within their boundaries. If Indigenous Peoples are recognized as "Peoples" then the former resolution would apply to them. Despite these two resolutions, the GA accepted the two International Human Rights Covenants in 1966 with the identical commitment in each Article 1 to the right to self-determination for all peoples. One legal commentator has observed:

> Which peoples are afforded rights under Article 1? What is the scope of the right granted? How is the right to be implemented? . . . The general spirit and context of Article 1 . . . applies to: (1) entire populations living in independent and sovereign states, (2) entire populations of territories that have yet to attain independence, and (3) populations living under foreign military occupation. It is thus apparent that the existence of a right of self-determination is not necessarily determined by reference to a territory's international political status.[50]

This notion was reinforced by the statement made by the British government representative during the debate on Article 1 of the International Covenant on Civil and Political Rights, Cassese notes:

> It is no accident that the first article of each of the international Covenants proclaims the right of self-determination. We should always remember that under the Covenants self-determination is a right of peoples and not of governments. Moreover, it is not only peoples suffering occupation by a foreign power which are deprived of their right to self-determination, accompanied by equally appalling violations of many other fundamental rights.[51]

State governments were aware of the implications of including the provision in the International Rights Covenants, which is, that by including the right to self-determination, Indigenous Peoples would want to leave the states which have oppressed them. The right to Self-determination is one which:

> exists under treaty law by virtue of Article 1 of the 1966 Covenants.

United Nations practice and the practice of the UN Committee on Human Rights show that for a long time there has been some resistance to move towards expanding customary law in order to discern any rights conferred by treaty law. . . . One of the reasons for customary law's resilience in the face of treaty law in this area is the fear on the part of the States that any action in the field would lead to undue interference in the domestic affairs of sovereign States. . . . The need to champion democratic values has all too often been subordinated to the desire to preserve intact the principle of State sovereignty.[52]

As outlined in the ICJ *Western Sahara* case the primary role and meaning of Self-determination requires a free and genuine expression of the will of the peoples concerned.[53] Indigenous Peoples pushed for the inclusion of Self-determination in the Draft Declaration in order to have their right to freely determine their future. This right has been denied to them since the doctrine of discovery subverted the course of international law. Indigenous delegates participating in the drafting of the Draft Declaration are promoting the right to self-determination within the UN and its subsidiary bodies. The principle of Self-determination lays down:

> the method by which States must reach decisions concerning peoples; this is by heeding their freely expressed will. In contrast, the principle neither points to the various specific areas in which Self-determination should apply, nor to the final goal of self-determination (internal self-government, independent statehood, association with or integration into another State).[54]

UN member states with Indigenous Peoples within their territory want to continue to control peoples as evident by ILO Convention 169. Indigenous Peoples are not peoples that states are prepared to recognize. International lawyer Richard Falk note that states take a "statist view of self-determination."[55] Having determined that states would be reluctant to recognize the rights of Indigenous Peoples' right of self-determination, Falk recognizes that:

> commentators have increasingly come to appreciate the overall human importance, ecologically and as an intrinsic benefit, of keeping indigenous peoples from being either extinguished through encroachment or by way of assimilation.[56]

A declaration is not binding on state governments and does not become a treaty with legal obligations on states. However, a declaration in a General Assembly resolution will be evidence of state practice and can contribute to evolution of customary international law. Therefore, inclusion of the right of self-determination in the Draft Declaration on the Rights of Indigenous Peoples should not be problematic.

An argument could be made for the customary application of the right of self– determination to colonized peoples, as articulated by the ICJ in the *Western Sahara* case. Indigenous Peoples want to have their right to freely determine their future recognized by the international community:

> The right of self-determination has been regarded by indigenous peoples as a prerequisite to the exercise of all other rights. The position of indigenous peoples has been that the Declaration must contain clear and explicit recognition of the fundamental right of self-determination, without discrimination or any other limitation. . . . It is clear that substantial progress has been made with respect to the right of self-determination, but many indigenous peoples have expressed concern about maintaining such language throughout the progression of the Draft Declaration within the United Nations.[57]

States such as Canada and the United States have expressed strong opposition to the inclusion of self-determination in the Draft Declaration. Their major objection seems to stem from the fear that explicit recognition of the right would allow Indigenous Peoples to exercise a right of political independence and separate from the states that surround them. The issue may prove a stumbling block for the future passage of a Declaration on the Rights of Indigenous Peoples, but it must be kept in mind that Canada and the United States have only 2 out of a possible 185 votes in the General Assembly. This issue will be covered more extensively in Chapter 5.

Rights to Land and Resources

Indigenous Peoples' requirement to return to self-determination is based on a factor that differs from the demands of other peoples–their relationship to their lands and territories. At the 1996 meeting held in Whitehorse on land rights, the expert participants determined that a link exists between self-determination and land rights.[58] Land rights cannot be separated from other rights that flow from exercising the right of self-determination. The basis for the requirement to return to self-determination is predicated on Indigenous Peoples' right to land and territory. To this day, Indigenous Peoples are affected by the consequences of having been deprived of their land and resource base, which is occupied by the colonizers. In his study, Martinez Cobo wrote:

> it must be recognized that Indigenous populations have their own identity rooted in historical factors which outweigh the phenomena of mere solidarity in the face of discrimination and exploitation, and that, by virtue of their very existence, they have a natural and original right to live freely on their own lands.[59]

Because land is central to the rights of Indigenous Peoples and, for the exercise of those rights, land rights are integral to the Draft Declaration.

Some common bonds helped Indigenous Peoples develop a consensus on the draft principles on land rights for the Declaration. In 1987 submission, six of the twenty draft principles referred to land rights,[60] most of which have been included in the Draft Declaration. There is one notable exception: sub-soil resources are not expressly included or excluded. However, as the right to the total environment of Indigenous Peoples is recognized in Article 26, it can be argued that the sub-soil is included.

Part VI of the Draft contains extensive provisions on land rights. Indigenous Peoples have the right to maintain and strengthen their distinctive spiritual and material relationship with the lands, territories, waters and coastal seas (Article 25). The drafting relates not only to lands in conventional Eurocentric terms, but to territories and waters. The Draft Declaration is unique in referring to the total environment as is customary for Indigenous Peoples. The challenge for Indigenous Peoples in the drafting was to include consensual Indigenous world view of their territories. For example, the Indigenous Peoples of the Amazon initially had difficulty understanding the need to protect sea-ice as requested by Inuit. At the same time, Inuit delegates initially did not perceive the need to protect tropical rainforests, as advocated by the Amazonian Indigenous Peoples. The consensus built amongst Indigenous Peoples over the integrated perception of land as territory is reflected in Article 26.

Article 27 relates to the right for Indigenous Peoples to have lands that have been confiscated, occupied, used, or damaged without their free and informed consent restored to them. Integral to the process of land protection is the right of Indigenous Peoples to conserve, restore and protect the total environment of their lands and territories (Article 28). In addition, the state must take effective measures to ensure that toxic wastes are not stored on or near Indigenous lands.

In another area related to property rights, the cultural and intellectual property of Indigenous Peoples is recognized (Article 29).[61] Indigenous Peoples' knowledge is intrinsically linked to the use of land and resources, and the value of Indigenous knowledge beyond Indigenous cultures has also become recognized in recent decades by Eurocentic scientists. Canada now includes Indigenous knowledge alongside science in federal reviews of impacts of development projects on Indigenous lands.

Even so, Indigenous Peoples have had to struggle against the specialized agencies of the UN[62] to have their cultural and intellectual property rights recognized:

The World Intellectual Property Organization (WIPO), the UN agency which protects patents, has told the UN Human Rights Centre that it does not recognize the standing of Indigenous Peoples. In a dismissive letter, the Director General of WIPO wrote to the Centre that intellectual property is distinguished by the type of intellectual creation and not by the group responsible for its creation. This position reflects WIPO's insistence on individual authorship as a prerequisite for patent protection.[63]

Article 29 of the Draft Declaration recognizes the Indigenous Peoples' right to full ownership, control and protection of their cultural and intellectual property.

The Draft Declaration also refers to the rights of Indigenous Peoples to determine and develop priorities and strategies for development and use of their lands according to their values. Consistent with maintaining Indigenous Peoples as objects in law, Indigenous lands have been perceived by states as available for development and exploitation without the Peoples' consent. As pointed out during the 1996 expert seminar on practical experiences regarding Indigenous land rights, one of the experts, Dr. Kenneth Coates wrote of the Canadian experience:

In the 19th century, the expansion of settler societies from Europe saw the incorporation of vast tracts of indigenous land into newcomer jurisdiction and mass dislocation of indigenous peoples. On all continents, the new arrivals used various methods to push the inhabitants aside. In some quarters, military conflicts and wars of extermination cleared the way for settlement; in others, formal treaties were signed with the First Peoples (and then often ignored), legally opening large areas for agricultural development. In still other areas, the indigenous people were simply neglected or shunted aside, not deemed worthy either of careful attention or military action. In rapid fashion, many of the world's underdeveloped temperate zones fell to the logger, farmer, rancher, or settler.[64]

The dispossession of Indigenous Peoples from their lands throughout the world began long before the nineteenth century; it began with the voyages of Columbus and the doctrine of discovery:

"The process of discovering America is still going on. We have cut down the forests and cleaned away the bushwood. We have settled it from ocean to ocean, and made it a part of the world; but there is something more to do–a much greater and more difficult task lies before us: to discover ourselves, what we are, what we stand for, and, through introspection, to justify the physical discovery of America."[65]

These are the words of sixteenth-century Spanish jurist Francisco de Vitoria writing at the time of Columbus, questioning Spain's ability to claim the land of the Indigenous Peoples. It was Vitoria's view that Indigenous Peoples were part of the family of nations where their rights to their lands and territories must be respected by the Spanish Crown:

> In Victoria's [sic] conception, the international community, composed of states without reference to geography, race or religion, replaced the large but still limited international community coexistence with Christendom; this is the opinion of the world today. . . . All this is not merely a consequence of Victoria's [sic] doctrine; it is the doctrine itself expressly and unmistakeably stated in classical terms four centuries before our modern world endeavoured to create by covenant what Victoria [sic] had proclaimed as a fundamental principle and which we would call the culmination of his law of nations.[66]

It has taken more than five hundred years for international law to come full circle. It norms are now moving toward the recognition of the Indigenous Peoples' land rights, through instruments like the Draft Declaration.

The primary difficulty with state governments accepting Indigenous Peoples into the family of nations relates to the way Indigenous Peoples hold and value their lands and territories. Since Indigenous Peoples share lands so that they are held collectively. In Eurocentic states, the acceptance of collective land rights poses some difficulty:

> Collective rights to land—at least so far as these are basic and not created through the exercise of individual rights—may be seen by some as incompatible with the liberal–individualistic political philosophy that most settler states at least officially embrace which is thought to underlie the Universal Declaration on Human Rights, as far as this philosophy is limited to individual rights. To determine whether these suspicions are grounded, one must become clearer about what is meant by "collective land rights" and what the justification for such rights is supposed to be.[67]

When Indigenous Peoples refer to land rights, they refer to lands and territories on which their people have been born since time began. Legal scholar Hurst Hannum, discussing what he calls myths about human rights, noted during the discussion on the Draft Declaration:

> The second myth is the myth of individualism, which holds that human rights are only individual and not collective in nature. Without entering fully into the discussion, I would simply note that many countries such as Colombia and the United States do recognize that indigenous nations have collective rights in their domestic law. All countries would at least agree on the collective nature of indigenous land ownership and use, which is fundamental to indigenous society. If the right to land can be held collectively, then there can be no philosophical or ideological objection to the possibility that other rights may have collective aspects as well.[68]

The collective right to land means that land has a value beyond being a commodity and is not to be purchased and exchanged. The broader value of land remains central to the lives and economies of Indigenous Peoples:

> Everything of consequence for indigenous peoples begins with their unique understanding of the ties between all life, the land and the seas. It is a "symbiotic relationship," a physical and spiritual unity, a seamless whole which [cannot] be divided into parts.' "My roots grow in jackpine roots," a Yukon Tlingit elder explained to her questioner. "I grow here. I branch here" . . . Indigenous peoples hold the land collectively, they do not own or claim it as individuals. . . .The Haudenosaunee, the Six Nations of the North American Iroquois Confederacy, describe the clash of perspectives between the "first peoples" and Europeans. Conquerors asserted the "doctrine of discovery." They "discovered lands" and the indigenous peoples became part of the "flora and fauna."[69]

In theory, it is difficult for Eurocentric models of land ownership to accept and coexist with the collective land holdings of Indigenous Peoples. A fundamental characteristic of Indigenous land rights is that lands cannot be sold, but—for the Peoples to be economically self-reliant—lands and the resources that the land promise are shared. However, the colonizers have chosen to disregard Indigenous use of the lands in order to promote Eurocentric concepts of economic development:

> Large-scale colonization, more than any other kind of economic development, raises the question of land rights. Officials and set-

tlers alike have little understanding of indigenous economics. They see Indigenous Peoples as aimlessly wandering through the forest or arbitrarily clearing and planting. Yet it is the complex social, economic, and cultural relationship of indigenous peoples with their environment which has allowed them to survive. What settlement schemes do is to discount this well established adaption to the environment and replace it with new forms of land use, carried out by settlers from regions which are ecologically quite different. . . . Inevitably there are conflicts, Indigenous Peoples see their land being occupied and, in their view, destroyed by the newcomers. The latter, however, only see the land as fertile, unexploited and unoccupied.[70]

Indigenous Peoples are trying to protect their lands and territories for future generations—a customary value characteristic of self-reliant peoples—through the provisions of the Draft Declaration. Land held in common by Indigenous Peoples is in trust for the next generations: a unique characteristic of Indigenous Peoples worldwide. Every year, Indigenous Peoples appear at the Working Group with information about loss of land from their traditional territories.

The restoration of the lands which were taken as a result of colonization is a critical aspect of land rights. Article 27 of the Draft Declaration provides for compensation if the land is not available for return. All the issues related to land are ultimately related to the right of Self-determination:

Collective land rights . . . are one important dimension of self-determination for indigenous peoples. . . . three justifications for indigenous peoples' collective land rights . . . can be "derived" from a general "right of Self-determination of all peoples" . . . (1) to the idea of collective land rights as an initial step in rectifying past unjust takings of territory; (2) to the principle of justice requires the restoration of pre-conquest indigenous collective property rights systems; and (3) to the instrumental role of collective land rights in protecting imperilled indigenous cultures. . . . Indigenous peoples' rights movement represents a challenge to the theory and practice of international law.[71]

Self–identification and Self-determination and land rights are interconnected: in order for Peoples to exercise the right of self-determination, they need to have a secure land base. Prior to colonization, Indigenous Peoples had territories over which they exercised all their rights. In the drafting process, the Working Group has attempted to re-establish the legal relationships that are critical to the survival of Indigenous Peoples. Peoples need territory:

A corollary of legal personality is the principle of territorial security. This means that Indigenous Peoples have defined historical territories—even within the borders of existing states—and the right to keep these territories physically intact, environmentally sound and economically sustainable in their own ways.[72]

Discussion of the Draft Declaration may seem to be premature, as it still has to pass through the internal UN system to the General Assembly. However, three elements distinguish the Draft Declaration from any other human rights instrument developed for review: legal personality, and territorial and international responsibility.[73]

Conclusion

In 1982, Indigenous Peoples participated directly in the first Working Group of the United Nations, a significant step toward recognition as subjects rather than objects of international law. The Working Group had a dual mandate to review recent developments and to begin working on standard-setting activities related to the protection of Indigenous Peoples. In less than twenty years, the Working Group—in cooperation with government representatives, intergovernmental organizations, specialized agencies and Indigenous Peoples organizations—developed a Draft Declaration. There are a number of key provisions of the Draft Declaration which make the instrument unique.

The drafting process was a contribution by Indigenous Peoples to development of the norms which are going to affect their lives. As active participants in the process, Indigenous Peoples moved towards their recognition as subjects in law rather than as objects. They have been active in pushing the UN to live up to the obligations set out in the Charter. In order to have a Draft Declaration completed in the Working Group, Indigenous Peoples worked against the opposition mounted by state governments.

The Draft as accepted by the members of the Working Group and the Sub-commission contains language which recognizes Indigenous Peoples as "peoples." In addition, the Draft Declaration contains explicit language on the right to self-determination for Indigenous Peoples. While some state governments have been against the inclusion of such language, the members of the Working Group felt that the time was right for the protection of Indigenous Peoples. Danilo Turk, a former expert in the Working Group, stated that the application of the right of self-determination does not define peoples to whom it applies, nor does it say what is the result of the application of the right. It is the recognition of the right of self-determination which is important for Indigenous Peoples who want to be able to determine freely their political future.

In order to assist state governments with the implementation of the Charter provisions, the General Assembly has passed numerous resolutions on territorial integrity, but resolutions of the GA are not binding instruments and have no specific legal authority. While resolutions are indicative of widely held views, they do not bind states. If "peoples" have a right to self-determination as set out in the UN Charter, then a General Assembly resolution cannot change that norm. Will state members of the UN recognize the rights of Indigenous Peoples? The test will come as the Draft Declaration makes its way through the UN system. Indigenous Peoples came to the UN in 1977 seeking changes to their status and rights in international law. Some of those changes could have a profound affect on the role of states and in the development of international law norms.

Footnotes

1. The Working Group on Indigenous Peoples was a result of resolution 47/75 of 14 December 1992 of the UN General Assembly, resolution 1993/30 of 5 March 1993 of the Commission on Human Rights and the recommendation of the 1993 World Conference on Human Rights (Vienna Declaration and Programme of Action, A/Conf.157/23, Part II, paragraphs 28-32) which requested it to complete the draft during its 11th session in July 1993. The push was to celebrate the recognition of the UN designated International Year for Indigenous People. The Working Group did not complete the draft during the Working Group session but rather during the Sub-commission meeting in August 1993. As a consequence, the formal acceptance of the Declaration took place in July 1994 with the reading of the final draft during its 12th session. The full discussion of the Sub-commission's consideration will be covered in Chapter 5.

2. *Study of the problems of Discrimination against Indigenous Populations* Special Rapporteur Jose R. Martinez Cobo, Volume V Conclusions, Proposals and Recommendations, (E/CN.4/Sub.2/1986/7/Add.4) at para.7 at 3 [hereinafter *Cobo Report*]. See, Chapters 2 and 3 for discussion on Cobo in relation to definition of Indigenous Peoples and his work as a special rapporteur of the Sub-commission.

3. Ibid. at para. 7 at 3.

4. Ibid. Final recommendations contained in add. 4.

5. UN Charter, *supra* note 1 Article 71 allows for the Economic and Social Council to make "suitable arrangements for consultation with non-governmental organization which are concerned with matters within its competence." There were thirty-six international organization which co-sponsored the meeting held in 1977. The number of organizations which participated in the 1981 meeting are not recorded.

6. "International NGO Conference on Discrimination Against Indigenous Peoples in the Americas—1977" (1977) 3 *American Indian Journal of the Institute for the Development of Indian Law* at 4 [hereinafter 1977 Conference Report].

7. Chapters XII and XIII of the UN Charter set up an international trusteeship system for the administration and supervision of territories placed thereunder by individual agreements. Article 76 set out the objectives of the trusteeship system while article 77 sets out under which circumstances a territory could be considered for placement under trusteeship.

8. 1977 Conference Report, *supra* note 6 at 5.

9. 1977 Conference Report, *supra* note 6 at 5.

10. Hurst Hannum, *Autonomy, Sovereignty, and Self-determination—The Accommodation of Conflicting Rights* rev.ed. (Philadelphia: University of Pennsylvania Press, 1996) at 83 [hereinafter Hannum, *Accommodation*].

11. Natan Lerner, *Group Rights and Discrimination in International Law* (Dordrecht: Martinus Nijhoff Publishers, 1991) [hereinafter Lerner, *Group Rights*].

12. Independent Commission on International Humanitarian Issues, *Indigenous Peoples —A Global Quest for Justice* (London: Zed Books Ltd., 1987) [hereinafter *Global Quest*].

13. Theo van Boven quoted in: B.G. Ramcharan, *The Concept and Present State of the International Protection of Human Rights Forty Years after the Universal Declaration* (Dordrecht: Martinus Nijhoff Publishers, 1989) at 207 [hereinafter Ramcharan].

14. Madame Erica–Irene Daes and Miguel Alfonso-Martinez attended the informal meeting. A formal presentation to the Working Group in 1986 included the minutes of the meeting contained in: Review of Developments: *Standard Setting Activities—Material Received From Non-Governmental Organizations in Consultative Status with the Economic and Social Council*, (E/CN.4/Sub.2/AC.4/WP.4/Add.1 (1987) [hereinafter *Informal meeting of the Working Group*] See also: *For the Record, Indigenous Peoples and Slavery in the United Nations A Special Report of the Two Working Groups of the Human Rights Sub-Commission August 1991* (Ottawa: Human Rights Centre 1991) at 7.

15. Lia Zanotta Machado "Indigenous Communitarianism as a Critique of Modernity and its Juridical Implications" in W.J. Assies and A.J. Hoekema eds., *Indigenous Peoples' Experiences with Self-Government* (Copenhagen: University of Amsterdam and IWGIA, 1994) at 73.

16. Meeting of Experts on Indigenous Self-Government, Nuuk, Greenland 24-28 September 1991 (E/CN.4/1992/42/Add.1) [hereinafter *Indigenous Government*].

17. Technical conference on Indigenous Peoples and the Environment held at Santiago, Chile in May 1992 (E/CN.4/Sub.2/1992/31 and Add. 1).

18. Report of the Expert Seminar on Practical Experiences Regarding Indigenous Land Rights and Claims, Whitehorse, Canada, 24–28 March 1996 (E/CN.4/Sub.2/AC.4/1996/6/Add. 1) -[hereinafter, *Land Rights*]

19. See the report of the Seminar (E/CN.4/1989/22).

20. Ibid.

21. Land Rights, *supra* note 17 at 6.

22. UN Charter, *supra* note 1, Articles 68, 69, 70 and 71 outline who may participate at meetings of the Economic and Social Council.

23. Report of the Working Group on Indigenous Populations on its first session (E/CN.4/Sub.2/1982/33) [hereinafter 1982 *Working Group Report*].

24. Hannum, *Accommodation*, supra note 10 at 84.

25. For a copy of the Draft Declaration, see Appendix I of this thesis.

26. Eyassu Gayim, *The UN Draft Declaration on Indigenous Peoples Assessment of the Draft Prepared by the Working Group on Indigenous Populations* (Rovaniemi: University of Lapland, 1994) at 9.

27. Of the three international instruments: Universal Declaration of Human Rights, International Covenant on Civil and Political Rights and International Covenant on Economic, Social and Cultural Rights, only Article 1 of both International Covenants refer to rights of a group, while Article 27 of the CCPR refers to the rights of individuals of minorities possessing rights.

28. Ian Brownlie,"The Rights of Peoples in Modern International Law" in James Crawford ed. *The Rights of Peoples* (Oxford: Clarendon Press, 1988) at 2.

29. Erica–Irene Daes, "Equality of Indigenous Peoples under the Auspices of the United Nations—Draft Declaration on the Rights of Indigenous Peoples" [1995] 7 *St. Thomas Law Review*, at 494 [hereinafter Daes, Equality].

30. Eyassu Gayim "The Draft Declaration on Indigenous Peoples: With Focus on the Rights to Self-Determination and Land" in Eyassu Gayim and Kristin Myntti eds., *Indigenous and Tribal Peoples' Rights—1993 and After* (Rovenaniemi: University of Lapland, 1995) at 20 [hereinafter Gayim, Focus on Self-Determination].

31. [1930] Permanent Court of International Justice Series B, No. 17 at 21.

32. Rudofo Stavenhagen, *The Ethnic Conflicts, Development, and Human Rights* (Tokyo: United Nations University Press, 1990) at 68.

33. Erica–Irene Daes, "Some Considerations on the Rights of Indigenous Peoples to Self-Determination", (1993) 3 *Transnational Law and Contemporary Problems* 1 at 5 [hereinafter Daes, *Rights*].

34. Erica–Irene Daes, "Working Paper by the Chairperson/Rapporteur on the Concept of 'indigenous people'" E/CN4/Sub.2/AC.4/1996/2 [hereinafter Daes, *Definition*].

35. Report of the Working Group on Indigenous Populations on its twelfth session (E/CN.4/Sub.2/ 1995/24) at 7 [hereinafter *1995 Working Group*] refers to Madame Daes's working paper on the criteria which might be applied when considering the concept of Indigenous Peoples (E/CN.4/AC.4/1995/3).

36. *1995 Working Group, supra* at note 35 at 13.

37. 1995 *Working Group, supra* at note 35 at 13.

38. 1995 *Working Group, supra* at note 35 at 33 in paragraph 3 of its resolution 1995/38 of 24 August 1995.

39. Discussed in detail in Chapter 5.

40. Article 8: Indigenous peoples have the collective and individual right to maintain and develop their distinct identities and characteristics, including the right to identify themselves as indigenous and to be recognized as such.

41. Daes, *Definition, supra* at note 34 at 13.

42. Daes, *Equality, supra* at note 29 at 496.

43. Indigenous Government meeting, *supra* at note at 20. See, also: Benedict Kingsbury,"Whose International Law? Sovereignty and Non–State Groups [1994] *American Society of International Law Proceedings* at 3 writes: "Features often associated with "indigenous peoples" include self–definition, common ethnicity, non-dominance in the state, existence in the territory or region prior to more recent arrivals who have become dominant, and particularly close connections with land."

44. *Report of the Committee on the Elimination of Racial Discrimination: General Recommendations* VII, UN GAOR, 45th Sess., Supp. No. 18, at 79.

45. James Crawford, "Outside the Colonial Context—Self-determination outside of the Colonial Context" in W. J. Allen Macartney, *Self-determination in the Commonwealth* (Aberdeen: The University Press, 1988) at 3 [hereinafter Crawford, *Colonial Context*].

46. Ibid. at 37.

47. A resolution of the General Assembly is "not binding document, and it has no specific legal authority; it is nonetheless indicative of widely held views on the subjects it deals with" ibid. at 6.

48. G.A. Resolution 1514 (XV), 14 December 1960.

49. G.A. Resolution 2625 (XXV) 24 October 1970.

50. Antonio Cassese, *Self-determination of peoples A legal reappraisal* (Cambridge: University of Cambridge, 1995) at 59 [hereinafter Cassese, *Self-determination*].

51. Crawford, *Colonial Context, supra* at note 44 at 6.

52. Cassese, *Self-determination, supra* note 49 at 102.

53. *Advisory Opinion of the International Court of Justice Concerning the Western Sahara*, [1975] ICJ Reports 12.

54. Cassese, *Self-determination, supra* note 49 at 320.

55. Richard Falk, "The Rights of Peoples (In Particular Indigenous Peoples)," in James Crawford, *The Rights of Peoples* (Oxford: Oxford University Press, 1988) at 24-27.

56. Ibid. at 36.

57. Dalee Sambo, 'Indigenous Peoples and International Standard–Setting Processes: Are State Governments Listening?" [1993] 3 *Transnational Law and Contemporary Problems* at 23-25.

58. *Land Rights, supra* note 17.

59. *Cobo Study, supra* note 2.

60. Draft Indigenous Principles, in *Informal meeting of the Working Group, supra* note 14.

61. For a discussion on these problems, see Darrell Posey, "Effecting International Change" (1991) 15 *Cultural Survival Quarterly* 29 who writes about the problem with WIPO and the protection of Indigenous Peoples Intellectual Property: "With songs and stories, emphasis on individual and Western corporate rights of property leave communal, easily copied 'property' vulnerable to use by anyone anywhere". Also see: Tom Greaves ed., *Intellectual Property Rights for Indigenous Peoples—A Source Book* (Oklahoma City: The Society for Applied Anthropology, 1994) which contains a number of essays on intellectual property rights of Indigenous Peoples and the work which is taking place on an international level with Indigenous Peoples within and outside of the United Nations [hereinafter Source Book]. In addition, Madame Daes undertook a study on the ownership and control of cultural property of Indigenous Peoples for the Sub-commission, see *Study on the Protection of the Cultural and intellectual property of Indigenous Peoples*, E/CN.4/Sub.2/1993/28 (1993). Intellectual property of Indigenous Peoples was discussed in the Charter of the Earth (also known as the Kari–Oca Declaration) which was tabled at the United Nations Conference on the Environment and Development (UNCED) in Rio in June 1992. This Charter was developed by Indigenous Peoples attending a conference prior to the World Conference. For more information on the Kari-Oca Declaration and the Indigenous Peoples meeting see: *International Work Group on Indigenous Affairs Newsletter,* No. 4, 1992 and Teresa Aparacio, "Indigenous Peoples in Rio: the Kari-Oca World Indigenous Conference, Ibid, at 53–56.. See also Sharon Venne, "Kari-Oca—An Indigenous Peoples' meeting" in (1993) *International Work Group on Indigenous Affairs Annual Report.* The Kari-Oca meeting was a significant step forward for Indigenous Peoples who developed their own agenda on development and the environment which was subsequently submitted to the UNCED meeting and included in the final report the General Assembly.

62. "In a comprehensive survey of such efforts [to protect the intellectual property of Indigenous Peoples] by Posey (1991), he reviews shortcomings in the multitude of efforts that have been broached by numerous agencies and organizations, including the United Nations World Intellectual Property Organization (WIPO), the Union for the Protection of New Varieties of Plants (UPOV), and the International Union for the Conservation of Nature (IUCN). Specifically, he observes that even though 123 United Nations members states have reached broad agreements on industrial property and trademark that these agreements have never been applied to indigenous knowledge or handicrafts" David J. Stephenson, Jr., "A Legal Paradigm for Protecting Traditional Knowledge" *Source Book, supra* at note 126 at 186.

63. Audrey R. Chapman," Human Rights Implications of Indigenous Peoples' Intellectual Property Rights" in *Source Book, supra* at note 59 at 214–215.

64. E/CN.4/Sub.2/AC.4/1996/6/Add.1 at 14.

65. James Brown Scott, *The Spanish Origin of International Law Francisco de Vitoria and His Law of Nations* (Oxford: Clarendon Press, 1934) at 18 [hereinafter Scott, *Vitoria*].

66. Ibid. at 283.

67. Allen Buchanan, "The Role of Collective Rights in the Theory of Indigenous Peoples' Rights", [1993] 3 *Transnational Law and Contemporary Problems* at 95 [hereinafter Buchanan, *Collective Rights*].

68. Hurst Hannum, "Procedural Aspects of International Law" [1996] 1 *International Work Group for Indigenous Affairs* 38.

69. Judith P. Zinsser, "A new partnership: indigenous peoples and the United Nations system (Paris: UNESCO, 1994) at 17.

70. *Global Quest, supra* at note 12 at 74.

71. Buchanan, *Collective Rights, supra* at note 65 at 106–107. Daes, Equality, supra at note 29 at 497.

72. Daes, *Equality, supra* note 29 at 496.

73. Daes, *Equality, supra* note 29 at 496.

5

The Responce of The UN To The Draft Declaration

Introduction

The Declaration developed by the Working Group was conceived as a statement of the minimum standard on the Rights of Indigenous Peoples, continuing the work of the past two decades by the UN to clarify those rights in relation to the UN Charter. A declaration is not like a treaty, which can be ratified by states and then become legally binding on them. In a legal opinion prepared for the CHR, the differences between an internal UN declaration and a recommendation were reviewed in relation to UN practice:

> A "declaration" is a formal and solemn instrument, suitable for rare occasions when principles of great and lasting importance are being enunciated, such as the Declaration of Human Rights. A "recommendation" is less formal. Apart from the distinction just indicated, there is probably no difference between a "recommendation" and a "declaration" in United Nations practice as far as strict legal principle is concerned. A "declaration" or a "recommendation" is adopted by resolution of a United Nations organ. As such it cannot be made binding upon Member States, in the sense that a treaty or convention is binding upon the parties to it, purely by the device of terming it a "declaration" rather than a "recommendation". However, in view of the greater solemnity and significance of a "declaration," it may be considered to impart, on behalf of the organ adopting it, a strong expectation that Members of the international community will abide by it. Consequently, in so far as the expectation is gradually justified by State practice, a "declaration" may by custom become recognized as laying down rules binding upon States.[1]

Thus, a resolution adopted by the GA, even in the form of a Declaration, is a recommendation only and is not binding on states. A Declaration is not considered to be a primary source of international law. However, a declaration becomes influential on the future role and action of states. Over time and with usage, a declaration can become accepted as an international law norm in that it becomes representative of customary international law. In some cases, a GA resolution's wording and format can be used at a later time as a basis for a convention:

> Without entering into details, we refer to further examples taken from the practice of the UN General Assembly to prove that the principles contained in the substantive resolutions of the General Assembly or in its declarations have provided a basis for the elaboration of a subsequent international conventional regulation. Thus, we can clearly recognize the impact which the Universal Declaration of Human Rights had upon the two Covenants adopted by the UN General Assembly on 16 December 1966 in respect of civil and political rights as well as economic, social and cultural rights, or upon the instruments adopted by the General Assembly on 21 December 1965 and entitled International Convention on the Elimination of All Forms of Racial Discrimination.[2]

The UN has a place to play in the process of formatting norms of international law. The intent of having a number of agencies and participants in the drafting of a declaration is to facilitate the drafting and acceptance of the instrument. In the case of the drafting process for the Declaration on the Rights of Indigenous Peoples, the participants included the Working Group on Indigenous Peoples, specialized agencies of the UN, state governments, legal writers and Indigenous Peoples and their organizations.

After six years of drafting and eight years of discussion, the Draft Declaration on the Rights of Indigenous Peoples[3] was ready to be moved from the Working Group on Indigenous Peoples toward the General Assembly (GA). The first step was review by the parent body of the Working Group, the Sub-commission on the Prevention of Discrimination and Protection of Minorities (Sub-Commission).[4] On 22 August 1994, Madame Erica-Irene Daes, Chairperson/Rapporteur of the Working Group introduced the document to the other members of the Sub-commission.

The work of the Sub-commission was to accept and/or amend the draft language proposed by the Working Group. In addition, the Commission on Human Rights (CHR) asked for recommendations on a possible course for future consideration of the draft.[5] In August, 1994 the Sub-commission recommended the Draft Declaration to the CHR without any reservation as to choice of language or terms. However, the Sub-commission resolution recommending the Draft Declaration to the CHR did not recommend the full participation of Indigenous Peoples in future discussions of the Draft Declaration.[6]

At the February-March 1995 meeting, CHR members decided not to accept the Draft Declaration as submitted by the Sub-commission. Instead, the members established an Open-ended Inter-sessional Working Group to elaborate a Draft Declaration. Once the Inter-sessional Working Group has completed its work, the revised Draft will be submitted to the CHR before it can be recommended to the larger UN bodies. Each of these processes will be reviewed in relation to two areas: (a) participation by Indigenous Peoples and (b) the evolution of international law standards in relation to Indigenous Peoples.

The Draft Declaration on the Rights of Indigenous Peoples is a precedent-setting international instrument. It is the first UN instrument to develop standards on Indigenous Peoples' rights. It is also the first UN instrument drafted with the direct participation by Indigenous Peoples in the process. Hundreds of Indigenous delegates over a long period of time attended and participated in the discussions leading to the final Draft Declaration. Consequently, the potential effect on the UN processes for developing international instruments on Indigenous Peoples and on international law norms are also likely to be precedent-setting, sweeping and significant. It is now impossible for international bodies to develop credible instruments affecting Indigenous Peoples without their direct and active participation. The drafting of a Declaration on the rights of Indigenous Peoples moved Indigenous Peoples towards being subjects of international law and away from being treated as objects.

Even if the Draft Declaration developed by the Working Group on Indigenous Peoples remains intact through the elaboration process in the Inter-sessional Working Group and is accepted by the members of the CHR, the draft instrument must be reviewed by members of the Economic and Social Council (ECOSOC) before it is transmitted to the General Assembly. The wording of the 1995 CHR resolution permits a complete redrafting of the document by the Inter–sessional Working Group. Indigenous Peoples would prefer that the rights in the current Draft Declaration are not amended,[7] while the state representatives are calling for major amendments and the redrafting of complete sections.[8] The process is perhaps understandable for such a precedent–setting legal instrument on the rights of Indigenous Peoples. At any place in the current process, substantial changes could be made to the Draft Declaration, with decreasing representation by Indigenous Peoples.

Participation by Indigenous Peoples in the drafting of this international standard on their rights has been as precedent-setting as the document itself. The resolution establishing the Inter-sessional Working Group also set up a complex set of procedures for participation by Indigenous Peoples. As a result, only seventy-eight Indigenous organizations[9] participated at the first Inter–sessional Working Group.[10] This chapter considers the participation of Indigenous Peoples throughout this process and its impact on international law. While discouraging, even this level of representation is progressive. In the final section of this chapter, progress of the Draft Declaration through the UN, as an example of the development of international standards by an international organization, will be reviewed. The Draft Declaration on the Rights of Indigenous Peoples has already set precedents for the UN, and has the potential for significant impacts on international law.

Drafting of The Declaration

Development of International Rights Standards

When the Working Group on Indigenous Peoples began its meetings in 1982, numerous issues[11] were placed before the members, including the development of standards which were considered a:

> complex matter and different interpretations of standards were possible: a) what are the standards to be applied?; b) to whom should these standards be applied?; and c) what would be the system of supervision of application of standards? One might distinguish 2 levels of standards: a) procedural and b) substantive standards.[12]

In the first session, the options for standards to be developed concerning the rights of Indigenous Peoples were reviewed:

> a) a statement of principles by the Working Group;
> b) a Declaration by another body of the United Nations, which will be more comprehensive and will not be legally binding; and
> c) an international convention [treaty], legally binding after adoption by States.[13]

In 1984, the Sub-commission[14] and then the CHR[15] recommended that the Working Group begin working on a declaration on substantive rights that could be adopted by the General Assembly.

By the third session of the Working Group in 1984, the expert members turned their attention to standard setting. It had been determined in the previous year "that standards concerning the rights of Indigenous populations should be considered as an evolutionary and not a static concept."[16] Indigenous delegates presented a consensus statement on the future role of the Working Group and the type of instrument to be drafted. Considering this statement to be important, the Working Group included it in its 1984 report to the Sub-commission:

> The Working Group should strive at this stage, to draft a Declaration of Indigenous Rights which should be considered for adoption by the appropriate bodies of the United Nations, and may subsequently form the basis of the multilateral treaty or covenant. In the same consensus text submitted to the Working Group those organizations suggested, as a method of proceeding to the drafting of such a Declaration, that the Working Group address each of the subjects in previously adopted plan of action, and begin to develop the elements of a declaration as these issues are discussed.[17]

The role of Indigenous delegates in the drafting process is discussed later in this chapter.

Based on the report of the Working Group and the resolution from the Sub-commission, the CHR directed the Working Group to begin drafting an instrument to elaborate standards for the protection of the rights of Indigenous Peoples. Within the UN system there were no existing instruments to protect the rights of Indigenous Peoples: "The view that existing instruments did not adequately respond to the needs of indigenous populations was endorsed by most speakers, including observers from Governments."[18]

At the 1985 meeting of the Working Group, the type of instrument to be drafted was discussed in greater detail. There was:

> more or less general agreement from all sides that the standards to be drafted by the Working Group should in the first instance form a declaration, eventually to be adopted by the General Assembly of the United Nations. The possibility of a convention was also mentioned, but there seemed to be general agreement, also on this point, that this kind of instrument would emerge further down the road, possibly with inspiration from the declaration.[19]

Having determined that the instrument would be a declaration, it was decided that Erica-Irene Daes, as chair of the Working Group, would serve as the Rapporteur for the drafting process.[20]

The Draft Declaration which will potentially be adopted by the GA would form part of the process inspired by the 1960 Declaration on Decolonization that condemned colonialism.[21] One member of the Working Group, seeing the drafting process as linked to the decolonization process for Indigenous Peoples, stated:

> the Group should draw inspiration from the influence which the

Declaration on the Granting of Independence to Colonial Countries and Peoples[22] has had on the decolonization process. Thanks to this Declaration, adopted by the General Assembly in 1960, millions of people all over the world now lived in freedom and independence. It was [this member's] belief that the recognition and the restoration of basic rights to indigenous populations and peoples would be hastened if an appropriate declaration could be drawn upon by the Working Group with the cooperation of all the parties concerned, bearing in mind that any future set of principles could only be adopted with the support of Governments.[23]

One member recognized that colonized Indigenous Peoples have a need to live in freedom and with independence. As reviewed in Chapter 1 of this book, Indigenous Peoples of the Americas were colonized with the arrival of Columbus in 1492 and their rights denied under the subsequent doctrine of discovery.[24]

In 1985, the Working Group introduced seven preliminary draft principles as follows:

1. The right to the full and effective enjoyment of the fundamental rights and freedoms universally recognized in existing international instruments, particularly in the Charter of the United Nations and the International Bill of Human Rights;
2. The right to be free and equal to all other human beings in dignity and rights, and to be free from discrimination of any kind;
3. The collective right to exist and to be protected against genocide, as well as the individual right to life, physical integrity, liberty, and security of person;
4. The right to manifest, teach, practice and observe their own religious traditions and ceremonies, and to maintain, protect, and have access to sites for these purposes;
5. The right to all forms of education, including the right to have access to education in their own languages, and to establish their own educational institutions;
6. The right to preserve their cultural identity and traditions, and to pursue their own cultural development; and
7. The right to promote intercultural information and education, recognizing the dignity and diversity of their culture. [25]

The Working Group followed the lead of Indigenous Peoples begun at the 1981 NGO conference, when the time, Indigenous Peoples were preparing principles in anticipation of the development of international rights standards. The development of these principles was an example of Indigenous involvement early in the Working Group's drafting process.

In 1985, twenty draft principles were prepared by Indigenous Peoples participating in preparatory meetings. While the members of the Working Group prepared seven very general principles, the Indigenous Declaration of Principles contains a wider variety of rights:

1. Indigenous nations and peoples have, in common with all humanity, the right to life, and to freedom from oppression, discrimination, and aggression.

2. All indigenous nations and peoples have the right to Self-determination, by virtue of which they have the right to whatever degree of autonomy or self–government they choose. This includes the right to freely determine their political status, freely pursue their own economic, social, religious and cultural development, and determine their own membership and/or citizenship, without external interference.

3. No State shall assert any jurisdiction over an indigenous nation or people, or its territory, except in accordance with the freely expressed wishes of the nation or people concerned.

4. Indigenous nations and peoples are entitled to the permanent control and enjoyment of their aboriginal ancestral–historical territories. This includes surface and subsurface rights, inland and coastal waters, renewable and non–renewable resources, and the economies based on these resources.

5. Rights to share and use land, subject to the underlying and inalienable title of the indigenous nation or people, may be granted by their free and informed consent, as evidenced in a valid treaty or agreement.

6. Discovery, conquest, settlement on a theory of terra nullius and unilateral legislation are never legitimate bases for States to claim or retain the territories of indigenous nations or peoples.

7. In cases where lands taken in violation of these principles have already been settled, the indigenous nation or people concerned is entitled to immediate restitution, including compensation for the loss of use, without extinction of original title. Indigenous peoples' desire to regain possession and control of sacred sites must always be respected.

8. No State shall participate financially or militarily in the involuntary displacement of indigenous populations, or in the subsequent economic exploitation or military use of their territory.

9. The laws and customs of indigenous nations and peoples must be recognized by the States' legislative, administrative and judicial institutions and, in case of conflicts with State laws, shall take precedence.

10. No State shall deny an indigenous nation, community, or peo-

ple residing within its borders the right to participate in the life of the State in whatever manner and to whatever degree they may choose. This includes the right to participate in other forms of collective action and expression.

11. Indigenous nations and peoples continue to own and control their material culture, including archeological, historical and sacred sites, artifacts, designs, knowledge, and works of art. They have the right to regain items of major cultural significance and, in all cases, to the return of the human remains of their ancestors for burial in accordance with their traditions.

12. Indigenous nations and peoples have the right to be educated and conduct business with States in their own languages, and to establish their own educational institutions.

13. No technical, scientific, or social investigations, including archeological excavations, shall take place in relation to indigenous nations or peoples, or their lands, without their prior authorization, and their continuing ownership and control.

14. The religious practices of indigenous nations and peoples shall be fully respected and protected by the laws of the States and by international law. Indigenous nations and peoples shall always enjoy unrestricted access to, and enjoyment of sacred sites in accordance with their own laws and customs, including the right of privacy.

15. Indigenous nations and peoples are subjects of international law.

16. Treaties and other agreements freely made with indigenous nations and peoples shall be recognized and applied in the same manner and according to the same international laws and principles as treaties and agreements entered into with other States.

17. Disputes regarding the jurisdiction, territories and institutions of an indigenous nation or people are a proper concern of international law, and must be resolved by mutual agreement or valid treaty.

18. Indigenous nations and peoples may engage in self–defence against State actions in conflict with their right to Self-determination.

19. Indigenous nations and peoples have the right to travel freely, and to maintain economic, social, cultural and religious relations with each other across State borders.

20. In addition to these rights, indigenous nations and peoples are entitled to the enjoyment of all the human rights and fundamental freedoms enumerated in the International Bill of Rights and other United Nations instruments. In no circumstances shall they be subject to adverse discrimination.[26]

In 1987, the Indigenous Peoples added two more principles to bring the total to twenty-two. The two new principles concerned traditional medicines and military service:

21. All indigenous nations and peoples have the right to their own traditional medicine, including the right to protection of vital medicinal plants, animals and minerals. Indigenous nations and peoples also have the right to benefit from modern medical techniques and services on a basis equal to that of the general population of the States within which they are located. Furthermore, all indigenous nations and peoples have the right to determine, plan, implement, and control the resources respecting health, housing, and other social services affecting them.

22. According to the right of self-determination, all indigenous nations and peoples shall not be obligated to participate in State military services, including armies, paramilitary or 'civil' organizations with military structures, within the country or in international conflicts.[27]

Although no official Working Group meeting was held in 1986 due to a UN financial crisis, an informal meeting co-sponsored by the WCIP and the Anti-Slavery Society for the Protection of Human Rights was held on 6-7 September, 1986. Two members of the Working Group attended the meeting and six governments sent representatives: Argentina, Australia, Canada, China, New Zealand and the United States of America. The report of the meeting was tabled at the fifth session of the Working Group.[28] During the informal meeting, some work was done to elaborate three of the draft principles for the Draft Declaration, which were favourably accepted when reported to the Working Group in 1987.[29]

At the next session held in 1987, the Working Group members returned to clarifications of principles to embrace the scope of the Declaration:

One member of the Working Group provided an overview of his thoughts on standard-setting relating to indigenous rights. He pointed out that this was a complex task which required a great deal of conceptual clarification and 'confidence building' necessary prior to the adoption of standards by the political bodies of the United Nations. In that connection, he identified three areas to be addressed: (a) the position of group rights in the context of United Nations human rights activities; (b) issues relating to autonomy, and (c) the possible relevance of new concepts, such as the right to development, to indigenous populations.[30]

Clearly, some members of the Working Group viewed the drafting of a Declaration as an exercise of identifying the collective or group rights of Indigenous Peoples, in contrast to most existing human rights instruments, which deal with rights through "the individualistic approach."[31] The Working Group compiled a list of rights which could be envisaged as collective rights:

> (a) the right to maintain and develop group characteristics and identity; (b) the right to be protected against attempts to destroy the group identity, including propaganda directed against the group; (c) the right to equality with other groups as regards the respect for and development of their specific characteristics; (d) the duty of the territorial State to grant the groups—within the resources available—the necessary assistance for the maintenance of their identity and their development; (e) the right to have their specific character reflected in the legal system and in the political institutions of their country, including cultural autonomy as well as administrative autonomy, wherever feasible; and (f) along with these general and common rights each category of groups and each group would be entitled to more specific rights. Thus, for instance, the land rights of indigenous peoples constitute a specific category of rights necessary for the development of this category of groups.[32]

The dilemma for the Working Group was to address the recommendations by Indigenous Peoples while trying to reconcile the individualistic focus of existing human rights instruments. It was also pointed out to the Working Group that UN instruments drafted to that date had been created without the participation or consent of the Indigenous Peoples. Existing rights instruments, therefore, reflected Eurocentric rather than Indigenous societal values—for example:

> The right to life and personal security which indigenous populations tied to the right to land, and the right to private property which was perhaps different from what indigenous populations meant or wanted when referring to the right to land.[33]

Collective or group rights are crucial to Indigenous Peoples, particularly in relation to self-determination as Indigenous delegates have indicated in their draft principles of 1985.

Participation by Indigenous Peoples

Indigenous preparatory meetings are held prior to every UN meeting in order to share information and discuss strategy. Many Indigenous Peoples who appear at such meetings have never attended before and do not know how to draft submissions or put their names on lists for speakers. Indigenous Peoples who have regularly attended the UN meetings brief the meeting on previous and future work in various areas. These preliminary meetings, which occur two or three days prior to a rgular meeting are usually informal. The main difficulty for Indigenous Peoples with such meetings involves translation. Many speak one of the colonizer languages along with their Indigenous language. In order to work effectively, translation is needed. In the past this has proven to be difficult. Often, support groups provide informal services. However, in 1996, the Greenland Home Rule government provided funds to hire official translators in three working languages: English, Spanish and Russian. At the end of the preparatory meetings, Indigenous participants prepare joint statements and resolutions to be tabled at the Working Group meetings. Delegates who cannot attend the preparatory meetings usually indicate their support for a particular resolution during their interventions.

While the final text of the Draft Declaration of the Working Group was some years away, Indigenous delegates were actively drafting principles for rights standards at every opportunity. It is significant that consensus was reached on these principles within four years of the establishment of the Working Group despite culture and language differences amongst Indigenous delegates. Discussion of these principles built on consensus was a first step toward securing universal language in the Draft Declaration supporting the process that would emerge within Working Group. Indigenous delegates and organizations then advocated support by Working Group members for the most vital principles: land rights, resource rights, self-determination, use of the word "Peoples" not "populations" and self-identification rather than imposed definition for Indigenous Peoples. These four key areas were itemized early in the process along with other areas relating to culture, education and social rights. Clearly, the focus was on political and not on cultural rights.

By the end of the fifth session, the Working Group agreed to develop a working paper as a "preliminary version" of the Declaration:

> It would likely contain square brackets with alternative texts, and it would as such be used for the Group's first and second readings of the draft declaration. . . . [The] working document would be a useful exercise. It would enable the Working Group to amplify still further the dialogue in which it is engaged and would indeed bring the adoption by the General Assembly of a "Universal Declaration on Indigenous Rights" one step closer.[34]

Based on Working Group sessions—and, in particular, the detailed discussions on group rights versus individual rights—the Chair/ Rapporteur was charged with developing the working text she presented at the 1988 session.[35] Madame Daes introduced the document pointing out the positive aspects of the draft:

> Those crucial issues included the use of the term "indigenous peoples" rather than "indigenous populations"; the combination of individual and collective rights with a special emphasis on the latter as an inherent and essential element of indigenous rights, the effective protection of indigenous identities as manifested in cultures, languages, religions, traditions, and customs; the introduction of indigenous autonomy with meaningful functions and powers; the reaffirmation of land and resource rights; and the absence of a definition of beneficiaries which she considered unnecessary for the adoption of a proper application of the declaration. Further, the Chairman/Rapporteur expected the debate to be general with a more specific debate [to take place in 1989].[36]

Indigenous Peoples generally accepted the 1988 working text as a necessary good first attempt for in areas of interest to them. In a statement from the Indigenous Peoples' preparatory meeting[37] held in Geneva in July 1988, a representative said:

> The Meeting's support for the Working Group's standard setting efforts which, he said, should be consistent with and in the context of the most fundamental rights of Indigenous Peoples, the right to Self-determination. The following constructive comments emanating from the 1988 [draft] were offered to the Working Group: (a) the right to self-determination was not adequately covered; (b) the collective right to lands and territories was not fully addressed; (c) the importance of lands and resources including surface and sub-surface resources had to be more extensively covered; and (d) the significance of treaties and treaty–making needed further elaboration.[38]

The four highlighted areas were the same principles outlined in the 1985 Indigenous draft principles which have consistently remained a priority for Indigenous participants.

At the sixth session of the Working Group, as a result of the Indigenous response to the 1988 draft, there was considerable discussion on collective rights versus individual rights and ways in which collective rights could coexist with existing UN instruments. Some time was spent reviewing Article 27 of the International Covenant on Civil and Political

Rights[39] and its relation to the Draft Declaration. Article 27 (discussed in Chapter 3) refers to rights of individuals within minorities within a state and, technically, is not an article which deals with collective rights. The members of the Working Group tried to find a connection between the two instruments but concluded that Indigenous Peoples are not minorities and consequently their collective rights to land and resources are not protected and guaranteed by Article 27.[40] On this point, the Working Group stated:

> Indigenous Peoples were indeed peoples and not minorities or ethnic groups. Although the concept of "peoples" had not been defined by the United Nations, state practice and other indications in national legislation showed that it could be used in the case of indigenous peoples.[41]

In the Indigenous draft principles submitted to the Working Group in 1985, the term "Indigenous Nations" was used along with "Indigenous Peoples." In later discussion, Indigenous participants agreed that "Peoples" was the more appropriate term, since it conforms with UN terminology.[42] The only places the word "Nation" is used in the UN Charter are the Preamble and Article 1(2).[43] Therefore, Indigenous participants agreed to forego the 1985 draft principle, that the term "Indigenous Nations" be recognized, agreeing instead with the UN terminology.

Indigenous participants effected a major change in the UN procedures during the responses to a general request from the Sub-commission (resolution 1988/18) to prepare a revised text of the Draft Declaration. This revision was to be based on comments made by state governments, specialized agencies, non-governmental organizations and Indigenous organizations.[44] By conventional UN procedures, such comments are written submissions. This revision process was postponed when the Working Group realized that Indigenous Peoples had not made any substantial written comments on the 1988 draft. As a result, the Chairman/Rapporteur decided to "restrict herself as much as possible to technical alterations of preambular and operative principles where she considered them appropriate and feasible rather than inserting more extensive and substantive revision."[45] Without the direct participation of the Indigenous Peoples, the Working Group considered the draft was incomplete in contrast to other standard-setting processes, such as development of the ILO Conventions. The Working Group's attempts to get written responses on the 1988 draft from delegates proved impractical since Indigenous Peoples preferred to be present and to be heard along with other representatives. It was a way to make the consensus– building process meaningful to Indigenous Peoples. The Working Group agreed and in 1989 succeeded in having the Sub-commission authorize the

Working Group meet in informal drafting groups for one week prior to the 1990 session. Indigenous Peoples did not consider the submitting of written texts to be full and active participation in which all views can be presented for response.

Only three informal groups were established to review the 1988 draft only. Group one was chaired by Miguel Alfonso-Martinez,[46] group two by Danilo Turk[47] and group three by Madame Daes.[48] Each group reviewing the Draft Declaration article by article included representatives of state governments, specialized agencies, non-governmental organizations and Indigenous organizations. This review process allowed for a wide range of discussion and contribution for developing consensus. The drafting groups allowed for "everyone [to] free[ly] submit, orally or in writing, any amendments which might improve, supplement or correct the existing text of the first revised text."[49] It was also agreed that any text in which "full consensus and agreement would be reached should appear in the present report of the Drafting Group."[50] Thus, the participation of Indigenous Peoples effected a significant change in the process for drafting and reviewing an international rights document.

As a result of the 1990 drafting exercise, the drafting process moved more easily and quickly from the informal oral process, and a complete revised text was presented to the 1991 Working Group meeting. The Working Group reported on the articles that had received broad agreement and those needing further consideration.[51] The areas requiring more work were those of paramount importance to Indigenous Peoples: articles relating to self-determination, land and resource rights, Indigenous governments and legal systems and use of the word "peoples" as opposed to "people" or "population." Further, the Chair/Rapporteur pointed out that articles marked as "adopted" or "recommended" signified only "that the provisions were agreed to by the participants in the respective informal Drafting Groups for submission to the Working Group for its evaluation and consideration."[52] However, the Working Group made few amendments to these articles, attesting to the strength of the consensus reached.

The 1991 Draft contained no language on the right of Self-determination for Indigenous Peoples as "the term 'self-determination' was unacceptable to governments because of its implicit reference to colonialism."[53] While states opposed the inclusion of language related to self-determination, Indigenous representatives maintained "their firm belief that the Declaration must mention directly or indirectly the concept of self-determination."[54] One member of the Working Group agreed with Indigenous Peoples that Self-determination must be included in the Draft Declaration, drawing attention to the principle and application of self-determination:

The principle of self-determination is indivisible; however, its application will differ in different circumstances. Any statement of the principle does not define the people to whom it applies nor does it say what the result of the application of self-determin-ation for any people may be. It was thus suggested . . . that a state-ment of the general principle of Self-determination could be included in the declaration without prejudicing the result of the application of the principle. Professor Turk commented further that present international law does not guarantee all states their territorial integrity; it only upholds that right for states that respect the general principle of self-determination. He suggested that the safeguards already present in international law were enough to allay the fears of states about giving the Indigenous Peoples with-in their countries a right of secession that they did not have previ-ously.[55]

As a result of the informal drafting discussion held by the Working Group and interventions by Indigenous Peoples, there was movement toward including the right of self-determination within the Draft Declaration to be submitted to the Sub-commission.

The rights identified by Indigenous Peoples since 1985 remained cen-tral to the drafting. Indigenous representatives were persuasive in encouraging the Working Group to find consensual language acceptable to states and to Indigenous organizations and NGO's. Following the discussion at the eighth session of the Working Group, the Chair/Rapporteur prepared a revised working paper[56] with a new draft operative paragraph 1 containing language specifically related to self-determination.[57]

After a general debate on the draft Declaration, the Working Group proceeded with a further elaboration of the provisions and a first reading of the Declaration article by article. Participants were invited to make amendments, revisions and suggestions to each draft article under consideration. This exercise was extremely difficult, taking into consideration the great number of participants and their different legal backgrounds. . . . On the basis of the fore-going discussion and the amendments and suggestions made by the participants, the Chairperson/Rapporteur proposed that the members of the Working Group should prepare a revised version of the preamble and first three parts of the draft declaration.[58]

By 1992 some state governments still resisted certain aspects of the Draft Declaration; the state representative from Canada was reported as point-ing out that:

several provisions of the text of the draft declaration were repetitive; certain concepts and terms such as "people," "Self-determination" as well as "lands and territories" were frequently used without definition and therefore would need further clarification.[59]

As a result, the Working Group prepared a final revised draft[60] along with an explanation of the points contained in the Draft Declaration.[61] The drafting process, which began as general discussions in 1985, was finalized in 1994. In eight sessions, the Working Group was able to take comments from a large number of participants and produce a document. For example, at the 1994 Working Group session there were:

> 44 observer Governments, 11 United Nations and intergovernmental organizations, 164 Indigenous nations, organizations and communities, and 83 non-governmental organizations and a large number of individual experts and scholars. . . . In total, 790 people had attended the Working Group.[62]

During drafting—especially during development of consensual language—the participation of Indigenous representatives became central to the process.

While the Working Group members had hoped to complete the text of the Draft Declaration during the eleventh session, they did not complete the work until 17 August 1993 during the Sub-commission meetings.[63] The complete Working Group draft was to be made available for the Sub-commission to consider. But, since it was not available for review during the 1993 Working Group meeting, the Chair/Rapporteur asked the Sub-commission for permission to allow Indigenous delegates to review the final Draft and make comments on it. These were not to request substantial amendments, in keeping with the Sub-commission request for general comments [that] "would not lead to formal changes to the Draft Declaration during the current session."[64] When all the comments had been made on the 1993 Draft, the members of the Working Group prepared the comments for Sub-commission review with the Draft Declaration. In addition, the Working Group made some strong recommendations about future review of the draft:

> The Working Group further recommended that the Sub-Commission urge the Commission on Human Rights to take the necessary steps to expedite the consideration of the draft declaration and to take the effective measures at its fifty-first session to ensure that the representatives of indigenous peoples were able to participate fully in the consideration of the text by the Sub-

Commission, if necessary, and the Commission. It also recommended to the Commission, through the Sub-Commission, to propose to the Economic and Social Council that it take steps to ensure that indigenous peoples could participate effectively in the consideration of the draft declaration, as they were able to do in the Working Group. **In the history of the United Nations, no other human rights instrument has enjoyed such diverse and constructive contributions by the peoples concerned, and that important partnership should continue.** At the same time, it was the view of the members of the Working Group that the effectiveness of the draft declaration, after its adoption, would depend fundamentally upon its credibility and legitimacy with indigenous peoples themselves and with the Governments concerned[65][emphasis added].

With the Working Group drafting of this international rights document, the Indigenous involvement was unprecedented in the history of drafting UN instruments. The peoples most affected by the Declaration were directly and fully involved in every step of the process, at times encouraging Working Group members to restructure their working methods to accommodate those of the Indigenous Peoples.' Oral interventions on key articles became acceptable where written submission were conventional. Indigenous Peoples were given opportunities to review and comment on the evolving drafts. Since the Working Group became open to Indigenous Peoples, the drafting process took on a more complex nature resulting in a more comprehensive text. When the Chair/Rapporteur attempted to draft a document using standard UN processes by having written interventions, she acknowledged that it would not work in this instance. Instead, the Working Group decided to draft in public with contributions from observer governments, experts, NGO's, and Indigenous Peoples. While it took the United Nations twenty years to draft the Covenants on Civil and Political Rights and on Social, Cultural and Economic Rights, it took only eight years to complete a draft of the Draft Declaration. Eight years is a very brief time in the histories of Indigenous Peoples.

During the drafting process, Indigenous participants, aware of their unprecedented involvement with the Working Group, maintained their preference for direct representation before other bodies of the UN when these bodies review the Draft Declaration. Indigenous Peoples had been able to participate in meetings of the Working Group without going through the formal ECOSOC accreditation process. As result, hundreds of Indigenous Peoples and their organizations were involved in the Working Group drafting process, which recommended continued participation for the peoples whose rights were the subject of the Declaration.

It will be a challenge for the UN system to ensure that Indigenous representatives have substantial involvement in any future consideration of the Draft.

> With regard to the subsequent consideration of the draft declaration by the parent bodies of the Working Group, a number of indigenous representatives called upon the Working Group to ensure that indigenous participation would be safeguarded during that review process to allow representatives of indigenous peoples without consultative status to continue to be involved in the drafting of the declaration.[66]

Although the Working Group did make a such recommendation to the Sub-commission, the resolution eventually passed by the Sub-commission did not allow for open registration of Indigenous delegates.[67]

The text of the Draft was acceptable to the expert members of the Sub-commission who immediately decided to send the Draft Declaration to the Commission for review. The draft resolution on its adoption of the Draft Declaration by the Sub-commission set out in part:

> (a) To adopt the draft United Nations declaration on the rights of indigenous peoples agreed upon by members of the Working Group as contained in the annex to the present resolution;
> (b) To submit the draft declaration to the Commission on Human Rights at its fifty-first session with the request that it consider the draft as expeditiously as possible;
> (c) To request the Secretary-General to transmit the text of the draft declaration to Indigenous peoples and organizations, governments and intergovernmental organizations and to include in the note of transmittal the information that the draft declaration is to be submitted to the Commission on Human Rights at its fifty-first session;
> 5. *Recommends* that the Commission on Human Rights and the Economic and Social Council take effective measures to ensure that representatives of indigenous peoples are able to participate fully in the consideration of the draft declaration by these two bodies, regardless of their consultative status with the Economic and Social Council.[68]

Considerable discussion on the participation by Indigenous Peoples proposed in paragraph 5 occurred as some members of the Sub-commission (Brazil and Bangladesh) did not want to include this recommendation in the resolution to the CHR. In order to have the resolution passed, a compromise was proposed wherein the word "fully" was removed from the resolution and it was to be adopted by consensus but without the consent of Indigenous Peoples. A consensus resolution was deemed to have stronger authority before the CHR. Sub-Commission resolution 1994/45 was amended to read: "Indigenous peoples are able to participate in the consideration," deferring to the CHR on the kind of participation Indigenous Peoples could have during the Declaration review. The resolution also deferred to states decisions about which Indigenous Peoples would participate in the process, rather than having Indigenous Peoples select their own representatives.

The Sub-Commission

On 22 August 1994, the Sub-commission turned its attention to the Draft Declaration on the Rights of Indigenous Peoples. Prior to their consideration, the Sub-commission had allowed for general comments during the twelfth Working Group on the 1993 Draft Declaration. Speakers from governments and Indigenous organizations made further suggestions on the 1993 Draft Declaration:

> The representatives of several indigenous peoples, including the Nobel Peace Prize Winner, Mrs. Rigoberta Menchu Tum, stated that the draft declaration, although not responding to all their concerns, constituted a useful and important document. . . . One indigenous representative said that it was necessary to be pragmatic and to unite to get approval for the draft declaration as it passed through the higher bodies of the United Nations, especially through lobbying at the national level.[69]

While Indigenous delegates were trying to encourage consensus for the rights in the Draft Declaration, many states were warning that the standards were not acceptable to them:

> The observer for Brazil expressed his concerns on several of the articles and the general language of the declaration. He argued that the use of the word "peoples," in the plural, would allow interpretation to the effect that indigenous people would be beneficiaries of the right of self-determination. That interpretation would make indigenous peoples the subject of international law, which was inconsistent with existing national constitutional and international law.[70]

State representatives from Canada and the United States had expressed concerns—similar to those of Brazil—on the language of the draft, in particular on the wording in Article 371 on the right to self-determination.

The general comments by all participants were recorded in a report to the Sub-commission.[72]

When the Draft Declaration was introduced to the Sub–commission, many members advocated moving it rapidly through the UN system, agreeing with the Working Group's assessment of the consequences of delay, that "every new proposal for delaying [should] be weighted soberly against the destruction of human life and ecosystems that another year or more of delay will bring."[73] The members of the Sub-commission decided to send the draft to the Commission without amendments. Some Sub-commission members were concerned with the reaction of governments:

> Fisseha Yimer, Sub-commission member from Ethiopia, said, "It is high time that we complete consideration of this document and submit it to the Commission right away." Asbjorn Eide, expert from Norway, said the reference to self-determination would undoubtedly draw comment, but that in this case "self-determination" meant not that indigenous peoples would have their own states so much as have autonomy—functional or territorial, or a combination of the two—within existing states. Claire Palley, expert from the United Kingdom noted that the draft Declaration was a significant piece of work which deserved great consideration. . . . The Sub-commission should warmly endorse the draft declaration and send it [to] the Commission. Louis Joinet, expert from France, said the drafting of the preambular section seemed more decisive and stronger than the drafting of the articles of the proposed Declaration. Since in seeking the best one often marred what was good, the Sub-commission should accept this draft declaration.[74]

The Draft Declaration, drafted by five human right expert members of the Working Group, with the assistance of hundreds of Indigenous delegates, moved to the CHR in the winter of 1995. The Sub–commission human rights experts, elected for their experience in human rights and international law, accepted the Draft Declaration on the Rights of Indigenous Peoples without amendments[75]–a significant acceptance of the Draft Declaration.

Commission on Human Rights

The first intergovernmental body to consider the Draft Declaration was the Commission on Human Rights (CHR), which serves as the principal policy organ in the field of human rights. When it was submitted to the CHR at its fifty-first session in 1995, there existed CHR requests,[76] from 1993 and 1994 , that the Sub-commission complete its consideration of the

Draft as rapidly as possible. The Sub-commission was instructed to submit any recommendations on the review process to be followed by CHR and ECOSOC. Consequently, the Sub-commission resolution became critical when the CHR prepared its own resolution on the Draft Declaration.

The CHR resolution was drafted by a member of the US delegation,[77] although the American delegation did not initially sponsor or co–sponsor it. The draft resolution was submitted on 28 February 1995[78] by Australia as the sponsor government, along with Canada and Finland as co-sponsors. Three observer governments[79]—Denmark, New Zealand and Norway—added their names as co-sponsors. Of the fifty-three members of the CHR, only three—all colonizer[80] states with Indigenous Peoples—sponsored the resolution. Fifty members—including all the Asian, Latin American, Eastern European and African countries—did not sponsor the resolution.

The draft resolution called, not for review of the Draft Declaration, but for the CHR to establish an Open–ended Inter–sessional Working Group:

> with the sole purpose of elaborating a draft declaration as contained in the annex of the resolution 1994/45 of 26 August 1994, entitled: "Draft United Nations declaration on the rights of indigenous peoples," for the consideration and adoption by the General Assembly within the International Decade of the World's Indigenous People.[81]

On 3 March 1995, the draft resolution was introduced before the Commission and explained by the sponsoring government, Australia. At that time, Chile, Mexico and the United States (members of the CHR) were added as co-sponsors. Thus, six members of the CHR supported the resolution, which was adopted without a vote.[82] No African or Asian member of the Commission added its name to the resolution.

A number of important points in the language of the resolution must be considered. First, the resolution refers to elaborating "a" draft declaration which does not restrict review to the existing Draft Declaration. A totally new declaration could be drafted by the Inter-sessional Working Group. Second, an "elaboration process" consists of more than just review: the resolution gives the Inter-sessional Working Group a mandate to open the Draft Declaration for substantive amendment. Third, there is no time limit on the process. The general request to finish the process within the UN Decade on Indigenous Peoples which ends in 2004, provides a time frame of up to eight years–the amount of time already spent on the current Draft. The resolution does not say that a draft declaration must be completed; it is simply a general request to have a declaration ready within the Decade and there are no contingency arrangements should the Inter-sessional Working Group not complete its draft by 2004. It is entirely within the parameters of the states participating in the Inter-sessional Working Group to determine the time frame. Fourth, as an open-ended Working Group, all state government members of the CHR can participate. State governments that have not attended the previous Working Group will have an opportunity to participate in the elaboration process. Fifth, as an Inter–sessional Working Group, it must hold sessions between meetings of the CHR and make reports to the next CHR meeting.[83]

The CHR resolution establishing the Inter-sessional Working Group also determined future participation by Indigenous Peoples' organizations. Fortunately, the UN Voluntary Fund which had been established to allow for Indigenous participation in the Working Group on Indigenous Peoples was amended to allow for monies to be made available for Indigenous delegates to attend the Inter–sessional Working Group.[84] The twelve NGOs with ECOSOC accreditation can participate, as the Inter-sessional Working Group would be part of ECOSOC.[85] The process for participation by Indigenous Peoples organizations without ECOSOC status was covered by procedures in an annex to the CHR Resolution. These procedures are complex and bureaucratic, unlike the more generous criteria used and recommended by the Working Group on Indigenous Peoples. Since the provisions are critical to the legal status of Indigenous Peoples as reflected, by their participation, the most relevant ones are presented:

> 3. Organizations of Indigenous people not in consultative status wishing to participate in the Working Group may apply to the Coordinator of the International Decade [Mr. I. Fall[86]]. Such application must include the following information concerning the organization concerned:
> (a) The name, headquarters or seat, address and contact person for the organization;
> (b) The aims and purposes of the organization (these should be in conformity with the spirit, purposes, and principles of the Charter of the United Nations);
> (c) Information on the programme and activities of the organization and of the country or countries in which they are carried out or to which they apply;
> (d) A description of the membership of the organization, indicating the total number of members.
> 4. Upon receipt of applications, the Coordinator of the International Decade should consult with any State concerned pursuant to Article 71 of the Charter of the United Nations and paragraph 9 of resolution 1296 (XLIV) of the Economic and Social

Council. The Coordinator should promptly forward all applications and information received to the Council Committee on Non-Governmental Organizations for its decision.

5. Authorization to participation shall remain valid for the duration of the Working Group subject to the relevant provisions of part VIII of the resolution 1296 of the Economic and Social Council.

8. Organizations of indigenous people may make written presentations which, however, will not be issued as official documents.[87]

The application procedures for Indigenous Peoples do no allow for self-identification without the consent of the state in which they live. Indigenous Peoples cannot attend Inter-sessional Working Group meeting through open registration. State governments, which must approve UN Council Committee applications for accreditation, can deny participation by Indigenous Peoples living in their state. The Council Committee is obligated under its rules of procedure to consult with state governments to determine if application information is accurate. At any stage, a state government can prevent an organization from becoming accredited to participate in the process.

During the first Inter-sessional Working Group meeting, some Indigenous organizations were refused accreditation because their state government did not recognize them as Indigenous accredited. Indigenous participants called for open registration to be approved.[88] While states have allowed for an open-ended process for themselves, they have severely restricted access for Indigenous Peoples. During the 1996 Working Group on Indigenous Peoples meeting, Mr. I. Fall indicated that just over one hundred applications from Indigenous organizations had been received by him and forwarded to the Committee for consideration.[89] This was far fewer than the hundreds of Indigenous Peoples who participated in the drafting of the 1993 Draft Declaration. Unless the process is changed, the most critical aspects of the elaboration of the Draft are likely to be undertaken without the beneficiaries present to contribute and share their worldview. This situation is reminiscent of the International Labour Organization (ILO) convention revision process widely denounced by Indigenous Peoples. Finally, if an Indigenous organization does get accredited, their statements and documented recommendations will not form part of the official record of the UN. Thus, future consideration of a Draft Declaration by larger UN bodies will not have the benefit of reasoning and evidence from Indigenous Peoples organizations on their rights.

Resolution 1995/32 of 3 March 1995 created a new Inter-sessional Working Group without giving the right of full participation to Indigenous delegates. The refusal by the Sub-commission to recommend to the CHR the kind of Indigenous participation in review of the Draft

Declaration provided CHR member states the opportunity, not only to delay review of the existing Draft Declaration, but also to diminish the status of the people the Declaration is intended to protect. The 1993 and 1994 CHR resolutions requested the Sub-commission's recommendation on procedures, but the human rights experts of the Sub-commission did not follow the Working Group on Indigenous Peoples' guidance to insist upon full participation by Indigenous delegates. The Sub-commission's omission may have lasting effects on the consideration of the Draft Declaration during the Inter-sessional Working Group elaboration process.

Inter-Sessional Working Group

The first meeting of the Inter-sessional Working Group was held in Geneva in November and December 1995. Mr. Jose Urrutia, Ambassador for Peru, was elected as Chair/Rapporteur by the thirty-six state governments represented. In addition, twenty-five observer governments sent representatives to the meeting. Its membership will change, as the members of the CHR are rotated by ECOSOC every three years. At its first meeting, the Inter-sessional Working Group in consultation with:

> Governments and indigenous organizations [accepted their proposed work plan] that the participants review the draft declaration part by part in order to identify where there was general consensus and which articles would require greater deliberations. In this respect, the Chairperson/Rapporteur proposed that, on completion of the debate on the scope of the application of the draft declaration, the Working Group consider first the title and preambular paragraphs, and then parts I to IX of the draft declaration. He proposed that, at this stage, the Working Group should not try to begin the process of drafting as such.[90]

This proposal seems to indicate that the Draft Declaration will undergo redrafting.

Indigenous Peoples and some state governments pushed for the acceptance by the Inter-sessional Working Group of the existing Draft Declaration as the basis for the discussions which was generally accepted. Every part of the Draft Declaration was considered, including the title as some state governments do not want the word "Peoples" with its implication of the right of Self-determination in the title. There was also a general discussion on the nature of declarations:

> Several Governments pointed out that a declaration has no legally binding force. Others added that although the draft declaration

was not legally binding it was politically binding and carried with it a great moral obligation to live by its provisions.[91]

Many state governments do not want a declaration. Some states want a declaration but only with their draft language.

As a result of the preliminary observations, the Chair/Rapporteur opened the discussion on the scope of the Draft Declaration. At this point, many state representatives wanted to have a definition of "Indigenous Peoples" prior to proceeding:

> It was stated by a number of delegates that the issue of defining "indigenous people" was crucial in the context of the declaration. The genesis of the issue in terms of its specificity to certain regions was referred to. Some Governments also referred to the process of decolonization which resulted in the birth of modern nations of ancient peoples, and deplored efforts to look for "indigenous populations" with indigenous nations. . . . Several Governments expressed the opinion that the absence of a definition of the term "indigenous people" in the draft declaration would lead to confusion and would limit the acceptability of the draft.[92]

The issue was diffused by Madame Daes who spoke at the eighth meeting, indicating that the Working Group on Indigenous Peoples would reconsider the issue of definition at its 1996 session. In the end, the members of the Inter-sessional Working Group agreed to consider the 1996 discussion by the Working Group on Indigenous Peoples on this issue at its session in October 1996. This group determined in its discussion that there should be no definition of Indigenous Peoples as such a definition would infringe on the right of self-identification.[93] The final report will be made available to the Inter-sessional Working Group where the response will be discussed.

The discussions in the first Inter-sessional Working Group meeting addressed the draft provisions and one government or another objected to most of the articles, indicating that the existing Draft will need to be reviewed in greater detail. No articles had broad support. The most contentious language is in the principles of greatest importance to Indigenous Peoples: use of the term "peoples," self-determination, land and resource rights and the collective rights[94] provisions. Many state governments were opposed to:

> the use of the term "peoples" since it would imply that indigenous peoples were considered to be subjects of international law and as such would be entitled to the right of self-determination and sovereignty over natural resources. Some Governments expressed the

concern that the use of the term "peoples" would also lead to a denial of the rights of individuals in favour of collective rights. In answer to the claim that collective rights did not exist in international human rights law, several Government and indigenous organizations stated that such rights existed in various international instruments and referred to the right of self-determination as reflected in the Charter of the United Nations and the International Covenants on Human Rights, the Convention on the Prevention and Punishment of the Crime of Genocide and the African Charter on Human and Peoples' Rights, as well as norms relating to peace and security, and environment and development.[95]

As a result of the general discussions, it became evident that state governments want to re-open all the articles and the preambular paragraphs for redrafting. At the next Inter-sessional Working Group, state members want to begin the redrafting process. Indigenous Peoples prefer the 1993 Draft Declaration developed by the Working Group on Indigenous Peoples.

Preparing For The General Assembly

Discussions are underway in some states to find ways to implement various articles of the 1993 Draft Declaration to widen state acceptance and practice. The Vice-President of Bolivia, Victor Hugo Cardenas, in a statement before the CHR in April 1996, called upon state governments to implement provisions of the Draft. Cardenas, an Indigenous Aymara, told the members of the CHR that the state of Bolivia was undergoing major structural reorganization to allow for the inclusion of Indigenous Peoples in all sectors of society. The Vice-President called for the quick passage of the 1993 Draft Declaration on the Rights of Indigenous Peoples as the least state governments could do to help begin to heal five hundred years of injustice under international law.[96]

Indigenous Peoples are organizing support for the 1993 Draft Declaration to promote its passage by the GA at the UN. A number of regional initiatives are taking place in North America, Central America, South America, Europe, Asia, Africa and the Pacific. In the fall of 1996, there were two major regional meetings (one in Finland and one in Fiji) where strategies related to the Draft are being developed.[97] The Fijian government sponsored a workshop by inviting Pacific Island delegates from Indigenous organizations and state governments to participate in discussions on the 1993 Draft Declaration. It is hoped that such discussions will lead to a wider acceptance of the Draft Declaration amongst the

Pacific Island states. Indigenous Peoples are involved in networks with intergovernmental agencies to promote training needs and communication of the Draft Declaration. In various workshops planned for the UN Decade, Indigenous Peoples have suggested that a key component be discussions related to the 1993 Draft Declaration and its significance.

In general, Indigenous Peoples have been very active internationally. One activity is the formation of networks. For example, there is an international network on mining and the effects of mining operations on Indigenous Peoples.[98] One of the significant aspects of the UN Working Group on Indigenous Peoples is that it has become the forum for Indigenous Peoples to meet yearly to share the situations in their territories. It is also an opportunity to form joint strategies in key areas.

Lawyers and scholars—particularly Indigenous lawyers and scholars —have been encouraged to write more articles on Indigenous Peoples. Gudmunder Alfredsson, former secretary to the Working Group, wrote that there is a literature explosion on the rights of Indigenous Peoples.[99] Universities have been encouraged to teach classes on the rights of Indigenous Peoples and international law. One such course is taught at the Waikato Law School in Hamilton, New Zealand.[100] Professor James Anaya, an Apache, teaches another class at York University and has recently published a book on the subject.[101] Other Indigenous Peoples have been publishing materials on the Draft Declaration and on the rights of Indigenous Peoples.[102] These initiatives help to educate state societies so that they can put pressure on their governments to recognize the rights of Indigenous Peoples. It is an educational process which is needed to get the 1993 Draft Declaration moved through the UN. Richard Falk has observed:

> At this stage it may be the indigenous peoples themselves who will be the major bearers of this emerging right of peoples. They must be the ones, I think, to give it most of its specific content, although subject to interaction with other viewpoints. The role of jurists is to validate and legitimate this enterprise, and to suggest that for vulnerable peoples to survive at the edge of modern civilization requires an enormous mobilization of moral, legal, and political energy. It will not happen on its own. It will not happen merely by waiting for it to happen, and waiting for the existing framework of laws and human rights to be applied and acted upon. A special circumstance of emergency must be acknowledged and acted upon. Only on this basis can we begin to do justice to this very fundamental challenge to our moral identity, and perhaps to our survival prospects as a species.[103]

The next step in the process involves lobbying in the Economic and Social

Council which consists of fifty-four members elected by the GA every three years.[104] ECOSOC has a number of different functions which have been set out in the UN Charter. The Council can make or initiate studies in relation to economic, social, cultural, educational, health and related matters.[105] In addition, ECOSOC can make recommendations for the purpose of promoting respect for, and observance of fundamental freedoms of all.[106] One important mandate of ECOSOC concerns their ability to draft conventions (treaties) for submission to the General Assembly.[107] Indigenous Peoples will lobby ECOSOC to have the members prepare a convention based on the Draft Declaration prepared by the Working Group on Indigenous Peoples.

When and if ECOSOC either approves the Draft Declaration on the Rights of Indigenous Peoples or drafts a treaty, it will need to proceed to the GA for final acceptance. The General Assembly will pass a resolution to accept the draft. The effect of such resolution can influence international law development. A declaration is "a basic or minimum standard for the international community as a whole."[108] When a declaration is passed by a GA resolution, such a declaration "is not an 'imposition' but an expression of commitment freely entered into by States in full sovereignty, and may not be disregarded."[109] A declaration leaves a state free to follow the principles contained in the instrument without having to comply with formal ratification and reporting procedures. A declaration is a modest attempt to set international norms. Nevertheless, a General Assembly resolution even in a declaration form, is not legally binding, it is of recommendatory effect only.[110] However, a General Assembly resolution may become evidence of customary international law:

> Resolutions of the General Assembly may constitute the practice of States; secondly, they may originate practice; thirdly that they may corroborate customary rules of International law; and fourthly, in appropriate cases, they may supply the opino juris sive necessitatis. . . . There are at least two other possible bases on which it might be claimed that United Nations resolutions are "lawmaking," namely as authoritative interpretation of the Charter and as statements of "general principles of law." . . . The principles or rules which eventually emerge as part of customary law will owe their force as law entirely to the two basic elements of customary law—usage and opinio juris—and only their formulation to the Assembly resolution.[111]

In the alternative, if a treaty is drafted, the General Assembly will confirm it by resolution. Notwithstanding, a treaty will not enter into force under international law unless a sufficient number of states sign and ratify it.

Conclusion

The Draft Declaration on the Rights of Indigenous Peoples has begun to make its way through the UN system. While the Sub-commission did not have any substantive amendments to the Draft prepared by the members of the Working Group, there was some discussion on the role of Indigenous Peoples in the future consideration of the Draft Declaration by the UN. While recommending that it be accepted by the CHR, there was no strong language to support the full participation of Indigenous Peoples in the process. As a result, the CHR established an Inter-sessional Working Group which did not allow for open registration for Indigenous participation.

At the 1996 Working Group on Indigenous Peoples, a consensus resolution from the Indigenous Preparatory meeting requested that the process be open. If the elaboration process continues for perhaps the next ten years, it appears that fewer and fewer Indigenous Peoples will be involved. It is simply a matter of economics. They cannot afford to be at the Working Group on Indigenous Peoples and at the Inter–sessional Working Group. As the process drags on, the state governments with all the resources will be able to elaborate a Draft Declaration which is acceptable to themselves.

State governments are concerned about the Draft Declaration which is not a treaty binding on states. The concern relates to the strong expectations which would be placed on states to abide by a declaration on the rights of Indigenous Peoples. International attention would be placed on those states violating the rights of Indigenous Peoples. As it presently stands, state governments are sensitive to criticism on their records in this area. Rigoberta Menchu Tum, Nobel Peace Prize winner, has been able to attract worldwide attention to the plight of the Maya Indigenous Peoples in Guatemala. Bolivia was forced to begin changing its attitude towards Indigenous People as was stated by the Vice-President during his presentation to the Commission on Human Rights.

Where will Indigenous Peoples be in the rest of the process? There is discussion amongst the Indigenous delegates to remove themselves from the Inter-sessional Working Group when the state governments move to delete Self-determination from the draft. Why? It would be a signal to Indigenous Peoples that state governments are not prepared to abide by the UN Charter and respect the equal rights and self-determination of peoples. The negative reception given to Indigenous Peoples by the colonizing state governments and their state organization—the UN—indicates that the doctrine of discovery remains a central foundation of international law.

Footnotes

1. Hanna Bokor–Szego, *The Role of the United Nations in International Legislation* (New York: North Holland Publishing Company, 1978) at 71–72 [hereinafter Bokor–Szego].

2. Ibid. at 79.

3. United Nations Draft Declaration on the Rights of Indigenous Peoples, E/CN.4/Sub.2/1994/2/Add.1 of 20 April 1994 [hereinafter Draft Declaration]. See appendix I for a copy of the Draft Declaration.

4. Discussed in Chapter 2 of this book.

5. Commission on Human Rights Resolution 1994/29 of 4 March 1994.

6. Sub–commission resolution E/CN.4/Sub.2/1994/45 [hereinafter Sub–commission resolution 1994/45].

7. "An Indigenous representative read a resolution, adopted by consensus by those Indigenous organizations which had attended a preparatory meeting, calling for the adoption by the Working Group of the draft declaration as adopted by the Sub-Commission. It was claimed that, as such, it reflected minimum standards for the survival of indigenous peoples" *Report of the Working Group established in accordance with Commission on Human Rights resolution* 1995/32 of 3 March 1995 E/CN.4./1996/84 [hereinafter *Inter–session Working Group*] at 6.

8. "Many Governments stated that, since a preamble is the philosophical and conceptual framework of the a draft declaration, it should be discussed after a detailed examination of the operative paragraphs of the draft declaration had taken place. They felt that this would be the only way by which contextual consistency between the substance of and the philosophy behind the draft declaration could be achieved. With reference to the term "peoples" and the concept of collective rights as contained in the title and the preamble of the draft declaration, some Governments added that these were substantial issues and should be discussed after a debate on the operative paragraphs had taken place" Ibid. at 8.

9. "By the start of the Commission Working Group, 99 applications had been received by the UN of which 78 had been approved" Andrew Gray, "Draft Declaration Reaches Government Levels", in Indigenous Affairs (Copenhagen: *International Work Group for Indigenous Affairs,* 1996) at 36 [hereinafter Gray, Reaches].

10. *Inter session Working Group, supra* note 7 at 3-4.

11. Ramcharan outlined the initial programme of action undertaken by the Working Group: "(a) Consideration of the right to autonomy, self-government and Self-determination, including political representation and institutions; (b) Consideration of the right and responsibility of indigenous populations, as of all others, to respect universally recognized human rights and fundamental freedoms; (c) Consideration of the right of indigenous populations to health, medical care, other social services and adequate housing; (d) Consideration of principles of equality and non-discrimination; (e) Consideration of the right to legal assistance and protection in administration and judicial affairs; (f) Consideration of the right to traditional productive activities, work, free choice of employment, just and favourable conditions of work, and join trade unions for protection of their interest; (g) Consideration of the right to freedom of peaceful assembly and association; (h)

Consideration of the right to social security; (i) Consideration of the right to trade and to maintain economic, technological, cultural and social relations" B.G. Ramcharan, *The Concept of Present Status of the International Protection of Human Rights Forty Years after the Universal Declaration* (Dordrecht: Martinus Nijhoff Publishers, 1989) at 209.

12. *Report of the Working Group on Indigenous Populations on its first session* (E/CN.4/Sub.2/1982/33) [hereinafter 1982 Working Group Report] at 2.

13. Ibid. at 14.

14. Sub–commission resolution 1984/35.

15. Commission on Human Rights Resolution 1985/21.

16. *Report of the Working Group on Indigenous Populations on its third session* (E/CN.4?Sub.2/ 1984/20) at 16 [hereinafter *1984 Working Group*].

17. Ibid. at 17.

18. *Report of the Working Group on Indigenous Populations on its fourth session,* (E/CN.4/Sub.2/ 1985/22) at 14 [hereinafter *1985 Working Group*].

19. Ibid. at 19.

20. Madame Daes, Greek expert of the Sub-commission, joined the Working Group in 1984 and assumed the Chair. She is the Western European representative on the Working Group. There are five members of the Working Group, one from each region: Western Europe which includes Canada, Australia, United States of America, and New Zealand, Eastern Europe, Africa, Asia and Latin America. In the same year, Madame Daes was elected to the Working Group, Miguel Alfonso-Martinez, Cuban expert from Latin America joined the Group. In 1996, Madame Daes and Mr. Martinez remain members of the Working Group and participated in the 1998 Working Group meeting held in July 1998. The other regions have changed members many times in the last ten years. As the Rapporteur, Madame Daes was charged with preparing the drafts of the Declaration for discussion in the private and public meetings of the Working Group.

21. "Thereby it resolved the contradiction that existed between the recognition of the right of self- determination and the provisions inconsistent with the implementation of this right, concerning non-self-governing territories. The resolution further laid down that colonization is contrary to the UN Charter, it being an impediment to the achievement of its primary purpose—the preservation of peace and co–operation among the peoples. By linking the issue of implementation of the right of Self-determination with the maintenance of international peace and security, the resolution also made it clear that the implementation of this right is a common affair of States" Bokor–Szego, *supra* note 1 at 54.

22. G.A. Resolution 1514 (XV) of 14 December 1960.

23. *1985 Working Group, supra* note 18 at 15.

24. "Most indigenous peoples have not only been attacked militarily but have subsequently seen their way of life systematically assaulted. Colonial powers and nineteenth–century states in the Americas attempted to conquer and exterminate hostile tribes, force the assimilation of more acculturated indigenous groups, erode traditional culture and landholdings, and expand private property at the expense of the collective or communal holdings of indigenous peoples" Hurst Hannum, *Autonomy, Sovereignty, and Self-determination—The Accommodation of Conflicting Rights rev. ed.* (Philadelphia: University of Pennsylvania Press,

1996) at 75.

25. E/CN.4/Sub.2/AC.4/1985/WP.4/Add.4 [hereinafter Draft Principles].

26. Ibid.

27. Ibid. at 32.

28. *Review of Consultative Status with the Economic and Social Council,* (E/CN.4/Sub.2/AC.2/WP.4/Add.1 (1987) [hereinafter *Informal meeting of the Working Group*].

29. *Report of the Working Group on Indigenous Populations on its fifth session,* (E/CN.4/Sub.2/1987 /22) at 17 [hereinafter 1987 Working Group].

30. Ibid. at 13.

31. Ibid. at 13.

32. Ibid. at 13.

33. Ibid. at 14.

34. Ibid. at 18.

35. Draft Universal Declaration on Indigenous Rights (E/CN.4/Sub.2/1988/25) was made available at the 1988 Working Group meeting. A copy of the document is also contained in the *Report of the Working Group on its sixth session* (E/CN.4/Sub.2/1988/24) [hereinafter *1988 Working Group*].

36. Ibid. at 18.

37. Draft Principles, *supra* note 25.

38. *1988 Working Group, supra* note 35 at 21.

39. (1966) 999 U.N.T.S. 171.

40. "This article [27] and the draft declaration should be seen as clearly distinct legal entities dealing with two different realities. Article 27 represented an expression of an international minimum standard, only indirectly relevant to the indigenous situation; it would be wrong if the draft declaration were viewed as an interpretation or general comment on article 27. Concerning the relationship between individual and collective rights, reference to article 27 could be useful although the draft declaration should strike a balance between individual and collective rights with an inevitable accent on the latter" *1988 Working Group, supra* note 35 at 19.

41. *1988 Working Group, supra* note 35 at 20.

42. *1988 Working Group, supra* note 35 at 21.

43. UN Charter preamble "to reaffirm faith in fundamental human rights, n the dignity and worth of the human person, in the equal rights of men and women and of nations large and small," and Article 1 (2); "To develop friendly relations among nations based on respect for the principles of equal rights and self-determination of peoples, and to take other appropriate measures to strengthen universal peace."

44. The document had been prepared for Madame Daes by the Secretariat of the Human Rights Centre which compiled all the analytical comments made by governments and non–governmental organizations and Indigenous organizations. (E/CN.4/Sub.2/1989/33/Add.1). There are thirty–five pages of general observations, comments on the preamble and then comments on each part as presented in 1988. There was an addendum containing more information released after the first revised text was tabled see: E/CN.4/Sub.2/1989/33/Add.3).

45. First revised text of the Draft Universal Declaration on Rights of Indigenous Peoples prepared by the Chairman–Rapporteur of the Working Group on Indigenous Populations, Mrs. Erica–Irene Daes, pursuant to Sub–commission resolution 1988/18 (E/CN.4/Sub.2./1989/33) at 3.

46. *Report of the informal drafting groups established to consider the first revised text of the draft declaration Universal Declaration on Indigenous Rights* (E/CN.4/Sub.2/AC.4/1990/7).

47. *Report of the informal drafting groups established to consider the first revised text of the draft declaration Universal Declaration on Indigenous Rights* (E/CN.4/Sub.2/AC.4/1990/7/Add. 1).

48. *Report of the informal drafting groups established to consider the first revised text of the draft declaration Universal Declaration on Indigenous Rights* (E/CN.4/Sub.2/AC.4/1990/7/Add. 2).

49. Ibid. at 2.

50. Ibid. at 2.

51. For a complete review of the process, see: Analytical commentary on the draft principles contained in the first revised text of the draft declaration on the rights of Indigenous peoples (E/CN.4/Sub.2/1989/36) elaborated by the Chairman/Rapporteur of the Working Group on Indigenous Populations, Ms. Erica-Irene A. Daes (E/CN.4/Sub.2/1990/39) [hereinafter Daes, *Analytical Commentary*].

52. *Report of the Working Group on Indigenous Populations on its eighth session* (E/CN.4/Sub.2/1990/42) at 14 [hereinafter *1990 Working Group*].

53. Daes, *Analytical Commentary, supra* note 51 at 23.

54. Daes, *Analytical Commentary, supra* note 51 at 23.

55. Catherine J. Iorns, "Indigenous Peoples and Self-Determination: Challenging State Sovereignty," [1992] 24 *Case Western Reserve Journal of International Law* at 220-221. Iorns makes a detailed review of the right of self-determination and the historical struggle Indigenous Peoples underwent in the Working Group to have the Right included in the draft.

56. Revised working paper submitted by the Chairman/Rapporteur, Ms. Erica–Irene Daes, pursuant to the Sub-commission on Prevention of Discrimination and Protection of Minorities resolution 1990/26 (E/CN.4/Sub.2/ 1991/36).

57. Ibid. at 41.

58. *Report of the Working Group on Indigenous Populations on its ninth session* (E/CN.4/Sub.2/1991/40) at 10 [hereinafter *1991 Working Group*].

59. Ibid. at 13.

60. Revised working paper on the draft declaration on Indigenous Peoples (E/CN.4/Sub.2/1993/26).

61. *Report of the Working Group on Indigenous Populations on its eleventh session* (E/CN.4/Sub.2/ 1993/29) [hereinafter *1993 Working Group*].

62. Ibid. at 12.

63. *Report of the Working Group on Indigenous Populations on its twelfth session* (E/CN.4/Sub.2/ 1994/30) at 11 [hereinafter *1994 Working Group*].

64. Ibid. at 13.

65. Ibid. at 30.

66. *1994 Working Group, supra* at note 63 at 15.

67. Sub-commission resolution 1994/45, *supra* note 6.

68. Sub-commission resolution 1994/45, *supra* note 10.

69. Ibid. at 14.

70. Ibid. at 14.

71. Draft Declaration, *supra* note 3, Article 3.

72. *Report of the Working Group on Indigenous Populations on its twelfth session* (E/CN.4/Sub.2/ 1994/30) [hereinafter *1994 Working Group*].

73. "Hundreds of Indigenous Peoples, a great number of representatives of the Observer Governments, representatives of specialized agencies of the UN system, hundred of representatives of NGO's, scholars, lawyers, participated actively and had the opportunity in a free, liberal and democratic environment to express their views, to propose amendments and to make their comments on the draft". Erica Irene-Daes, "Introductory statement on the United Nations Draft Declaration on the rights of Indigenous Peoples in the Sub-commission on Prevention of Discrimination and Protection of Minorities at its forty-sixth session 22 August 1994." A copy of the statement is on file with the author [hereinafter Daes, Introductory Statement].

74. United Nations Office in Geneva Information Service, HR/SC/94/30, 22 August 1994.

75. See discussion of the Sub-commission and its composition in Chapter 2 of this thesis. "The members of the Sub-Commission have been so assertive at times that its superior bodies have tried to suppress its activity, ignore its projects, change its mandates, or change its membership. It has been more willing than its superiors to use public pressure on states. It has sought to do as much as it can on a number of problems" David P. Forsythe, *The Internationalization of Human Rights* (Lexington: Lexington Books, 1991) at 64.

76. Commission on Human Rights Resolutions 1993/31 and 1994/29.

77. This information was recorded by the author who was one of the two Indigenous delegates present during the discussions on the draft resolution. During the negotiations, the United States' representative took over the drafting process. The resolution requesting that the CHR consider an open registration for Indigenous participation in the Commission's

Working Group; passed at the preparatory meeting in 1994 was presented to the representative. This request was made to ensure that a just and knowledgable consideration be given to the Draft Declaration.

78. E/CN.4/1995/L.62 [hereinafter *Commission Resolution*].

79. Rule 69, paragraph 3 of the rules of procedure of the functional commissions of the Economic and Social Council allow for observer governments to add their names to the list of sponsors.

80. For a detailed discussion on Canada as an evolving colonial entity created by colonial interests see: Joyce A. Green, "Towards A Detente With History Confronting Canada's Colonial Legacy" (1995) 12 *International Journal of Canadian Studies* 85.

81. *Commission resolution*, supra at note 78.

82. Commission on Human Rights Report to ECOSOC indicated that the resolution was adopted without a vote (E/CN.4/1995).

83. The mandate from ECOSOC is on a yearly basis. Every year, ECOSOC must take the report of the previous Inter-sessional Working Group, then determine if the next meeting is necessary. There is no blanket resolution which permits the Inter–sessional Working Group to continue. As a result, the UN cannot schedule the meeting until ECOSOC has met. In 1996, ECOSOC met in June and July. Therefore, it was not possible to schedule the Inter–sessional Working Group prior to the Working Group on Indigenous Peoples, or when the Subcommission began its four week meeting to take up the resources in translation and meeting services.

84. In 1985, the General Assembly resolution 40/131 created a Voluntary Fund whereby Indigenous Peoples would be able to apply for funds to attend the Working Group on Indigenous Peoples. By G.A. Resolution 50/156 of 21 December 1995 the Voluntary Fund was opened to allow for funds to assist representatives of Indigenous communities and organizations to participate in the Inter-sessional Working Group.

85. *Commission resolution, supra* at note 78: "These procedures are consistent with the procedures set forth in resolution 1296 (XLIV) of 23 May 1968 of the Economic and Social Council on NGO accreditation and do not constitute a precedent in any other situation. They shall apply only to the Working Group created by Council resolution . . . and they shall remain in effect for the duration of the Working Group."

86. Mr. I. Fall is the Under–Secretary General for Human Rights and Director of the Human Rights Centre. He was appointed by the Secretary–General of the UN as the coordinator of the UN Decade on the Rights of Indigenous Peoples.

87. *Commission resolution, supra* at note 78.

88. In a joint statement from the preparatory meeting, Indigenous delegates deplored the failure of the process for accreditation of Indigenous delegates. The Indigenous Peoples called for the Inter–sessional Working Group to approved Indigenous Peoples' organizations and ask the Commission on Human Rights to have an open registration procedure for the future Inter-sessional Working Group meetings.

89. *Report of the Working Group on Indigenous Populations on its fourteenth session* (E/CN.4/Sub.2/ 1996/32) [hereinafter *1996 Working Group*].

90. *Inter-session Working Group, supra* at note 7 at 5.

91. *Inter-session Working Group, supra* at note 7 at 5.

92. *Inter-session Working Group, supra* at note 7 at 6–7.

93. The discussion of definition took place in the Working Group on Indigenous Peoples in July 1996. A summary of the discussion is covered in chapter 4 of this thesis.

94. "Another major debate at the beginning of the meeting centered around whether collective rights are recognized in international law and whether they should be applied to indigenous peoples. Leading the attack against indigenous collective rights was the United States. In spite of reasoned critiques by eminent lawyers in the room that collective rights are recognized throughout international law, the individual emphasis was kept up for the remainder of the meeting by a group consisting of the USA, Japan and France" Gray, *Reaches, supra* at note 9 at 36.

95. *Inter-session Working Group, supra* at note 7 at 9.

96. A copy of his statement is on file with the author. It is only available in Spanish. Statement made on 18 April 1996. The author of this thesis was present during his presentation which received a standing ovation—a unique occurrence in such a UN meeting.

97. From personal communication by the author who was invited to participate in both conferences in an advisory capacity.

98. In May, 1996, the World Council of Churches helped facilitate a workshop of fifty Indigenous representatives who formed an international communications network to facilitate information about mining operations on Indigenous lands. One of the initiatives was to publish a "hot spots" list of critical areas under present danger. As a result of the publication, a number of initiatives by mining companies have been started. In Papua New Guinea, the mining company has tried to settle with the Indigenous land owners and to put in place environmental safeguards against pollution from mining activities. There is also an international Rainforest movement to protect the rainforest. In September, 1996, there was an organizational meeting held in Geneva, Switzerland to establish an international network of all Indigenous Peoples affected by forestry operations. The Lubicon Cree were invited to attend the meeting. There is also an international network of Indigenous Women who are monitoring the Human Genome Diversity Project which has targeted Indigenous Peoples' genetic materials for patenting. These networks work outside of the UN structure but use the Working Group on Indigenous Peoples' meeting to have informal strategy meetings on the next year's activities. All this information is from the personal communication by the author who has participated in the informal meetings and in the formal meetings which have structured the international networks.

99. Bernadette Kelly Roy and Gudmunder Alfredsson, "Indigenous Rights: The Literature Explosion" (1987) 13 *Transnational Perspectives* 19.

100. In July 1995, the author gave two lectures on the history of the Draft Declaration and its progress through the UN in that class.

101. James Anaya, *Indigenous Peoples in International Law* (Oxford: Oxford University Press, 1996).

102. Robert Williams, *The American Indian in Western Legal Thought: The Discourse of Conquest* (New York: Oxford University Press, 1990); Oren Lyons ed., *Exiled in the Land of the Free,*

Democracy, Indian Nations and the U.S. Constitution (Sante Fe: Clear Light Publishers, 1992); Vine Deloria Jr., *Red Earth and White Lies, Native Americans and the Myth of Scientific Fact* (New York: Scribner, 1995) are just a sample of the books written by Indigenous authors on the issue. Also see, the bibliography of this thesis under Articles.

103. Richard Falk, "The Rights of Peoples (In Particular Indigenous Peoples)" in James Crawford ed., *The Rights of Peoples* (Oxford: Clarendon Press, 1988) at 36.

104. UN Charter, Article 61(1), (2) and (3). "The amendment of Article 61 of the Charter, decided upon in Resolution 2847(XXVI), establishes five categories of members corresponding to the following groups: African, Asian, Latin-American, W. European and other, E. European. Article 69 gives a right of participation to any member of the UN "on matters of particular concern to that Member," but without a right of vote" D. W. Bowett, *The Law of International Institutions 4th ed.* (London: Stevens & Sons, 1982) at 61.

105. UN Charter, Article 62(1).

106. UN Charter, Article 62(1).

107. UN Charter, Article 62(3): "It may prepare draft conventions for submission to the General Assembly, with respect to matters falling within its competence".

108. Patrick Thornberry, "Some Implications of the UN Declaration on Minorities for Indigenous Peoples" in Eyassu Gayim and Kristian Myntti ed., *Indigenous and Tribal Peoples' Rights —993 and After* (Rovaniemi: University of Lapland, 1995) at 7.

109. Ibid.

110. Also see, (1996) ICJ *Advisory Opinion on Legality of Nuclear Weapons*, July 1996 para. 68-73 on discussion of the use of General Assembly resolutions as evidence of custom.

111. H.W.A. Thirlway, *International Customary Law and Codification—An examination of the continuing role of custom in the present period of codification of international law* (Leiden: A.W. Sijthoff, 1972) at 63–64.

Bibliography
Primary Sources
United Nations Documents
And
Other Human Rights Material

General UN Documents

Covenant of the League of Nations, 22 Consolidated Treaty Series 195, 28 June 1919.

Charter of the United Nations, 1 United Nations Treaty Series xvi; (1946).

Statute of the International Court of Justice, 59 Statute 1031, Treaty Series No. 993, 24 October 1945.

Convention on the Prevention and Punishment of the Crime of Genocide, United Nations Treaty Series 77 (1948).

Universal Declaration of Human Rights, General Assembly Resolution 217 A(III), Adopted 10 December 1948.

Declaration on the Granting of Independence to Colonial Territories and Peoples, General Assembly Resolution 1514 (XV) of 14 December 1960.

International Convention on the Elimination of all Forms of Racial Discrimination, 660 United Nations Treaty Series 212.

Declaration on Principles of International Law Concerning Friendly Relations and Cooperation among States in accordance with the Charter of the United Nations, General Assembly Resolution 2625 (XXV) of 24 October 1970.

International Covenant on Civil and Political Rights (1966) 999, United Nations Treaty Series 171, in force 3 January 1976.

First Optional Protocol to the International Covenant on Civil and Political Rights (1966) 999, United Nations Treaty Series 302, in force 23 March 1976.

Second Optional Protocol to the International Covenant on Civil and Political Rights aiming at the Abolition of the Death Penalty, General Assembly Resolution 15 December 1989, in force 11 July 1991.

International Covenant on Economic, Social and Cultural Rights, 993, United Nations Treaty Series 171, in force 23 March 1976.

Study on the Rights of Person Belonging to Ethnic, Religious and Linguistic Minorities, Francesco Caportori, Special Rapporteur, (New York: United Nations 1979) E/CN.4/ Sub.2/384/Add.1–7.

Vienna Convention on the Law of Treaties (1969) 1155, United Nations Treaty Series 331, in force 27 January 1980.

Report of the World Conference to Combat Racism and Racial Discrimination, A/CONF./92/40 (1979).

The Historical and Current Development of the Right to Self-determination on the Basis of the United Nations and other instruments adopted by United Nations, Aureliu Cristescu, Special Rapporteur, (New York: United Nations, 1981) E/CN.4/Sub.2/404.

Implementation of United Nations Resolutions Relating to the Right of Peoples under Colonial and Alien Domination to Self-determination, Hector Gros Espiell, Special Rapporteur, (New York: United Nations, 1981) E/CN.4/Sub.2/405.

Study of the problem of discrimination against indigenous populations, Economic and Social Council Resolution 1982/34.

Second World Conference on Racism and Racial Discrimination, A/CONF./119/26. (1983).

Proposal Concerning a Definition of the term 'Minority,' Jules Deschenes, Special Rapporteur, E/CN.4/Sub.2/1985/31.

Study of the Problems of Discrimination against Indigenous Populations, Martinez Cobo, Special Rapporteur, E/CN.4/Sub.2/1986/Add.1–8.

The Report United Nations Seminar on the Effects of Racism and Racial Discrimination on the Social and Economic Relations between Indigenous Peoples and States, E/CN.4/Sub.2/ 1988/22.

Report of the Committee on the Elimination of Racial Discrimination: General Recommendations, A/45/18 (1990).

Study on treaties, agreements and other constructive arrangements between states and indigenous populations, preliminary report (Miguel Alfonso-Martinez, Special Rapporteur), E/CN.4/Sub.2/1991/33.

Report of the Meeting of Experts to Review the Experience of Countries in the Operation of Schemes of Internal Self–Government for Indigenous Peoples, Nuuk, Greenland, E/CN.4/ 1992/42.

Indigenous Peoples Earth Charter, E/CN.4/Sub.2/AC.4/1994/12 (adopted 30 May 1992).

Rio Declaration on Environment and Development, A/CONF.151/5/Rev.1 (June, 1992). A text of the Declaration in 31 *International Legal Materials*, 874.

Agenda 21: Chapter 26, Recognizing and Strengthening the Role of Indigenous Peoples and Their Communities, UN Conference on Environment and Development, Rio de Janeiro, 13 June 1992 A/CONF. 151/26(vol. 3) at 16, Annex 2.

Study on treaties, agreements and other constructive arrangements between states and indigenous populations, First Progress Report (Miguel Alfonso–Martinez, Special Rapport– eur), E/CN.4/Sub.2/1992/32.

Report of the United Nations Technical Conference on Practical Experience in the Realization of Sustainable and Environmental Sound Self–Development of Indigenous Peoples, Santiago, Chile, E/CN.4/Sub.2/1992/31.

UN Declaration on the Rights of Persons Belonging to National or Ethnic, Religious and Linguistic Minorities, G.A. Res. 47/135 of 18 December 1992. A text of the Declaration is in: *Human Rights: A Compilation of International Instruments Vol. 1* (New York: United Nations, 1993) 140.

Vienna Declaration and Programme of Action, Report of the World Conference on Human Rights, A/Conf.157/24 (1993) 25 June 1993.

UN Conference on Population and Development, Cairo, 5–13 September, 1994 (ST/ESA/ SER.A/149/1995).

Study on treaties, agreements and other constructive arrangements between states and indigenous populations, second progress report (Miguel Alfonso–Martinez, Special Rapporteur), E/CN.4/Sub.2/1995/27.

Study on treaties, agreements and other constructive arrangements between states and indigenous populations, third progress report (Miguel Alfonso–Martinez, Special Rapporteur), E/CN.4/Sub.2/1996/23.

Report of the Expert Seminar on Practical Experience Regarding Indigenous land Rights and Claims, Whitehorse 1996, E/CN.4/Sub.2/AC.4/1996/6.

International Labour Organization

Statute of the International Labour Organization includes amendments adopted up to 1964, United Kingdom Treaty Series No. 59.

Convention Concerning the Protection and Integration of Indigenous and Other Tribal and Semi–Tribal Populations in Independent Countries, 328, United Nations Treaty Series 247 (1959).

International Labour Organization Convention on Indigenous Populations No. 169 of 27

June 1989, reprinted in International Labour Organization, Provisional Record, International Labour Conference, 76th Sess. Geneva, No. 25 also reprinted (1989) 28 *International Legal Materials* 1382.

International Labour Conference 75th Session, *Report VI(1) Partial revision of the Indigenous and Tribal Populations Convention, 1957 (No. 107)* (Geneva: International Labour Office, 1988).

International Labour Conference 75th Session, *Report VI(2) Partial revision of the Indigenous and Tribal Populations Convention, 1957 (No. 107)* (Geneva: International Labour Office, 1988).

International Labour Conference 76th Session, *Report IV(1) Partial revision of the Indigenous and Tribal Populations Convention, 1957 (No. 107)* (Geneva: International Labour Office, 1989).

International Labour Conference 76th Session, *Report IV(2A) Partial revision of the Indigenous and Tribal Populations Convention, 1957 (No. 107)* (Geneva: International Labour Office, 1989).

International Labour Conference 76th Session, *Report IV(2B) Partial revision of the Indigenous and Tribal Populations Convention, 1957 (No. 107)* (Geneva: International Labour Office, 1989).

International Labour Conference 75th Session, *Provisional Record (No. 32) — Sixth item on the agenda: Partial revision of the Indigenous and Tribal Populations Convention, 1957 (No. 107)* (Geneva: International Labour Office, 1988).

International Labour Conference 75th Session, *Provisional Record (No. 36) — Thirty–fourth sitting: Report of the Committee on Convention 107: Submission –Partial revision of the Indigenous and Tribal Populations Convention, 1957 (No. 107)* (Geneva: International Labour Office, 1988).

International Labour Conference 76th Session, *Provisional Record (No. 25) — Fourth item on the agenda: Partial revision of the Indigenous and Tribal Populations Convention, 1957 (No. 107)* (Geneva: International Labour Office, 1989).

International Labour Conference 76th Session, *Provisional Record (No. 32) — Thirty–sixth sitting: Final record vote on the Convention concerning Indigenous and Tribal Peoples in Independent Countries at 32/6* (Geneva: International Labour Office, 1989).

International Labour Office, *A Guide to ILO Convention No., 169 on Indigenous and Tribal Peoples* (Geneva: International Labour Office, 1995).

International Labour Office, *Indigenous and Tribal Peoples and the ILO* (Geneva: International Labour Office, 1994).

World Bank

World Bank, *Operational Directive 4.20: Indigenous Peoples* (World Bank: World Information Centre, 1991).

Cindy M. Buhl, *A Citizens' Guide to the Multilateral Development Banks and Indigenous Peoples* (World Bank: The Bank Information Centre, 1994).

Working Group on Indigenous Peoples

Report of the Working Group on Indigenous Populations on its first session, E/CN.4/Sub.2/1982/33.

Report of the Working Group on Indigenous Populations on its second session, E/CN.4/Sub.2/1983/22.

Report of the Working Group on Indigenous Populations on its third session, E/CN.4/Sub.2/1984/20.

Report of the Working Group on Indigenous Populations on its fourth session, E/CN.4/Sub.2/1985/22.

Review of Developments Standard–Setting Activities – Material Received from Non–Governmental Organizations in Consultative Status with the Economic and Social Council E/CN.4/Sub.2/AC.4/WP4/Add. 1 (1987).

Report of the Working Group on Indigenous Populations on its fifth session, E/CN.4/Sub.2/1987/22.

Report of the Working Group on Indigenous Populations on its sixth session, E/CN.4/Sub.2/1988/24.

Universal Declaration on Indigenous Rights: A Set of Draft Preambular Paragraphs and Principles, E/CN.4/Sub.2/1988/25.

Discrimination Against Indigenous Peoples: Analytical Compilation of Observations and Comments Received Pursuant to Sub–Commission Resolution 1988/18, E/CN.4/Sub.2/1989/33/Add.1.

First Revised Text of the Draft Declaration on the Rights of Indigenous Peoples Prepared by the Chairman–Rapporteur of the Working Group on Indigenous Populations, Mrs. Erica– Irene Daes, Pursuant to Sub–Commission Resolution 1988/18, E/CN.4/Sub.2/1989/33.

Analytical compilation of observations and comments received pursuant to Sub–Commission resolution 1988/18, E/CN.4/Sub.2/1989/33/Add.3.

Report of the Working Group on Indigenous Populations on its seventh session, E/CN.4/ Sub.2/1989/36

Analytical compilation of observations and comments received pursuant to Sub–Commission resolution 1988/18, E/CN.4/Sub.2/1989/33/Add.1.

Analytical Commentary on the Draft Principles Contained in the First Revised Text of the Draft Declaration on the Rights of Indigenous Peoples, (E/CN.4/Sub.2/1989/36) elabo-rated by the Chairman/Rapporteur of the Working Group on Indigenous Populations, Mrs. Erica– Irene Daes, E/CN.4/Sub.2/1990/39.

Report of the Working Group on Indigenous Populations on its eighth session, E/CN.4/ Sub.2/1990/42.

Standard–Setting Activities: Evolution of Standards Concerning the Rights of Indigenous Peoples – Information Received from Governments, E/CN.4/Sub.2/AC.4/1990.

Standard–Setting Activities: Evolution of Standards Concerning the Rights of Indigenous Peoples – Information Received from Intergovernmental Organizations, E/CN.4/Sub.2/ AC.4/1990/2 & Add. 1.

Standard–Setting Activities: Evolution of Standards Concerning the Rights of Indigenous Peoples – Information Received From Non–Governmental Organizations, E/CN.4/Sub.2/ AC4/1990/3 & Add. 1–2.

Report of the Informal Drafting Group I, Chaired by Mr. Miguel Alfonso–Martinez, E/CN.4/ Sub.2/AC.4/1990/7.

Report of the Informal Drafting Group II, Chaired by Mr. Danilo Turk, E/CN.4/ Sub.2/AC.4/1990/7/Add.1.

Report of the Informal Drafting Group III, Chaired by Mrs. Erica–Irene Daes, E/CN.4/ Sub.2/AC.4/1990/7/Add.2.

Report of the Working Group on Indigenous Populations on its ninth session, E/CN.4/Sub.2/1991/40.

Draft Declaration on the Rights of Indigenous Peoples, Revised Working paper submit-ted by the Chairperson/Rapporteur, Mrs. Erica–Irene Daes, pursuant to Sub–Commission on Prevention of Discrimination and Protection of Minorities resolu-tion 1990/26, E/CN.4/ Sub.2/1991/36.

Report of the Working Group on Indigenous Populations on its tenth session, E/CN.4/Sub. 2/1992/33.

Report of the Working Group on Indigenous Populations on its eleventh session, E/CN.4/ Sub. 2/1993/29.

Draft Declaration on the Rights of Indigenous Peoples, Revised Working Paper Submitted by the Chairperson/Rapporteur, Mrs. Erica–Irene Daes, E/CN.4/Sub.2/1993/26.

Explanatory Note Concerning the Draft Declaration on the Rights of Indigenous Peoples, E/CN.4/Sub.2/1993/26/Add.1.

Report of the Working Group on Indigenous Populations on its twelfth session, E/CN.4/ Sub. 2/1994/30.

Technical Review of the United Nations draft declaration on the rights of Indigenous Peoples, E/CN.4/Sub.2/1994/2.

Report of the Working Group on Indigenous Populations on its thirteenth session, E/CN.4/ Sub.2/1995/24.

Note by the Chairperson–Rapporteur, Mrs. Erica–Irene Daes, on criteria which might be applied when considering the concept of indigenous peoples, (E/CN.4/Sub.2/AC.4/1995/3).

Principles and Guidelines for the Protection of the Heritage of Indigenous Peoples, proposed by the Chairperson/Rapporteur of the Working Group on Indigenous Populations, (E/CN.4/ Sub.2/1995/26).

Report of the Working Group established in Accordance with Commission on Human Rights resolution 1995/32, E/CN.4/1996/84.

Standard Setting Activities: Evolution of Standards Concerning the Rights of Indigenous People, Working Paper by the Chairperson–Rapporteur, Mrs. Erica–Irene Daes, on the concept of "indigenous people", E/CN.4/Sub.2/AC.4/1996/2.

Report of the Working Group on Indigenous Populations on its fourteenth session, E/CN.4/ Sub.2/1996/21.

Other instruments

American Declaration on the Rights and Duties of Man, 119, United Nations Treaty Series 48, Resolution XXX, Final Act of the Ninth International Conference of American States, Bogota, Colombia 30 March – 2 May 1948.

American Convention on Human Rights, (1970) 9 International Legal Materials, 65.

European Convention for the Protection of Human Rights and Fundamental Freedoms, 213 UNTS 221. Signed on 4 November 1950 and entered into force on 3 September 1953.

Council of Europe: Framework Convention for the Protection of National Minorities (1995) 34, *International Legal Materials* 351.

African Charter on Human and Peoples' Rights (1981) 21, *International Legal Materials*, 59.

Resolution on Action required internationally to provide effective protection for Indigenous Peoples, Adopted by the European Parliament in its plenary session, Strasbourg, France, 9 February 1994. European Parliament Doc. PV 58(II) (1994).

Draft of the Inter–American Declaration on the Rights of Indigenous Peoples, OEA/Ser /L/V/II.90 Doc.9 rev.1 21 September 1995.

International Court of Justice

Greco–Bulgarian "Communities" Case (1930) Permanent Court of International Justice Reports 503.

Interpretation of the Peace Treaties with Bulgaria, Hungary and Romania [1951] International Court of Justice Reports 3.

Reservation to the Convention on Genocide Case [1951] International Court of Justice Reports, 15.

Right of Passage over Indian Territory Case [1960] International Court of Justice Reports, 6.

International Status of South–West Africa [1971] International Court of Justice Reports, 16.

Western Sahara: Advisory Opinion [1975] International Court of Justice Reports, 12.

Case Concerning East Timor (Portugal v. Australia) [1995] International Court of Justice Reports, 1.

North Sea Continental Shelf Cases, Federal Republic of Germany v. Denmark and v. Netherlands' [1969] International Court of Justice Reports, 3.

Legality of Nuclear Weapons Advisory Opinion [1996] International Court of Justice Reports, 1.

Human Rights Committee Cases

Edgar A. Canon Garcia v. Ecuador, Communication No., 319/1988, UN GOAR 47th Sess. Supp. No. 40 at 298, UN Doc. A/47/40 (Adopted 1992).

Kitok v. Sweden, Communication No. 197/1985, UN GOAR, 43 rd Sess. Supp. No. 40 at 207, UN Doc. A/43/40 Annex 7(G) (Adopted 1988).

Sandra Lovelace v. Canada, Communication No. R 6/24, Report of the Human Rights Committee, UN GOAR, 36th Sess. Supp. No. 40, UN Doc. A/36/40 Annex 18 (Adopted 29 December 1977).

Mikmaq Tribal Society v. Canada, Communication No. 78/1980, UN GOAR, 39th Sess. Supp.. No. 40, UN Doc. A/39/40, Annex 16 (Adopted in 1984).

Mikmaq People v. Canada, Communication No. 205/1986, UN GOAR, 47th Sess. Supp. No. 40 at 213 UN Doc. A/47/40 Annex 9(A) (1992) (Adopted 3 December 1991).

Ominayak v. Canada, Communication No. 167/1984, UN GAOR, 45th Sess. Supp. No. 40, vol. 2, UN Doc. A/45/40 (Adopted 26 March 1990).

Secondary Sources

Books

African Law Association, *The African Charter on Human and Peoples' Right: Development, Context, Significance Papers of a Symposium* (Marburg/Lahn: S. & W. Druckerei und Verlag GmbH, 1991).

Kuljit Ahluwalia, *The Legal Status, Privileges and Immunities of the Specialized Agencies of the United Nations and Certain Other International Organizations* (The Hague: Martinus Nijhoff, 1964).

Antony Alcock, *History of the International Labor Organization* (New York: Octagon Books, 1971).

Charles Henry Alexandrowicz, *The Law–Making Functions of the Specialized Agencies of the United Nations* (Sydney: Angus & Robertson (Publishers) Pty Ltd., 1973).

Charles Henry Alexandrowicz, *An Introduction to the History of the Law of Nations in the East Indies – 16th, 17th and 18th Centuries* (Oxford: Clarendon Press, 1967).

Charles Henry Alexandrowicz, *The Law–Making Function of the Specialized Agencies of the United Nations* (Sydney: Angus & Robertson (Publishers)Pty Ltd. 1973).

Charles Henry Alexandrowicz, *The European–African Confrontation* (Leiden: A.W.Wright, 1993).

Charles Henry Alexandrowicz ed., *Grotian Society Papers 1968 Studies in the History of the Law of Nations* (The Hague: Martinus Nijhoff, 1970).

Philip Alston ed., *The United Nations and Human Rights A Critical Appraisal* (Oxford: Clarendon Press, 1992).

Samir Amin, *Eurocentrism* (New York: Monthly Review Press, 1989).

Samir Amin, *Culture and Imperialism* (New York: A. A. Knopf, 1993).

S. James Anaya, *Indigenous Peoples in International Law* (New York: Oxford Press, 1996).

James Armitage, *Comparing the Policy of Aboriginal Assimilation: Australia, Canada, and New Zealand* (Vancouver: University of British Columbia Press, 1995).

Ralph Arnold, *Treaty Making Procedure: A Comparative Study of The Methods Obtaining in Different States* (Oxford: Oxford University Press, 1993).

Obed Y. Asamoah, *The Legal Significance of the Declarations of the General Assembly of the United Nations* (The Hague: Martinus Nijhoff, 1966).

W. J. Assies and A. J. Hoekema ed., *Indigenous Peoples' Experiences with Self-Government* (Copenhagen: IWGIA & University of Amsterdam, 1994).

Peter R. Baehr, *The Role of Human Rights in Foreign Policy* (New York: St. Martin's Press, 1994).

Sydney D. Bailey, *The General Assembly of the United Nations: A Study of Procedure and Practice* (New York: Frederick A. Praeger, 1960).

Gordon Bennett, *Aboriginal Rights in International Law* (London: Royal Anthropological Institute of Great Britain and Ireland, 1978).

Norman Bentwich, and Andrew Martin, *A Commentary on the Charter of the United Nations* (New York: Kraus Reprint Co., 1969).

Dennison Berwick, *Savages—The Life and Killing of the Yanomami* (Toronto: MacFarlane Walter & Ross, 1992).

Greta Bird, Gary Martin & Jennifer Nielson ed., *Majah Indigenous Peoples and the Law* (Annandale, NSW: The Federation Press, 1996).

Nicholas B. Birks ed., *Colonialism and Culture* (Ann Arbor: University of Michigan Press 1992).

James M. Blaut, *1492—The Debate on Colonialism, Eurocentrism and History* (Trenton, N.J.: Africa World Press, Inc).

James M. Blaut, *The Colonizer's Model of the World: Geographical Diffusionism and Eurocentric History* (New York: Guilford Press, 1993).

Hanna Bokor-Szego, *The Role of the United Nations in International Legislation* (Amsterdam: North-Holland Publishing Company, 1978).

D. W. Bowett, *The Law of International Institutions* (London: Stevens & Sons, 1982). Catherine Brolmann, Rene Lefeber and Majoleine Zieck, eds., *Peoples and Minorities in International Law* (Dordrecht: Martinus Nijhoff Publishers, 1993).

Jens Brosted ed., *Native Power: The Quest for Autonomy and Nationhood of Indigenous Peoples* (Universitelsforlaget, 1985).

Ian Brownlie, *Principles of Public International Law* 4th ed. (Oxford: Clarendon Press, 1990).

Ian Brownlie, ed., *Basic Documents in International Law* 4th ed. (Oxford: Clarendon Press, 1995).

Lee C. Buchhett, *Secession: The Legitimacy of Self-determination* (New Haven: Yale University Press, 1978).

Carnegie Endowment for International Peace Conference on International Law, *Papers and Proceedings, The Concept of Jus Cogens in International Law* (Geneva: Carnegie Endowment for International Peace, 1967).

Sarah Carter, *Lost Harvests: Prairie Indian Reserve Farmers and Government Policy* (Montreal & Kingston: McGill–Queen's University Press, 1990).

Antonio Cassese, *Current Problems of International Law, Essays on U.N. Law, and on the Law of Armed Conflict* (Milano: Dott. A. Giuffre Editore, 1975).

Antonio Cassese, Self-determination *of peoples—A legal reappraisal* (Cambridge: Cambridge University Press, 1995).

James Crawford, *The Creation of States in International Law* (Oxford: Clarendon Press, 1979).

B.S. Chimni, *International Law and World Order: A Critique of Contemporary Approaches* (Newbury Park, California: Sage Publications Inc, 1993).

Rey Chow, *Writing Diaspora Tactics of Intervention in Contemporary Cultural Studies* (Indianapolis: Indiana University Press, 1993).

Ward Churchill, *From a Native Son: Selected Essays on Indigenism, 1985–1995* (Boston: South End Press, 1996).

Ward Churchill, *Since Predator Came: Notes from the Struggle for American Indian Liberation* (Boulder: Westview Press, 1995).

Ward Churchill, *A Little Matter of Genocide Holocaust and Denial in the Americas 1492 to the Present* (San Francisco: City Lights Books, 1997).

Inis L. Claude, Jr., *Self-determination within the Community of Nations* (Leyden: A. W. Sijthoff, 1967).

Robert T. Coulter, *The Evolution of International Human Rights Standards: Implications for Indigenous Populations of the Americas* (Washington, D.C.: Indian Law Resource Center, 1986).

Maurice Cranston, *What are Human Rights?* (Toronto: The Bodley Head, 1973).

James Crawford ed., *The Rights of People* (Oxford: Clarendon Press, 1988).

Cultural Survival, *State of Peoples: A Global Human Rights report on Societies in Danger* (Boston: Beacon Press, 1993).

Anthony D'Amato, *International Law: Process and Prospect* (New York: Transnational Publishers, Inc., 1995).

Anthony D'Amato, *International Law and Political Reality Collected Papers, Volume One* (The Hague: Kluwer Law International, 1995)

Scott Davidson, *The Inter–American Court of Human Rights* (Dartmouth, England: Dart– mouth Publishing Company Ltd., 1992).

Scott Davidson, *Human Rights* (London: Biddles Lt., 1993).

Denys Deleage, *Better Feast: Amerindians and Europeans* (Vancouver: University of British Columbia Press, 1994).

Vine Deloria, Jr., *Red Earth and White Lies, Native Americans and the Myth of Scientific Fact* (New York: Scribner, 1995).

Vine Deloria, Jr. and C. Lytle, *American Indians, American Justice* (Austin: University of Texas Press, 1983).

Vine Deloria, Jr. and C. Lytle, *The Nations Within: The Past and Future of American Indian Sovereignty* (New York: Pantheon Books, 1984).

R. P. Dhokalia, *The Codification of Public International Law* (Dobbs Ferry: Oceana Publications Inc., 1970).

Brian Dippie, *The Vanishing American: White Attitudes and the U.S. Indian Policy* (Mid– dleton: Wesleyan University Press, 1982).

Jack Donnelly, *International Human Rights* (Boulder: Westview Press, 1993).

Gary L. Dorsey, *Beyond the United Nations Changing Discourse in International Politics and Law* (Lanham, MD: University Press of America, 1986).

James E. Falkowski, *Indian Law/Race Law—A Five Hundred Year History* (New York: Praeger, 1992).

Alain Fenet, Genevieve Koubi, Isabelle Schulte–Tenckhoff et Tatjana Ansbach, *Le Droit et Les Minorities—Analyses et Textes* (Bruxelles: Bruylant, 1995).

R. Brian Ferguson and Neil L. Whitehead, *War in the Tribal Zone: Expanding States and Indigenous Welfare* (Sante Fe: School of American Research Press, 1992).

George A. Finch, *The Sources of Modern International Law* (Washington: Carnegie Endowment for International Peace, 1937).

Peter Fitzpatrick, *The Mythology of Modern Law* (London & New York: Routledge, 1992).

David P. Forsythe, *The Internationalization of Human Rights* (Lexington, Massachusetts: Lexington Books, 1991).

Eyassu Gayim, *The UN Draft Declaration on Indigenous Peoples' Assessment of the Draft Declaration Prepared by the Working Group on Indigenous Populations* (Rovaniemi, University of Lapland, 1994).

Eyassu Gayim and Kristian Myntti ed., *Indigenous and Tribal Peoples' Rights—1993 and After* (Rovaniemi: University of Lapland, 1995).

S. R. Gibbons and R. Morican, *The League of Nations and UNO* (London: Longman Group Limited, 1970).

Tom Greaves ed., *Intellectual Property Rights for Indigenous Peoples — A Source Book* (Oklahoma City: Society for Applied Anthropology, 1994).

Gustavo Gutierrez, *Las Casas—In Search of the Poor of Jesus Christ* (New York: Orbis Books, 1993).

Ernst B. Haas, *Beyond the Nation–State Functionalism and International Organization* (Stanford: Stanford University Press, 1964).

William T. Hagan, *American Indians, 3rd ed.* (Chicago: University of Chicago Press, 1993).

Peter I. Hajnal, *Guide to United Nations Organization, Documentation & Publishing For Students, Researchers, Librarians* (Dobbs Ferry, New York: Oceana Publications, Inc., 1978).

Morton H. Halperin and David J. Scheffer, *Self-determination in the New World Order* (Washington: Carnegie Endowment for International Peace, 1992).

Lauri Hannikainen, *Peremptory Norms (Jus Cogens) In International Law* (Helsinki Finland: Lakimiesliiton Kustannus, 1988).

Hurst Hannum ed., *Guide to International Human Rights Practice* (Philadelphia: University of Pennsylvania Press, 1984).

Hurst Hannum, *Autonomy, Sovereignty, and Self-determination—The Accommodation of Conflicting Rights*, rev. ed. (Philadelphia: University of Pennsylvania Press, 1996).

Kayleen M. Hazlehurst, ed., *Legal Pluralism and the Colonial Legacy: Indigenous experiences of justice in Canada, Australia, and New Zealand* (Brookfield, Vermont: Ashgate Publishing Company, 1995).

John P. Humphrey, *Human Rights and the United Nations, A Great Adventure* (Dobbs Ferry, New York: Transnational, Publishers, Inc., 1984).

George T. Hunt, *The War of the Iroquois—A Study in Intertribal Trade Relations* (Madison: University of Wisconsin Press, 1940).

International Centre for Human Rights and Democratic Development, *Essays on Human Rights and Democratic Development of People or Peoples: Equality, Autonomy and Self-Determination: The Issues at Stake of the International Decade of the World's Indigenous People* (Montreal: International Centre for Human Rights and Democratic Development, 1996).

International Labour Office, *Constitution of the International Labour Organization and Standing Orders of the International Labour Conference* (Geneva: International Labour Office, 1974).

International Labour Office, *The Impact of International Labour Conventions and Recommendations* (Geneva: International Labour Office, 1976).

Francis G. Jacobs, *The European Convention on Human Rights* (Oxford: Clarendon Press, 1975).

Grand Council of the Crees, *Sovereign Injustice—Forcible Inclusion of the James Bay Crees and Cree Territory into a Sovereign Quebec* (Montreal: Nemaska, 1995).

C. Wilfred Jenks, *Social Justice in the Law of Nations—The ILO Impact After Fifty Year* (Oxford: Oxford University Press, 1970).

Francis Jennings, *The Founders of America* (New York: W.W. Morton, 1993).

G. A. Johnston, *The International Labour Organization Its Work For Social and Economic Progress* (London: Europa Publications, 1970)

Harold S. Johnson, *Self-determination within the Community of Nations* (Leyden: A. W. Sijthoff, 1967).

Klans E. Knorr, *British Colonial Theories 1570–1850* (Toronto: University of Toronto Press, 1994).

W. Ofuatey–Kodjoe, *The Principle of Self-determination in International Law* (New York: Nellen Publishing, Co. Inc., 1977).

Dr. Min-Chuan Ku, *A Comprehensive Handbook of the United Nations: A Documentary Presentation in Two Volumes, Volume 1* (New York: Monarch Press, 1978).

Vassilis Lambropoulos, *The Rise of Eurocentrism, Anatomy of Interpretation* (Princeton, Princeton University Press, 1993).

Fernand van Langehover, *The Question of Aborigines before the UN: The Belgian Thesis* (Brussels: Royal Colonial Institute of Belgium, Section of Social and Political Sciences, 1954).

Sir Hersch Lauterpacht, *The Development of International Law by the International Court* (Cambridge: Grotius Publications Ltd., 1982).

Natan Lerner, *Group Rights and Discrimination in International Law* (Norwell, Ma.: Kluwer Academic Publishers, 1991).

Michael D. Leven (ed.), *Ethnicity and Aboriginality Case Studies in Ethnonationalism* (Toronto: University of Toronto Press, 1993).

Mark F. Lindley, *The Acquisition and Government of Backward Territory in International Law Being a Treaties on the Law and Practice Relating to Colonial Expansion* (New York: Negro Universities Press, 1969). Reissued, based upon the original text of 1926.

Oren Lyons ed., *Exiled in the Land of the Free, Democracy, Indian Nations, and the U.S. Constitution* (Sante Fe: Clear Light Publishers, 1992).

George Manuel and Michael Posluns , *The Fourth World* (Toronto: Collier Macmilan, 1974).

P. K. Menon, *The Law of Treaties Between States and International Organizations* (Lewiston: The Edwin Mellen Press, 1992).

Allan McCartney, ed., *Self-Determination in the Commonwealth* (Aberdeen: The University Press, 1988).

Dominic McGoldrick, *The Human Rights Committee: Its Role in the Development of the International Covenant on Civil and Political Rights* (Oxford: Clarendon Press, 1991).

W. D. McIntyre, *Colonies into Commonwealth* (London: Blandford Press, 1966).

Warwick McKean, *Equality and Discrimination under International Law* (Oxford: Clarendon Press, 1993).

Bradford W. Morse and Gordon R. Woodman (eds.) *Indigenous Law and The State* (Dordrecht, Holland: Foris Publications, 1988).

David A. Morse, *The Origin and Evolution of I.L.O. and Its Role in the World Community* (New York: New York State School of Industrial and Labour Relations, 1969).

James Muldoon ed., *The Expansion of Europe: The First Phase* (Philadelphia: University of Pennsylvania Press, 1977).

James Muldoon, *The Americas in the Spanish World Order—The Justification for Conquest in the Seventeenth Century* (Philadelphia: University of Pennsylvania Press, 1994).

Benyamin Neuberger, *National Self-Determination in Postcolonial Africa* (Boulder: Lynne Rienne Publishers Inc., 1986).

L. Oppenheim, ed., *The Collected Papers of John Westlake on Public International Law* (Cambridge: University Press, 1914).

Organization of American States: *The Contribution of the OAS Inter–American Juridical Committee Towards Development and Codification of International Law* (Washington: General Secretariat of the Organization of American States, 1993).

Ebere Osieke, *Constitutional Law and Practice in the International Labour Organisation* (Dordrecht: Martinus Nijhoff Publishers, 1985).

Albert C. Outler, Thomas S. K. Scott–Craig, Edwin W. Patterson, Arthur L. Harding eds., *Natural Law and Natural Rights* (Dallas: Southern Methodist University Press, 1955).

Clive Parry, *The Sources and Evidence of International Law* (Manchester: The University Press, 1965).

Chris Maina Peter, *Human Rights in Africa A Comparative Study of the African Human and Peoples' Rights Charter and the New Tanzanian Bill of Rights* (New York: Greenwood Press, 1990).

Katherine Pettipas, *Severing the Ties that Bind—Government Repression of Indigenous Religious Ceremonies on the Prairies* (Winnipeg: University of Manitoba Press, 1994).

Robert Phillimore, *Commentaries upon International Law* (Littleton, Colorado: Fred B. Rothman & Co., 1985). Reissued based upon the original text of 1854.

Michla Pomerance, *Self-determination in Law and Practice—The New Doctrine in the United Nations* (The Hague: Martinus Nijhoff Publishers, 1982).

Cecilia Medina Quirocga, *The Battle of Human Rights Gross, Systematic Violations and the Inter-American System* (Utrecht: Martinus Nijhoff Publishers, 1988).

Jose Rabassa, *Inventing A–M–E–R–I–C–A: Spanish Historiography and the Formation of Eurocentrism* (Norman Oklahoma: University of Oklahoma Press, 1993).

B. G. Ramcharan, *The Concept of Present Status of the International Protection of Human Rights Forty Years after the Universal Declaration* (Dordrecht: Martinus

Nijhoff Publishers, 1989).

Alison Derondes Renteln, *International Human Rights* (Newbury Park: Sage, 1990).

Henry Reynolds, *Aboriginal Sovereignty—Reflections on race, state and nation* (St. Leonards: Allen & Unwin Pty Ltd., 1996)

Henry Reynolds, *Law of the Land* (Sydney: Penguin Press, 1992).

Boyce Richardson ed., *Drum Beat—Anger and Renewal in Indian Country* (Toronto: Summerhill Press Ltd., 1989).

Christos Rosenstein-Rozakis, *The Peremptory Norms of General International Law (Jus Cogens) Under the Vienna Convention on the Law of Treaties* (Urbana, Illinois: University of Illinois, 1973)

Norbert Rouland, *Legal Anthropology* (Stanford: Stanford University Press, 1994).

Francis Stephen Ruddy, *International Law in the Enlightenment—The Background of Emmerich de Vattel's Le Droit des Gens* (Dobbs Ferry, New York: Oceana Publications, Inc., 1975).

Edward Said, *Culture and Imperialism* (New York: Random House, 1994).

S. Sampat–Mahta, *Minority Rights and Obligations* (Ottawa: Canada Research Bureau, 1993).

James Brown Scott, *The Spanish Origin of International Law: Francisco de Vitoria and His Law of Nations* (Oxford: At the Clarendon Press, 1934).

Malcolm Shaw, *Title to Territory in Africa—International Legal Issues* (Oxford: Clarendon Press, 1986).

P. Sieghart, *The Lawful Rights of Mankind* (Oxford: Oxford Press, 1986).

Jay A. Sigler, *Minority Rights—A Comparative Analysis* (Westport, Connecticut: Green– wood Press, 1983).

Ian Sinclair, *The Vienna Convention on the Law of Treaties* (Manchester: Melland Schill Fund, 1984).

Georges E. Sioui, *For an Amerindian Autohistory—An Essay on the Foundations of a Social Ethic* (Montreal & Kingston: McGill & Queen's University Press, 1992).

Audrey Smedley, *Race in North America Origin and Evolution of a Worldview* (Boulder: Westview Press, 1993).

Alpheus Henry Snow, *The Question of Aborigines in the Law and Practice of Nations* (Northbrook, Illinois: Metro Books Inc., 1972).

Fiona J. Stafford, *The Last of the Race* (Oxford: Clarendon Press, 1994).

Rodolfo Stavenhagen, The Ethnic Question: Conflicts, Development, and Human Rights (Tokyo: United Nations University Press, 1990).

Rodolfo Stavenhagen, *Ethnic Conflicts and the Nation-State* (London: St. Martin's Press, 1996).

Mara Stickland, *Colonialism and Development in the Contemporary World* (New York: Mansell Publishers 1991).

Joseph Story, *Commentaries on the Constitution of the United States With a Preliminary Review of the Constitutional History of the Colonies and States before the Adoption of the Constitution, Volume I* (New York: Da Capa Press, 1970). Reissued based upon the original text of 1833.

A. Rigo Sureda, *The Evolution of the Right of Self-determination—A Study of United Nations Practice* (Leiden: Sijthoff, 1973).

Jerzy Sztucki, *Jus Cogens and the Vienna Convention on the Law of Treaties A Critical Appraisal* (New York: Springer–Verlag 1974).

H. W. A. Thirlway, *International Customary Law and Codification—An examination of the continuing role of custom in the present period of codification of international law* (Leiden: A. W. Sijthoff, 1972).

Nicholas Thomas, *Colonialism's Culture: Anthropology; Travel and Government* (Princeton: Princeton University Press, 1994).

Ruth Thompson ed., *The Rights of Indigenous Peoples in International Law: Selected Essays on Self-determination* (Saskatoon: University of Saskatchewan Native Law Centre, 1987).

Patrick Thornberry, *International Law and the Rights of Minorities* (Oxford: Oxford Press, 1991).

Brian Titley, *A Narrow Vision—Duncan Campbell Scott and the Administration of Indian Affairs in Canada* (Vancouver: University of British Columbia Press, 1986).

Christian Tomuschat ed., *Modern Law of Self-Determination* (Dordrecht, The Netherlands: Martinus Nijhoff Publishing, 1993).

William Twining ed., *Issues of Self-Determination* (Aberdeen: Aberdeen University Press, 1991).
Prof. N. Valticos, *International Labour Law* (The Netherlands: Kluwer, 1979).

Sharon Venne and Ward Churchill eds., *Islands in Captivity: The Record of the International Tribunal on the Rights of Indigenous Hawaiians* (3 volumes) (1997).

Mark E. Villiger, *Customary International Law and Treaties* (Dordrecht, The Netherlands: Martinus Nijhoff Publishers, 1985).

Jack McIver Weatherford, *Savages and Civilization—Who will Survive?* (New York: Crown Publishers Inc., 1994).

Urban G. Whitaker Jr., *Politics and Power—A Text in International Law* (New York: Harper & Row, 1964).

Franck Wilmer, *The Indigenous Voice in World Politics: Since Time Immemorial* (Newbury Park California: Sage, 1993).

Robert A. Williams Jr., *The American Indian In Western Legal Thought: The Discourses of Conquest* (New York: Oxford University Press, 1990).

United Nations' Office of Public Information, *Everyman's United Nations The Structure, Functions and Work of the Organization and its Related Agencies during the Years 1945–1962 and a United Nations Chronology for 1963* (New York: United Nations, 1964).

Tony J. M. Zuijdwijk, *Petitioning the United Nations—A Study in Human Rights* (New York: St. Martin's Press, 1982).

Alfred Zimmern, *The League of Nations and the Rule of Law 1918-1935* (New York: Russell and Russell, 1939, reissued 1969).

Judith P. Zinsser, *A new partnership: indigenous peoples and the United Nations system* (Paris: UNESCO Publishing, 1994).

Articles

Richard Abel, "Custom, Rules, Administration, Community" (1984) 28. *Journal of African Law* , 6.

Gudmunder Alfredsson, "International Law, International Organizations, and Indigenous Peoples" (1982) 36. *Journal of International Affairs*, 113.

Gudmunder Alfredsson, "Fourth Session of the Working Group on Indigenous Populations" (1986) 55. *Nordic Journal of International Law,* 22.

A.N. Allott, "What is to be Done with African Customary Law? The Experience of Problems and Reforms in Anglophone Africa from 1950" (1984) 28. *Journal of African Law*, 56.

Philip Alston, "Conjuring Up New Human Rights: A Proposal For Quality Control" (1984) 78. *American Journal of International Law,* 607.

S. James Anaya and et al., "Comment on the Working Group Report and Draft Declaration" (1991) 8. *Arizona Journal of International and Comparative law*, 221.

S. James Anaya, " Indigenous Rights Norms in Contemporary International Law" (1991) 8. *Arizona Journal of International and Comparative Law*, 1.

S. James Anaya, "A Contemporary Definition of the International Norm of Self–Determination" (1993) 3. *Transnational Law & Contemporary Problems*, 131.

S. James Anaya and S. Todd Crider, "Indigenous Peoples: The Environment, and Commercial Forestry in Developing Countries: The Case of Awas Tingni, Nicraragua" (1996) 18. *Human Rights Quarterly*, 345.

Ellen Anderson, "The Saskatchewan Indians and Canada's New Constitution," (1982) 36. *Journal of International Affairs*, 125.

Tatjana Ansbach, "Impunity–Revenge–Justice? An Eastern European Point of View" [1993] Geneva: *Impunite, Impunity, Imprimidad*, 58.

Nelly Arvelo–Jimenez, "The Political Struggle of the Guyana Region's Indigenous Peoples" (1982) 36. *Journal of International Affairs*, 43.

Karen W. Baer, "A Theory on Intellectual Property and the Biodiversity Treaty" (1995) 21. *Syracuse Journal of International Law and Commerce*, 279.

Russel Lawrence Barsh, "The Omen: Three Affiliated Tribes v. Moe and the Future of Tribal Self–Government" (1977) 5. *American Indian, 1.*

Russel Lawrence Barsh, "Indigenous Peoples: An Emerging Object of International Law" (1986) 80. *American Journal of International Law*, 369.

Russel Lawrence Barsh, "United Nations Seminar on Indigenous Peoples and States" (1989) 83. *American Journal of International Law*, 599.

Russel Lawrence Barsh, "An Advocate's Guide to the Convention on Indigenous And Tribal Peoples" (1990). *Oklahoma City University Law Review*, 209.

Russel Lawrence Barsh, "The Challenge of Indigenous Self-determination" (1993) 26. *University of Michigan Journal of Law Reform*, 277.

Russel Lawrence Barsh, "Indigenous Peoples: An Emerging Object of International Law", (1986) 80. *American Journal of International Law*, 369.

Russel Lawrence Barsh, "Indigenous Peoples in the 1990s. From Object to Subject of International Law" (1994) 7. *Harvard Human Rights Journal*, 33.

R.R. Baxter, "International Law—Her Infinite Variety" (1980) 29. *International and Comparative Law Quarterly*, 549.

A. F. Bayefsky, "The Human Rights Committee and the Case of Sandra Lovelace" (1982) 20. *Canadian Yearbook of International Law*, 244.

Howard Berman, "The International Labour Organization and Indigenous Peoples: Revision of ILO Convention 107 at the 75th session of the I.L.O. Conference, 1988" 41. *International Commission of Jurist Review*, 48.

Curtis G. Berkey, "International Law and Domestic Courts: Enhancing Self-Determination for Indigenous Peoples" (1992) 5. *Harvard Human Rights Journal*, 65.

Lea Brilmayer, "Secession and Self-determination: A Territorial Interpretation" (1991) 16. *Yale Journal of International Law*, 177.

Allen Buchanan, "The Right to Self-Determination: Analytical and Moral Foundations" (1991) 8. *Arizona Journal of International and Comparative Law*, 41.

Allen Buchanan, "Self-Determination and the Right to Secede" (1992) 45. *Journal of International Affairs*, 347.

Allen Buchanan, "The Role of Collective Rights in the Theory of Indigenous Peoples' Rights" (1993) 3. *Transnational Law & Contemporary Problems*, 89.

Thomas Buergenthal, "International Human Rights Law and Institutions: Accomplishments and Prospects" (1968) 63. *Washington Law Review*, 1.

Thomas Buergenthal, "The Inter-American Court, Human Rights and the OAS" (1986) 7. *Human Rights Law Journal*, 157.

Deborah Z. Cass, "Re-Thinking Self-Determination: A Critical Analysis of Current International Law Theories" (1992) 18. *Syracuse Journal of International Law and Commerce*, 21.

Duane Champagne, "Beyond Assimilation as a Strategy for National Integration: The Persistence of American Indian Political Identities" (1993) 3. *Transnational Law & Contemporary Problems*, 109.

C. M. Chinkin, "The Challenge of Soft Law: Development and Change in International Law" (1989) 38. *International and Comparative Law Quarterly*, 850.

Ward Churchill and Winona LaDuke, "Radioactive Colonization and the Native American" (1986) 13. *The Insurgent Sociologist*, 34.

John Claydon, "International Human Rights Law and the Interpretation of the Canadian Charter of Rights and Freedoms" (1982) 4. *Supreme Court Law Review*, 287.

John Howard Clinebell and Jim Thomson, "Sovereignty and Self-determination: The Rights of Native Americans Under International Law" (1978) 27. *Buffalo Law Review*, 669.

Robert N. Clinton, "The Rights of Indigenous Peoples as Collective Group Rights"

(1990) 32. *Arizona Law Review*, 739.

Cindy A. Cohn, "The Early Harvest: Domestic Legal Changes Related to the Human Rights Committee and the Covenant on Civil and Political Rights" (1991) 13. *Human Rights Quarterly*, 295.

J. J. Corntassel and T. Hopkins Primeau, "Indigenous 'Sovereignty' and International Law: Revised Strategies for Pursuing 'Self-Determination'" (1995) 17. *Human Rights Quarterly*, 343.

Dean Cycon, "When Worlds Collide: Law, Development and Indigenous Peoples" (1991) 25. *New England Law Review*, 761.

Erica-Irene Daes, "Native Peoples' Rights (1986) 27. *Cahiers de Droit*, 123.

Erica–Irene Daes, "Some Considerations on the Rights of Indigenous Peoples to Self– Determination" (1993) 3. *Transnational Law & Contemporary Problems*, 1.

Erica–Irene Daes, "Equality of Indigenous Peoples Under the Auspices of the United Nations—The Draft Declaration on the Rights of Indigenous Peoples" (1995) 7. *St. Thomas Law Review*, 493.

H. Elizabeth Dallam, "The Growing Voice of Indigenous Peoples: Their Use of Story Telling and Rights Discourse to Transform Multilateral Development Bank Policies" (1991) 8. *Arizona Journal of International and Comparative Law*, 117.

Roy Stone de Montpensier, "The British Doctrine of Parliamentary Sovereignty: A Critical Inquiry" (1966) 26. *Louisana Law Review*, 753.

Stanley Diamond, "The Rule of Law vs. the Order of Custom" (1971) 38. *Social Research*, 387.

Yoram Dinstein, "Collective Human Rights of Peoples and Minorities" (1976) 25. *International and Comparative Law Quarterly*, 103.

Isaak I. Dore, "United Nations Measures to Combat Racial Discrimination Progress and Problems in Retrospect" (1981) 10. *Journal of International Law and Policy*, 299.

John Dugard, "South Africa's "Independent" Homelands: An Exercise in Denationalization" (1980) 10. *Journal of International Law and Policy*, 11.

E. Eggleston, "Prospects for United Nations protection of the human rights of indigenous minorities" (1970–73) 5. *Australian Yearbook of International Law*, 68.
Leslie G. Espinoza, "Masks and Other Disguises: Exposing Legal Academia" (1990) 103. *Harvard Law Review*, 1878.

Graham Flack, Ajeet Kang, Michele Leighton and David Preger, "The International Legal Right of Self-Determination Four Legal Approaches and Their

Textual Foundations" (1992) 1. *Dalhousie Journal of Legal Studies*, 189.

A. Belden Fields and Wolf–Dieter Narr, "Human Rights as a Holistic Concept" (1992) 14. *Human Rights Quarterly*, 1.

Robert E. Frankel, "Recognizing Self-determination in International Law-Kuwait's Conflict with Iraq" (1992) 14. *Loyala Los Angeles International and Comparative Law*, 359.

Lesley Karen Friedman, "Native Hawaiian, Self-Determination and the Inadequacy of the State Land Trusts" (1992) 14. *University of Hawai'i Law Review*, 519.

Ton Gardeniers, Hurst Hannum and Janice Kruger, "The 1981 Session of the UN Sub-Commission on Prevention of Discrimination and Protection of Minorities" (1982) 76. *American Journal of International Law*, 405.

E. Gayim, "United Nations law on self-determination of indigenous peoples" (1982) 51. *Nordisk Tidsskrift*, 53.

P.R. Ghandhi, "The Human Rights Committee and the Right of Individual Communication" (1986) 57. *British Yearbook of International Law*, 201.

Richard Gittleman, "The African Charter on Human and Peoples' Rights: A Legal Analysis" (1982) 22. *Virginia Journal of International Law*, 667.

Joyce A. Green, "Towards A Detente With History—Confronting Canada's Colonial Legacy" (1993) 12. *International Journal of Canadian Studies*, 85.

Daniel R. Gross, "The Indians and the Brazilian Frontier" (1982) 36. *Journal of International Affairs*, 1.

Tadeusz Gruchalla-Wesierski, "A Framework for Understanding "Soft Law" [1984] *McGill Law Review*, 37.

Isabelle R. Gunning, "Modernizing Customary International Law: The Challenge of Human Rights" (1991) 31. *Virginia Journal of International Law*, 213.

Jean Guiart, "One of the Last Colonies: New Caledonia" (1982) 36. *Journal of International Affairs*, 105.

Patricia K. Hall, "Military rule threatens Guatemala's Highland Maya Indians (1986) 10. *Cultural Survival Quarterly*, 48.

Hurst Hannum, "New Developments in Indigenous Rights" (1988) 28. *Virginia Journal of International Law*, 649.

Joan F. Hartman, "Derogation from Human Rights Treaties in Public Emergencies—A Critique of Implementation by the European Commission and Court of Human Rights and the Human Rights Committee of the United Nations"

(1981) 22. *Harvard International Law Journal*, 1.

Richard J. Harvey, "The Right of the People of the Whole of Ireland to Self-Determination, Unity, Sovereignty and Independence" (1990) 11. *New York Law School Journal of International and Comparative Law*, 167.

Alexis Heraclides, "Secession, Self-Determination and Nonintervention: In Quest of a Normative Symbiosis" (1992) 45. *Journal of International Affairs*, 399.

Richard Herz, "Legal Protection For Indigenous Cultures: Sacred Sites and Communal Rights" (1993) 79. *Virginia Law Review*, 691.

George R. Hesse, "Securing Tangible Results of Self-determination: A Scheme to Solicit Support From the International Boundary and Water Commission for Indigenous Peoples' Water Rights Claims" (1991) 8. *Arizona Journal of International and Comparative Law*, 149.

Lord Lester of Herne Hill, "Non–Discrimination in International Human Rights Law" (1993) 19. *Commonwealth Law Bulletin*, 1653.

D.C. Hodgson, "Aboriginal Australian and the World Court, Sovereignty by Conquest, The Advisory Jurisdiction of the World Court" [1985] *New Zealand Law Journal*, 33.

Rhoda Howard, "Evaluating Human Rights in Africa: Some Problems of Implicit Comparison" (1984) 6. *Human Rights Quarterly*, 160.

Richard F. Iglar, "The Constitutional Crisis in Yugoslavia and the International Law of Self-Determination: Slovenia's and Croatia's Right to Secede" (1992) 15. *Boston College International and Comparative Law Review*, 213.

Catherine J. Iorns, "Indigenous Peoples and Self-Determination Challenging State Sovereignty" (1992) 24. *Case Western Reserve Journal of International Law*, 199.

Ferrokh Jhabvala, "The Practice of the Covenant's Human Rights Committee, 1976–82: Review of the State Party Reports" (1984) 6. *Human Rights Quarterly*, 81.

Darlene M. Johnston, "Native Rights as Collective Rights: A Question of Group Self– preservation" (1989) 2. *Canadian Journal of Law and Jurisprudence*, 19.

Christopher C. Joyner, "The Historical Status of American Indians Under International Law (1978) 11. *The Indian Historian*, 30.

Shelly Kellman, "The Yanomamis: Their Battle for Survival" (1982) 36. *Journal of International Affairs*, 15.

Benedict Kingsbury, "Claims by Non-State Groups in International Law" (1992) 25. *Cornell International Law Journal*, 481.

Benedict Kingsbury, "Self-Determination and "Indigenous Peoples" (1992) *The American Society of International Law, 86th Annual Meeting,* 383.

Benedict Kingsbury, "Whose International Law? Sovereignty and Non-State Groups" (1994). *The American Society of International Law, 88th Annual Meeting,* 1.

Michael Kirby, "Decision of the Permanent Tribunal of Peoples in its Session on Tibet Strasbourg, France, November 1992" [1994]. *Australian Law Journal,* 135.

Frederic L. Kirgis Jr., "The Degrees of Self-determination in the United Nations Era" (1994) 88. *American Journal of International Law,* 304.

Alexandre Kiss, "The Peoples' Right to Self-Determination" (1986) 7. *Human Rights Law Journal,* 165.

Richard N. Kiwanuka, "The Meaning of "People" in the African Charter on Human and Peoples' Rights" (1988) 82. *American Journal of International Law,* 80.

Michael A.G. Korengold, "Lessons in Confronting Racial Speech: Good Intentions, Bad Results, and Article 4(a) of the Conventions on the Elimination of All Forms of Racial Discrimination" (1993) 77. *Minnesota Law Review,* 719.

Fae L. Korsmo, "Nordic Security and the Saami Minority: Territorial Rights in Northern Fennoscandia" (1988). *Human Rights Quarterly,* 509.

Martti Koskenniemi, "National Self-determination Today: Problems of Legal Theory and Practice" (1994) 43. *International and Comparative Law Quarterly,* 241.

Josef L. Kuns, "Chapter XI of the United Nations Charter in Action" (1954) 48. *American Journal of International Law,* 103.

Edward A. Laing, "The Norm of Self-determination, 1941–1991" (1992) 22. *California Western International Law Journal,* 209.

Maivan Clech Lam, "Making Room for Peoples at the United Nations: Thoughts Provoked by Indigenous Claims to Self-determination" (1992) 25. *Cornell International Law Journal,* 603.

Ruth Lapidoth, "Sovereignty in Transition" (1992) 45. *Journal of International Affairs,* 325.

Sir Hersch Lauterpacht, "Codification and Development of International Law" (1955) 49. *American Journal of International Law,* 16.

Andree Lawrey, "Contemporary Efforts to Guarantee Indigenous Rights Under International Law" (1990) 23. *Vanderbilt Journal of Transnational Law,* 703.

Matthew Lippman, "Human Rights Revisited: The Protection of Human Rights under the International Covenant on Civil and Political Rights" (1980) 10.

California Western International Law Journal, 450.

Janet E. Lord,"The United Nations High Commissioner for Human Rights: Challenges and Opportunities" (1995) 17. *Loyala Los Angeles International and Comparative Law Journal*, 329.

Eric Lucas, "Towards an International Declaration on Land Rights" (1984) 33. *The Review International Commission of Jurists*, 61.

Drew Mahalic and Joan Gambee Mahalic, "The Limitation Provisions of the International Convention on the Elimination of All Forms of Racial Discrimination" (1987) 9. *Human Rights Quarterly*, 74.

Louise Mandell, "Indian Nations not minorities" (1986) 27. *Cahiers de Droit*, 101.

Gregory Marchildon "Quebec's Right of Secession Under Canadian and International Law" (1992) 32. *Virginia Journal of International Law*, 583.

Jean-Bernard Marie, "Relations Between Peoples' Rights and Human Rights: Semantic and Methodological Distinctions" (1986) 7. *Human Rights Law Journal*, 195.

G.C. Marks, "Indigenous Peoples in International Law: The Significance of Francisco de Vitoria and Bartoloma de Las Casas" [1993]. *Australian Yearbook of International Law*, 1.

Geoffrey Marshall, "Parliamentary Sovereignty: A Recent Development" (1967) 12. *McGill Law Journal*, 523.

J.G. McGilp, "The Relations of Canadian Indians and Canadian Governments" (1963) 6. *Canadian Public Administration*, 299.

Kent McNeil, "The Decolonization of Canada: Moving Toward Recognition of Aboriginal Governments" (1994) 7. *Western Legal History*, 113.

Theodor Meron, "The Meaning and Reach of the International Convention on the Elimination of All Forms of Racial Discrimination" (1985) 79. *American Journal of International Law*, 283.

Theodor Meron, "Reform of Lawmaking in the United Nations: The Human Rights Instance" (1985) 79. *American Journal of International Law*, 664.

Henry Minde, "The Making of an International Movement of Indigenous Peoples (1996) 4. *Scandivanian Journal of History*, 40.

J.D.B. Mitchell, "Sovereignty of Parliament—Yet Again" (1963) 79. *Law Quarterly Review*, 196.

Glenn T. Morris, "In Support of the Right of Self-Determination for Indigenous

Peoples Under International Law" (1986) 29. *German Yearbook of International Law*, 277.

Erick Mose and Torkel Opsahl, "The Optional Protocol to the International Covenant on Civil and Political Rights" (1981) 21. *Santa Clara Law Review*, 271.

Wendy Moss, "Indigenous Self-Government in Canada and Sexual Equality Under the Indian Act: Resolving Conflicts Between Collective and Individual Rights" (1990) 15. *Queen's Law Journal*, 279.

Alexander J. Motyl, "The Modernity of Nationalism: Nations, States and Nation-States in the Contemporary World" (1992) 45. *Journal of International Affairs*, 307.

Ved. P. Nanda, "Self-Determination Under International Law Validity to Claims to Secede" (1981) 13. *Case Western Reserve Journal of International Law*, 257.

Frank C. Newman, "Introduction: The United States Bill of Rights, International Bill of Human Rights, and Other 'Bills' "(1991) 40. *Emory Law Journal*, 731.

Garth Nettheim, "Seminar on the Rights of Indigenous Peoples under Law and Practice" (1986) 60. *Australian Law Journal*, 416.

B. Obinna Okere, "The Protection of Human Rights in Africa and the African Charter on Human and Peoples' Rights: A Comparative Analysis with the European and American Systems" (1984) 6. *Human Rights Quarterly*, 141.

John O'Manique, "Development, Human Rights and Law" (1992) 14. *Human Rights Quarterly*, 383.

John A. Onorato, "Saving Grace or Saving Face: The Roman Catholic Church and Human Rights" (1989) 8. *Dickinson Journal of International Law*, 81.

Tia Oroa, "Religious Freedom an American Illusion for Natives" [1994]. *The Circle*, 5.

Dianne Otto, "A Question of Law or Politics? Indigenous Claims to Sovereignty in Australia" (1995) 21. *Syracuse Journal of International Law and Commerce*, 65.

Anthony G. Pazzanika, "Legal Aspects of Membership In the Organization of African Unity: The Case of the Western Sahara" (1984) 17. *Case Western Reserve Journal of International Law*, 123.

John T. Paxman, "Minority Indigenous Populations and Their Claims for Self-determination" (1989) 21. *Case Western Reserve Journal International Law*, 185.

Monroe E. Price, "Lawyers on the Reservation: Some Implications for the Legal Profession" [1969]. *Arizona State Law Journal*, 162.

Proceedings of 79th Annual meeting of the American Society of International Law, Panel discussion on: "Indigenous Populations Entitled to International Juridical Personality" 26. April 1985, 189.

Proceedings of 81st Annual Meeting of the American Society of International Law, Panel discussion on: "International Human Rights Standards Setting: The Case of Indigenous Peoples" 8-11 April 1987, 277.

Proceedings of 87th Annual Meeting of the American Society of International Law, Panel discussion: "Indigenous Peoples and the Right to Self-Determination", 31 March-3 April 1993, 190.

Proceedings of 87th Annual Meeting of the American Society of International Law, Panel discussion: "Communities in Transition: Autonomy, Self–Governance and Independence" 31 March-3 April 1993, 248.

Proceedings of 88th Annual Meeting of the American Society of International Law, Panel discussion: "Indigenous Peoples—Sovereignty and Non-State Groups" 1994, 1.

Philip Vuciri Ramaga, "The Bases of Minority Identity" (1992) 14. *Human Rights Quarterly*, 409.

W. Michael Reisman, "Sovereignty and Human Rights in Contemporary International Law" (1990) 84. *American Journal of International Law,* 866.

W. Michael Reisman, "Protecting Indigenous Rights in International Relations" (1995) 89. *American Journal of International Law,* 350.

Osborne M. Reynolds Jr., "Agua Caliente Revisited: Recent Developments as to Zoning of Indian Reservations" (1977) 4. *American Indian Law Review,* 249.

W. Riphagen, "From soft law to jus cogens and back" (1987) 17. *Victoria University of Wellington Law Review* at 81.

Carl Bryant Rogers, "Zoning: A Rebuttal to "Village of Euclid Meets Agua Caliente" (1977) 4. *American Indian Law Review,* 141.

Shabtai Rosenne, "Article 27 of the Statute of the International Court of Justice" (1991) 32. *Virginia Journal of International Law,* 213.

June M. Ross, "Limitation on Human Rights in International Laws: Their Relevance to the Canadian Charter of Rights and Freedoms" (1984) 6. *Human Rights Quarterly,* 180.

Bernadette Kelly Roy and Gudmunder Alfredsson, "Indigenous Rights: The Literature Explosion (1987) 13. *Transnational Perspectives,* 19.

Frank Salomon, "The Andean Contrast", (1982) 36. *Journal of International Affairs,* 56.

Dalee Sambo,"Indigenous Peoples and International Standard-Setting Processes: Are State Governments Listening?" (1993) 3. T*ransnational Law & Contemporary Problems,* 13.

Douglas Sanders, "The Re-emergence of Indigenous Questions in International Law" [1984.] *Canadian Human Rights Yearbook of International Law*, 3.

Douglas Sanders, "Another Step: The UN Seminar on Relations Between Indigenous Peoples and States" [1989]. *Canadian Native Law Reporter*, 7.

Douglas Sanders, "Revised Draft Universal Declaration on Rights of Indigenous Peoples", [1989]. *Canadian Native Law Reporter*, 44.

Douglas Sanders, "International Labour Organization Convention 169–Concerning Indigenous and Tribal Peoples in Independent Countries" [1989]. *Canadian Native Law Reporter*, 49.

Douglas Sanders, "The UN Working Group on Indigenous Populations" (1989) 11. *Human Rights Quarterly*, 406.

Douglas Sanders, "Collective Rights" (1991) 13. *Human Rights Quarterly*, 368.

Douglas Sanders and Mary Ellen Turpel, "The Draft Declaration on the Rights of Indigenous Peoples" [1994]. *Canadian Native Law Reporter*, 40.

Douglas Sanders, "Indigenous Peoples at the United Nations: An Overview" [1996] 2. *Canadian Native Law Reporter*, 20.

Oscar Schachter, "United Nations Law" (1994) 88. *The American Journal of International Law*, 1.

Isabelle Schulte-Tenckhoff, "Reassessing the Paradigm of Domestication: The Problematic of Indigenous Treaties" (1997) Vol. IV, No. 2. *Review of Constitutional Studies*, 239.

Isabelle Schulte-Tenckhoff, "The Function of Otherness in Treaty-Making: Re–reading Charles H. Alexandrowicz" in *Sovereignty, Legitimacy and Power in West African Societies*, (Lit-Verlag: Hamburg, Germany, 1998) (In Print).

Isabelle Schulte-Tenckhoff, "The Irresistible Ascension of the United Nations Draft Declaration on the Rights of Indigenous Peoples: Stopped short in its tracks?" (1995) 9. *European Review of Native American Studies* , 5.

Isabelle Schulte-Tenckhoff, "Inquiry and Analysis of Materials Necessary for the Study on Treaties, Agreements and Other Constructive Arrangements between Indigenous Peoples and States: Selected Case Studies II" (1995) United Nations Centre for Human Rights (Unpublished research report).

Isabelle Schulte-Tenckhoff, "Inquiry and Analysis of Materials Necessary for the Study on Treaties, Agreements and Other Constructive Arrangements between Indigenous Peoples and States: Selected Case Studies II" (1994) United Nations Centre for Human Rights (Unpublished research report).

Isabelle Schulte-Tenckhoff, "Inquiry and Analysis of Materials Necessary for the Study on Treaties, Agreements and Other Constructive Arrangements between Indigenous Peoples and States: Selected Case Studies II" (1993) United Nations Centre for Human Rights (Unpublished research report).

Isabelle Schulte-Tenckhoff, "Inquiry and Analysis of Materials Necessary for the Study on Treaties, Agreements and Other Constructive Arrangements between Indigenous Peoples and States: Selected Case Studies II" (1992) United Nations Centre for Human Rights.

Craig Scott, "The Interdependence and Permeability of Human Rights Norms: Towards a Partial Fusion of the International Covenants on Human Rights" (1989) 27. *Osgoode Hall Law Journal*, 769.

Claude-Armand Sheppard, "Is Parliament Still Sovereign?" (1964) 7. *Canadian Bar Journal*, 39.

Ibrahim F. I. Shihata, "The World Bank and Non-Governmental Organizations" (1992) 25. *Cornell International Law Journal*, 623.

William Andrew Shutkin, "International Human Rights Law and the Earth: The Protection of Indigenous Peoples and the Environment" (1991) 31. *Virginia Journal of International Law*, 479.

Jean M. Silveri, "A Comparative Analysis of the History of United States and Canadian Federal Policies Regarding Native self-government" (1993) 16. *Suffolk Transnational Law Review*, 618.

Bruno Simma and Philip Alston, "The Sources of Human Rights Law: Custom, Jus Cogens, and General Principles" (1992) 12. *Australian Yearbook of International Law*, 82.
Richard Chase Smith, "Liberal Ideology and Indigenous Communities in Post–Independence Peru" (1982) 36. *Journal of International Affairs*, 73.

Luis B. Sohn, "The New International Law: Protection of the Rights of Individuals Rather than States" (1982) 32. *American University Law Review*, 1.

Luis B. Sohn, "'Generally Accepted' International Rules" (1986) 61. *Washington Law Review*, 1073.

J. Sonarajah, "Internal Colonialism and Humanitarian Intervention" (1981) 11 *Georgia Journal of International and Comparative Law*, 45.

Elsa Stamatopoulou, "Indigenous Peoples and the United Nations: Human Rights as a Developing Dynamic" (1994) 16. *Human Rights Quarterly*, 58.

Rodolfo Stavenhagen, "Challenging the Nation-State in Latin America" (1995) 45. *Journal of International Affairs*, 421.

Laura Stomski, "The Development of Minimum Standards for the Protection and Promotion of Rights For Indigenous Peoples" (1991) 16. *American Indian Law Review,* 575.

Dean B. Suagee, "Self-determination For Indigenous Peoples at the Dawn of the Solar Age" (1992) 25. *University of Michigan Journal of Law Reform,* 671.

Frances Svennsson, "Comparative Ethnic Policy on the American and Russian Frontiers" 1982) 36. *Journal of International Affairs,* 83.

Lee Swepston, "The Indian in Latin America: Approaches to Administration, Integration, and Protection" (1978) 27. *Buffalo Law Review,* 715.

Lee Swepston, "A New Step in the International Law on Indigenous and Tribal Peoples: ILO Convention No. 169 of 1989" (1990) 15. *Oklahoma City University Law Review,* 677.

Lee Swepston and Roger Plant, "International Standards and the Protection of the Land Rights of Indigenous and Tribal Populations" (1985) 124. *International Labour Review,* 91.

Walter Tarnopolsky, "The Canadian Experience with the International Covenant on Civil and Political Rights Seen From the Perspective of a Former Member of the Human Rights Committee" (1987) 20. *Akron Law Review,* 611.

Chris Tennant, "Indigenous Peoples, International Institutions, and the International Legal Literature from 1945–1993" (1994) 16. *Human Rights Quarterly,* 1.

Patrick Thornberry, "Self-determination, Minorities, Human Rights: A Review of International Instruments" (1989) 38. *International and Comparative Law Quarterly,* 687.

Raidza Torres, "The Rights of Indigenous Populations: The Emerging International Norm" (1991) 16. *Yale Journal of International Law,* 127.

Charmain Edwards Toussaint, "The Colonial Controversy in the United Nations" [1956]. *The Year Book of World Affairs,* 170.

Mililani B. Trask, "Historical and Contemporary Hawaiian Self-determination: A Native Hawaiian Perspective" (1991) 8. *Arizona Journal of International and Comparative Law,* 77.

D.C. Turack, "The African Charter on Human and Peoples' Rights: some preliminary thoughts" (1984) 17. *Akron Law Review,* 489.

Mary Ellen Turpel, "Indigenous Peoples' Rights of Political Participation and Self-Determination: Recent International Legal Developments and the Continuing Struggle for Recognition" (1992) 25. *Cornell International Law Journal,* 579.

Vogesh Tyaagi, "Cooperation Between the Human Rights Committee and Non–governmental Organizations: Permissibility and Propositions" (1983) 18. *Texas International Law Journal*, 272.

O. U. Umozurike, "The African Charter on Human and Peoples' Rights" (1983) 77. *American Journal of International Law*, 902.

Theo van Boven, "The Relations Between Peoples' Rights and Human Rights in the African Charter" (1986) 7. *Human Rights Law Journal*, 183.

Johan D. van der Vyver, "Sovereignty and Human Rights in Constitutional and International Law" (1991) 5. *Emory International Law Review*, 321.

Sharon H. Venne, "The New Language of Assimilation: A Brief Analysis of ILO Convention 169" (1990)Washington, D.C.: *Without Prejudice*, 53.

Sharon H. Venne, (ed.), Honour Bound: Onion Lake and the Spirit of Treaty Six – The International Validity of Treaties with Indigenous Peoples (Copenhagen: IWGIA Document No. 84, 1997).

Sharon H. Venne, "Understanding Treaty Six: An Indigenous Perspective" in M. Asch, ed., *Aboriginal and Treaty Rights in Canada* (Vancouver: University of British Columbia Press, 1997).

Sharon H. Venne, "Self-determination Issues in Canada: A First Person's Overview" in *Self-determination—International Perspectives,* ed. Donald Clark and Robert Williamson (1996 London: St. Martins Press) 291.

Anna M. Vradenburgh, "The Chapter VII: Powers of the United Nations Charter: Do They "Trump" Human Rights Law?" (1992) 14. *Loyala of Los Angeles International and Comparative Law*, 175.

William M. Walker, "The Remedies of Law of the International Covenant on Civil and Political Rights: Current Trends and a Conceptual Framework for the Future" (1988) 20. *International Law and Politics*, 525.

Burns H. Weston, "Human Rights" (1984) 6. *Human Rights Quarterly*, 257.

Anthony Whelan, "Wilsonian Self-determination and the Versailles Settlement" (1994) 43. *International and Comparative Law Quarterly*, 99.

Carol Weisbrod, "Minorities and Diversities: The "Remarkable Experiment" of the League of Nations" (1993) 8. *Connecticut Journal of International Law*, 359.

Robert Williams Jr., "Columbus's Legacy: Law as an Instrument of Racial Discrimination Against Indigenous Peoples' Right of Self-Determination" (1991) 8. *Arizona Journal of International and Comparative Law*, 51.

Robert Williams Jr., "Encounters on the Frontiers of International Human Rights Law: Redefining the Terms of Indigenous Peoples' Survival in the World" [1990]. *Duke Law Journal*, 660.

APPENDIX I

Draft Declaration as Agreed Upon by The Members of The Working Group at Its Eleventh Session

Affirming that indigenous peoples are equal in dignity and rights to all other peoples, while recognizing the right of all peoples to be different, to consider themselves different, and to be respected as such,

Affirming also that all peoples contribute to the diversity and richness of civilizations and cultures, which constitute the common heritage of humankind,

Affirming further that all doctrines, policies and practices based on or advocating superiority of peoples or individuals on the basis of national origin, racial, religious, ethnic or cultural differences are racist, scientifically false, legally invalid, morally condemnable and socially unjust,

Reaffirming also that indigenous peoples, in the exercise of their rights, should be free from discrimination of any kind,

Concerned that indigenous peoples have been deprived of their human rights and fundamental freedoms, resulting, *inter alia*, in their colonization and dispossession of their lands, territories and resources, thus preventing them from exercising, in particular, their right to development in accordance with their own needs and interests,

Recognizing the urgent need to respect and promote the inherent rights and characteristics of indigenous peoples, especially their rights to their lands, territories and resources, which derive from their political, economic and social structures and from their cultures, spiritual traditions, histories and philosophies,

Welcoming the fact that indigenous peoples are organizing themselves for political, economic, social and cultural enhancement and in order to bring an end to all forms of discrimination and oppression wherever they occur,

Convinced that control by indigenous peoples over development affecting them and their lands, territories and resources will enable them to maintain and strengthen their institutions, cultures and traditions, and to promote their development in accordance with their aspirations and needs,

Recognizing also that respect for indigenous knowledge, cultures and traditional practices contributes to sustainable and equitable development and proper management of the environment,

Emphasizing the need for demilitarization of the lands and territories of indigenous peoples, which will contribute to peace, economic and social progress and development, understanding and friendly relations among nations and peoples of the world,

Recognizing in particular the right of indigenous families and communities to retain shared responsibility for the upbringing, training, education and well-being of their children,

Recognizing also that indigenous peoples have the right freely to determine their relationship with States in a spirit of coexistence, mutual benefit and full respect,

Considering that treaties, agreements and other arrangements between States and indigenous peoples are properly matters of international concern and responsibility,

Acknowledging that the Charter of the United Nations, the International Covenant on Economic, Social and Cultural Rights and the Covenant on Civil and Political Rights affirm the fundamental importance of the right of self-determination of all peoples, by virtue of which they freely determine their political status and freely pursue their economic, social and cultural development,

Bearing in mind that nothing in this Declaration may be used to deny any peoples their right of Self-determination,

Encouraging States to comply with and effectively implement all international instruments, in particular those related to human rights, as they apply to indigenous peoples, in consultation and cooperation with the peoples concerned,

Emphasizing that the United Nations has an important and continuing role to play in promoting and protecting the rights of indigenous peoples.

Believing that this Declaration is a further important step forward for the recognition, promotion and protection of the rights and freedoms of indigenous peoples and in the development of relevant activities of the United Nations system in this field,

Solemnly proclaims the following United Nations Declaration on the Rights of Indigenous Peoples:

PART I

Article 1

Indigenous Peoples have the right to the full and effective enjoyment of all human rights and fundamental freedoms recognized in the Charter of the United Nations, the Universal Declaration of Human Rights and international human rights law.

Article 2

Indigenous individuals and peoples are free and equal to all other individuals and peoples in dignity and rights, and have the right to be free from any kind of adverse discrimination, in particular that based on their indigenous origin or identity.

Article 3

Indigenous Peoples have the right of Self-determination. By virtue of that right they freely determine their political status and freely pursue their economic, social and cultural development.

Article 4

Indigenous Peoples have the right to maintain and strengthen their distinct political, economic, social and cultural characteristics, as well as their legal systems, while retaining their rights to participate fully, if they so choose, in the political, economic, social and cultural life of the State.

Article 5

Every indigenous individual has the right to a nationality.

PART II

Article 6

Indigenous peoples have the collective right to live in freedom, peace and security as distinct peoples and to full guarantees against genocide or any other act of violence, including the removal of indigenous children from their families and communities under any pretext.

Article 7

Indigenous Peoples have the collective and individual right not to be subjected to ethnocide and cultural genocide, including prevention of and redress for:

(a) Any action which has the aim or effect of depriving them of their integrity as distinct peoples, or of their cultural values or ethnic identities;

(b) Any action which has the aim or effect of dispossessing them of their lands, territories or resources;

(c) Any form of population transfer which has the aim or effect of violating or undermining any of their rights;

(d) Any form of assimilation or integration by other cultures or ways of life imposed on them by legislative, administrative or other measures;

(e) Any form of propaganda directed against them.

Article 8

Indigenous Peoples have the collective and individual rights to maintain and develop their distinct identities and characteristics, including the right to identify themselves as indigenous and to be recognized as such.

Article 9

Indigenous Peoples and individuals have the right to belong to an indigenous community or nation, in accordance with the traditions and customs of the community or nation concerned. No disadvantage of any kind may arise from the exercise of such a right.

Article 10

Indigenous Peoples shall not be forcibly removed from their lands or territories. No relocation shall take place without the free and informed consent of the indigenous peoples concerned and after agreement on just and fair compensation and, where possible, with the option to return.

Article 11

Indigenous peoples have the right to special protection and security in periods of armed conflict.

States shall observe international standards, in particular the Fourth Geneva Convention of 1949, for the protection of civilians populations in circumstances of emergency and armed conflict and shall not:

(a) Recruit indigenous individuals against their will into the armed forces and, in particular, for use against other indigenous peoples;

(b) Recruit indigenous children into the armed forces under any circumstances;

(c) Force indigenous individuals to abandon their lands, territories or means of subsistence, or relocate them in special centres for military purpose;

(d) Force indigenous individuals to work for military purposes under any discriminatory conditions.

PART III

Article 12

Indigenous peoples have the right to practice and revitalize their cultural traditions and customs. This includes the right to maintain, protect and develop the past, present and future manifestations of their cultures, such as archaeological and historical sites, artifacts, designs, ceremonies, technologies and visual and performing arts and literature, as well as the right to the restitution of cultural, intellectual, religious and spiritual property taken without their free and informed consent or in violation of their laws, traditions and customs.

Article 13

Indigenous peoples have the right to manifest, practise, develop and teach their spiritual and religious traditions, customs and ceremonies; the right to maintain, protect, and have access in privacy to their religious and cultural sites; the right to the use and control of ceremonial objects; and the right to the repatriation of human remains.

States shall take effective measures, in conjunction with the indigenous peoples concerned, to ensure that indigenous sacred places, including burial sites, be preserved, respected and protected.

Article 14

Indigenous peoples have the right to revitalize use, develop and transmit to future generations their histories, languages, oral traditions, philosophies, writing systems and literatures, and to designate and retain their own names for communities, places and persons.

States shall take effective measures, whenever any right of indigenous peoples may be threatened, to ensure this right is protected and also to ensure that they can understand and be understood in political, legal and administrative proceedings, where necessary through the provision of interpretation or by other appropriate means.

PART IV

Article 15

Indigenous children have the right to all levels and forms of education of the State. All indigenous peoples also have this right and the right to establish and control their educational systems and institutions providing education in their own languages, in a manner appropriate to their cultural methods of teaching and learning.

Indigenous children living outside their communities have the right to be provided access to education in their own culture and language.

States shall take effective measures to provide appropriate resources for these purposes.

Article 16

Indigenous peoples have the right to have the dignity and diversity of their culture, traditions, histories and aspirations appropriately reflected in all forms of education and public information.

States shall take effective measures, in consultation with the indigenous peoples concerned, to eliminate prejudice and discrimination and to promote tolerance, understanding and good relations among indigenous peoples and all segments of society.

Article 17

Indigenous peoples have the right to establish their own media in their own languages. They also have the right to equal access to all forms of non-indigenous media.

Article 18

Indigenous peoples have the right to enjoy fully all rights established under international labour law and national labour legislation.

Indigenous individuals have the right not to be subjected to any discriminatory conditions of labour, employment or salary.

PART V

Article 19

Indigenous peoples have the right to participate fully, if they so choose, at all levels of decision-making in matters which may affect their rights, lives and destinies through representatives choose by themselves in accordance with their own procedures, as well as to maintain and develop their own indigenous decision-making institutions.

Article 20

Indigenous peoples have the right to participate fully, if they so choose, through procedures determined by them, in devising legislative or administrative measures that may affect them.

States shall obtain the free and informed consent of the peoples concerned before adopting and implementing such measures.

Article 21

Indigenous peoples have the right to maintain and develop their political, economic and social systems, to be secure in the enjoyment of their own means of subsistence and development, and to engage freely in all their traditional and other economic activities. Indigenous peoples who have been deprived of their means of subsistence and development are entitled to just and fair compensation.

Indigenous peoples have the right to special measures for the immediate, effective and continuing improvement of their economic and social conditions, including in the areas of employment, vocational training and retraining, housing, sanitation, health and social security.

Particular attention shall be paid to the rights and special needs of indigenous elders, women, youth, children and disabled persons.

Article 23

Indigenous peoples have the right to determine and develop priorities and strategies for exercising their right to development. In particular, indigenous peoples have the right to determine and develop all health, housing and other economic and social programmes affecting their own institution.

Article 24

Indigenous peoples have the right to their traditional medicines and health practices, including the right to the protection of vital medicinal plants, animals and minerals.

They also have the right to access, without any discrimination, to all medical institutions, health services and medical care.

PART VI

Article 25

Indigenous peoples have the right to maintain and strengthen their distinctive spiritual and material relationship with the lands, territories, waters and coastal seas and other resources which they have traditionally owned or otherwise occupied or used, and to uphold their responsibilities to future generations in this regard.

Article 26

Indigenous peoples have the right to own, develop, control and use the lands and territories, including the total environment of the lands, air, waters, coastal seas, sea–ice, flora and fauna and other resources which they have traditionally owned and otherwise occupied or used. This includes the right to the full recognition of their laws, traditions and customs, land-tenure systems and institutions for the development and management of resources, and the right to effective measures by States to prevent any interference with, alienation of or encroachment upon these rights.

Article 27

Indigenous peoples have the right to the restitution of the lands, territories and resources which they have traditionally owned or otherwise occupied or used, and which have been confiscated. Where this is not possible, they have the right to just and fair compensation. Unless otherwise freely agreed upon by the peoples concerned, compensation shall take the form of lands, territories and resources equal in quality, size and legal status.

Article 28

Indigenous peoples have the right to the conservation, restoration and protection of the total environment and the productive capacity of their lands, territories and resources, as well as to assistance for the purpose from States and through international cooperation. Military activities shall not take place in the lands and territories of indigenous peoples, unless otherwise freely agreed upon by the peoples concerned.

States shall take effective measures to ensure that no storage or disposal of hazardous materials shall take place in the lands and territories of indigenous peoples.

States shall also take effective measures to ensure, as needed, that programmes for monitoring, maintaining and restoring the health of indigenous peoples, as developed and implemented by the peoples affected by such materials, are duly implemented.

Article 29

Indigenous peoples are entitled to the recognition of the full ownership, control and protection of their cultural and intellectual property.

They have the right to special measures to control, develop and protect their sciences, technologies and cultural manifestations, including human and other genetic resources, seeds, medicines, knowledge of the properties of fauna and flora, oral traditions, literatures, designs and visual and performing arts.

Article 30

Indigenous peoples have the right to determine and develop priorities and strategies for the development or use of their lands, territories and other resources, including the right to require that States obtain their free and informed consent prior to the approval of any project affecting their lands, territories and other resources, particularly in connection with the development, utilization or exploitation of mineral, water or other resources. Pursuant to agreement with the indigenous peoples concerned, just and fair compensation shall be provided for any such activities and measures taken to mitigate adverse environmental, economic, social, cultural or spiritual impact.

PART VII

Article 31

Indigenous peoples, as a specific form of exercising their right to Self-determination, have the right to autonomy or self–government, in matters relating to their internal and local affairs, including culture, religion, education, information, media, health, housing, employment, social welfare, economic activities, land and resources management, environmental and entry by non–members, as well as ways and means for financing these autonomous functions.

Article 32

Indigenous peoples have the collective right to determine their own citizenship in accordance with their customs and traditions. Indigenous citizenship does not impair the right of indigenous individuals to obtain citizenship of the States in which they live.

Article 33

Indigenous peoples have the right to promote, develop and maintain their institutional structures and their distinctive juridical customs, traditions, procedures and practices, in accordance with internationally recognized human rights standards.

Article 34

Indigenous peoples have the collective right to determine the responsibilities of individuals to their communities.

Article 35

Indigenous peoples, in particular those divided by international borders, have the right to maintain and develop contacts, relations and cooperation, including activities for spiritual, cultural, political, economic and social purposes, with other peoples across borders.

States shall take effective measures to ensure the exercise and implementation of this right.

Article 36

Indigenous peoples have the right to the recognition, observance and enforcement of treaties, agreements and other constructive arrangements concluded with States or their successors, according to their original spirit and intent, and to have States honour and respect such treaties, agreements and other constructive arrangements. Conflicts and disputes which cannot otherwise be settled should be submitted to competent international bodies agreed to by all parties concerned.

PART VII

Article 37

States shall take effective and appropriate measures, in consultation with the indigenous peoples concerned, to give full effect to the provisions of this Declaration. The rights recognized herein shall be adopted and included in national legislation in such a manner that indigenous peoples can avail themselves of such right in practice.

Article 38

Indigenous peoples have the right to have access to adequate financial and technical assistance, from States and through international cooperation, to pursue freely their political, economic, social, cultural and spiritual development and for the enjoyment of the rights and freedoms recognized in this Declaration.

Article 39

Indigenous peoples have the right to have access to and prompt decision through mutually acceptable and fair procedures for resolution of conflicts and disputes with States, as well as to effective remedies for all infringements of their individual and collective rights. Such decision shall take into consideration the customs, traditions, rules and legal systems of the indigenous peoples concerned.

Article 40

The organs and specialized agencies of the United Nations system and other intergovernmental organizations shall contribute to the full realization of the provisions of this Declaration through the mobilization, inter alia, of financial cooperation and technical assistance. Ways and means of ensuring participation of indigenous peoples on issues affecting them shall be established.

Article 41

The United Nations shall take the necessary steps to ensure the implementation of this Declaration including the creation of a body at the highest level with special competence in this field and with the direct participation of indigenous peoples. All United Nations bodies shall promote respect for and full application of the provisions of this Declaration.

PART IX

Article 42

The rights recognized herein constitute the minimum standards for the survival, dignity and well–being of the indigenous peoples of the world.

Article 43

All the rights and freedoms recognized herein are equally guaranteed to male and female indigenous individuals.

Article 44

Nothing in this Declaration may be construed as diminishing or extinguishing existing or future rights indigenous peoples may have or acquire.

Article 45

Nothing in this Declaration may be interpreted as implying for any State, group or person any right to engage in any activity or to perform any act contrary to the Charter of the United Nations.

APPENDIX II

Draft of the Inter–American Declaration on the Rights of Indigenous Peoples.

PREAMBLE

1. Indigenous institutions and the strengthening of nations

The member States of the Organization of American States (hereafter the States),

Recalling that the indigenous peoples of the Americas constitute an organized, distinctive and integral segment of their population and are entitled to be part of the countries' national identity, and have a special role to play in strengthening the institutions of the State and in establishing national unity based on democratic principles; and,

Further recalling that some of the democratic institutions and concepts embodied in the Constitutions of American States originate from institutions of the indigenous peoples, and that in many instances their present participatory systems for decision–making and the internal authority of the indigenous peoples contribute to improving democracies in the Americas.

2. Erradication of poverty

Recognizing the severe and widespread poverty afflicting indigenous peoples in many regions of the Americas, and that their living conditions and social services are generally deplorable; and concerning that indigenous peoples have been deprived of their human rights and fundamental freedoms, resulting inter alia in their colonization and the dispossession of their lands, territories and resources, thus preventing them from exercising, in particular, their right to development in accordance with their own needs and interests.

Recalling that in the Declaration of Principles issued by the Summit of the Americas, in December 1994, the Heads of State and Governments declared that in observance of the International Decade of the World's Indigenous People, they will focus their energies on improving the exercise of democratic rights and the access to social services by indigenous peoples and their communities.

3. Indigenous culture and ecology

Appreciating the respect for the environment accorded by the cultures of indigenous peoples of the Americas, and considering the special relationship between the indigenous peoples and the land on which they live.

4. Harmonious relations, respect and the absence of discrimination

Mindful of the responsibility of all States and peoples of the Americas to participate in the struggle against racism and racial discrimination.

5. Enjoyment of community rights

Recalling the international recognition of rights that can only be enjoyed when exercised in community with other members of a group.

6. Indigenous survival and control of their territories

Considering that in many indigenous cultures, traditional collective systems for control and use of land and territory, including bodies of water and coastal areas, are a necessary condition for their survival, social organization, development and their individual and collective well–being; and that the form of such control and ownership is varied and distinctive and does not necessarily coincide with the systems protected by the domestic laws of States in which they live.

7. Demilitarization of indigenous areas

Noting the presence of armed forces in many areas of the lands and territories of the indigenous peoples, and emphasizing the importance of withdrawing them from where they are not strictly needed for their specific functions.

8. Human rights instruments and other advances in international law

Recognizing the preeminence and applicability of the American Declaration of the Rights and Duties of Man, the American Convention on Human Rights and international human rights law, to the States and peoples of the Americas; and

Mindful of the progress achieved by the States and indigenous organizations in codifying indigenous rights, especially in the sphere of the United Nations and the International Labor Organization, and in this regard recalling the ILO Agreement 169 and the Draft UN Declaration on the subject.

Affirming the principle of the universality and indivisibility of human rights, and the application of international human rights to all individuals.

9. Advances in the provisions of national instruments

Noting the constitutional and legislative progresses achieved in some countries of the Americas in guaranteeing the rights and institutions of indigenous peoples.

Declare:

Section One: `Indigenous Peoples'

Art. 1 Definition

1. In this Declaration indigenous peoples are those who embody historical continuity with societies which existed prior to the conquest and settlement of their territories by Europeans. (alternative I) [, as well as peoples brought involuntarily to the New World who freed themselves and re–established the cultures from which they have been torn]. (alternative 2) [,as well as tribal peoples whose social, cultural and economic conditions distinguish them from other sectors of the national community, and whose status is regulated wholly or partially by their own customs or traditions or by special laws or regulations].

2. Self–identification as indigenous or tribal shall be regarded as a fundamental criterion for determining the groups to which the provisions of this Declaration apply.

3. The use of the term "peoples" in this Instrument shall not be construed as having any implication with respect to any other rights that might be attached to that term in inter– national law.

Section Two: `Human Rights'

Art. II Full observance of human rights

1. Indigenous peoples have the right to full and effective enjoyment of the human rights and fundamental freedoms recognized in the Charter of the OAS, the American Declaration on the Rights and Duties of Man, the American Convention on Human Rights, and international human rights law; and nothing in this Declaration shall be construed as in any way limiting or denying those rights or authorizing any action not in

accordance with the instruments of international law including human rights law.

2. The States shall ensure for all indigenous peoples the full exercise of their rights.

3. The States also recognize that the indigenous peoples are entitled to collective rights insofar as they are indispensable to the enjoyment of the individual human rights of their members. Accordingly they recognize the right of the indigenous peoples to collective action, to their culture, to profess and practice their spiritual beliefs and to use their language.

Art. III Right to belong to an indigenous community or nation

Indigenous peoples and individuals have the right to belong to an indigenous community or nation, in accordance with the traditions and customs of the community or nation concerned. No disadvantage of any kind may arise from the exercise of such a right.

Art. IV No forced assimilation

The States shall ensure that within their legal system personality is attributed to communities of indigenous peoples.

Art. V Special guarantees against discrimination

1. The States recognize that, where circumstances so warrant, special guarantees against discrimination may have to be instituted to enable indigenous peoples to fully enjoy internationally and nationally–recognized human rights; and that indigenous peoples must participate fully in the prescription of such guarantees.

2. The States shall also take the measures necessary to enable both indigenous women and men to exercise, without any discrimination, civil, political, economic, social and cultural rights. The States recognize that violence exerted against persons because of their gender prevents and nullifies the exercise of those rights.

Section Three: 'Culteral Development'

Art. VII. Right to Cultural Integrity

1. States shall respect the cultural integrity of indigenous peoples, their development in their respective habitats and their historical and

archeological heritage, which are important to the identity of the members of their groups and their ethnic survival.

2. Indigenous peoples are entitled to restitution in respect of property of which they have been dispossessed, or compensation in accordance with international law.

3. States shall recognize, and respect, indigenous life–styles, customs, traditions, forms of social organization, use of dress, language and dialects.

Art. VIII Philosophy, outlook and language

1. States recognize that indigenous languages, philosophy and outlook are a component of national and universal culture, and as such shall respect them and facilitate their dissemination.

2. The States shall take measures to see to it that broadest radio and television programs are broadcast in the indigenous languages, in the regions where there is a strong indigenous presence, and to support the creation of indigenous radio stations and other media.

3. The States shall take effective measures to enable indigenous peoples to understand administrative, legal and political rules and procedures and to be understood in relation to these matters. In areas where indigenous peoples wish, education systems shall be conducted in the indigenous languages and incorporate indigenous content, and that shall also provide the necessary training and means for complete mastery of the official language or languages.

Art. IX Education

1. Indigenous peoples shall be entitled to: a) establish and set in motion their own educational programs, institutions and facilities; b) to prepare and implement their own educational plans, programs, curricula and materials; c) to train, educate and accredit their teachers and administrators. The States shall endeavour to ensure that such systems guarantee equal educational and teaching opportunities for the entire population and complementarity with national education system.

2. States shall ensure that those educational systems are equal in all ways to that provided to the rest of the population.

3. States shall provide financial and any other type of assistance needed for the implementation of the provisions of this Article.

Art. X Spiritual and religious freedom

1. Indigenous peoples have the right to liberty of conscience, freedom of religion and spiritual practice for indigenous communities and their

members, a right that implies freedom to conserve them, change them, profess and propagate them, both publicly and privately.

2. States shall take necessary measures to ensure that attempts are not made to forcibly convert indigenous peoples or to impose on them beliefs against the will of their communities.

3. In collaboration with the Indigenous peoples concerned, the States shall adopt effective measures to ensure that their sacred sites, including burial sites, are preserved, respected and protected. When sacred graves and relics have been appropriated by state institutions, they shall be returned.

Art. XI Family Relations and family ties

1. Families are a natural and basic component of societies and must be respected and protected by the State. Consequently the State shall protect and respect the various established forms of indigenous organizations relating to family and filiation.

2. In determining the child's best interest in matters relating to the protection and adoption of children of members of indigenous peoples, and in matters of breaking of ties and other similar circumstances, consideration shall be given by Courts and other relevant institutions to the views of those peoples, including individual, family and community views.

Art. XII Health and wellbeing

1. The States shall respect indigenous medicine, pharmacology, health practices and promotion, including prevention and rehabilitative practices.

2. They shall facilitate the dissemination of those medicines and practices of benefit to the entire population.

3. Indigenous peoples have the right to the protection of vital medicinal plants, animals and minerals.

4. Indigenous peoples shall be entitled to use, maintain, develop and manage their own health services, and they shall also have access, without any discrimination, to all health institutions and services and medical care.

5. The states shall provide the necessary means to enable the indigenous peoples to eliminate such health conditions in their communities which fall below international accepted standards.

Art. XIII Right to environmental protection

1. Indigenous peoples are entitled to a healthy environment, which is an essential condition for the enjoyment of the right to life and

well–being.

2. Indigenous peoples are entitled to information on the environment, including information that might ensure their effective participating in actions and policies that might affect their environment.

3. Indigenous peoples shall have the right to conserve, restore and protect their environment, and the productive capacity of their lands, territories and resources.

4. Indigenous peoples shall participate fully in formulating and applying governmental programmes of conservation of their lands and resources.

5. Indigenous peoples shall be entitled to assistance from their states for purposes of environmental protection, and may request assistance from international organizations.

Section Four: 'Organizational and Political Rights'

Art. XIV Rights of association, assembly, freedom of expression and freedom of thought

1. The States shall promote the necessary measures to guarantee to indigenous communities and their members their right of association, assembly and expression in accordance with their usages, customs, and ancestral traditions, beliefs and religions.

2. The States shall respect and enforce the right to of assembly of indigenous peoples and to the use of their sacred and ceremonial areas, as well as the right to full contract and common activities with sectors and members of their ethnic groups living in the territory of neighbouring states.

Art. XV Right to self–government, management and control of internal affairs

1. States acknowledge that indigenous peoples have the right to freely determine their political status and freely pursue their economic, social and cultural development, and that accordingly they have the right to autonomy or self–government with regard to their internal and local affairs, including culture, religion, education, information, media, health, housing, employment, social welfare, economic activities, land and resources management, the environment and entry by nonmembers; and to the ways and means for financing these autonomous functions.

2. Indigenous populations have the right to participate without discrimination, if they so decide, in all decision–making, at all levels, with

regard to matters that might affect their rights, lives and destiny. They may do so through representatives elected by them in accordance with their own procedures. They shall also have the right to maintain and develop their own indigenous decision–making institutions, as well as equal opportunities to access to all national fora.

Art. XVI Indigenous Law

1. Indigenous law is an integral part of the States' legal system and of the framework in which their social and economic development takes place.
2. Indigenous peoples are entitled to maintain and reinforce their indigenous legal systems and also to apply them to matters within their communities, including systems pertaining to ownership of real property and natural resources, resolution of conflicts within and between indigenous communities, crime prevention and law enforcement, and maintenance of internal peace and harmony.
3. In the jurisdiction of any State, procedures concerning indigenous peoples or their interests shall be conducted in such a way as to ensure the right of indigenous peoples to full representation with dignity and equality before the law. This shall include observance of indigenous law and customs and, where necessary, use of the native language.

Art. XVII National incorporation of indigenous legal and organizational systems

1. The States shall promote the inclusion, in their national organizational structures, of institutions and traditional practices of indigenous peoples.
2. The institutions of each state in areas that are predominately indigenous or that are serving in those communities, shall be designed and adapted as to reflect and reinforce the identity, culture and organization of those populations, in order to facilitate their participation.

Section Five: 'Social, Economic and Property Rights'

Art. XVIII Traditional forms of ownership and ethnic survival. Rights to land and territories

1. Indigenous peoples have the right to the legal recognition of the various and specific forms of control, ownership and enjoyment of territories and property by indigenous peoples.

2. Indigenous peoples have the right to the recognition of their property and ownership rights with respect to lands and territories they have historically occupied, as well as to the use of those to which they have historically had access for their traditional activities and livelihood.

3. Where property and user rights of indigenous peoples arise from rights existing prior to the creation of those States, the States shall recognize the titles of indigenous peoples relative thereto as permanent, exclusive, inalienable, imprescriptible and indefeasible. This shall not limit the right to of indigenous peoples to attribute ownership within the community in accordance with their customs, traditions, uses and traditional practices, nor shall it affect any collective community right over them. Such titles may only be changed by mutual consent between the State and respective indigenous people when they have full knowledge and appreciation of the nature or attributes of such property.

4. The rights of indigenous people to existing natural resources on their lands must be especially protected. These rights include the right to the use, management and conservation of such resources.

5. In the event that ownership of the minerals or resources of the subsoil pertains to the State or that the State has rights over other resources on the lands, the governments must establish or maintain procedures for the participation of the peoples concerned in determining whether the interests of these people would be adversely affected and to what extent, before undertaking or authorizing any program for tapping or exploiting existing resources on their lands. The peoples concerned shall participate in the benefits of such activities, and shall receive compensation in accordance with international law, for any damages which they may sustain as a result of such activities.

6. The States shall not transfer or relocate indigenous peoples except in exceptional cases, and in those cases with the free, genuine and informed consent of those populations, with full and prior indemnity and prompt replacement of lands taken, which must be of similar or better quality and which must have the same legal status; and with guarantees of the right to return if the causes that give rise to the displacement cease to exist.

7. Indigenous peoples have the right to the restitution of the lands, territories and resources which they have traditionally owned or otherwise occupied or used, and which have been confiscated occupied, used or damaged, or the right to compensation in accordance with international law when restitution is not possible.

8. The States shall take all measures, including the use of law enforcement personnel, to avert, prevent and punish, if applicable, any intrusion or use of those lands by unauthorized persons or by persons who take advantage of indigenous peoples or their lack of understanding of the laws, to take possession or make use of them. The States shall give max-

imum priority to the demarcation of properties and areas of indigenous use.

Art. XIX Workers rights

1. Indigenous peoples shall have the right to full enjoyment of the rights and guarantees recognized under international labor law or domestic labor law; they shall also be entitled, where circumstances so warrant, to special measures to correct, redress and prevent the discrimination to which they have historically been subject.

2. Where circumstances so warrant, the States shall take such special measures as may be necessary to:

a. protect effectively the workers and employees who are members of indigenous communities in respect of fair and equal hiring and terms of employment, insofar as general legislation governing workers overall does not provide;

b. to improve the work inspection service in regions, companies or paid activities involving indigenous workers or employees;

c. ensure that indigenous workers:

i. enjoy equal opportunity and treatment as regards all conditions of employment, job promotion and advancement;

ii. are not subject to racial, sexual or other forms of harassment;

iii. are not subjected to coercive hiring practices including servitude for debts or any other form of servitude, even if they have their origin in law, custom or a personal or collective arrangement which shall be deemed absolutely null and void in each instance;

iv. are not subjected to working conditions that endanger their health, particularly as a result of their exposure to pesticides or other toxic or radioactive substances;

v. receive special protection when they serve as seasonal, casual or migrant workers in agriculture or in other activities and also when they are hired by labor contractors in order that they benefit from national legislation and practice which must, itself be in accordance with firmly established international human rights standards in respect of seasonal workers, and

vi. ensure that indigenous workers or employees are provided with full information on their rights, consistent with such national legislation and international standards, and on resources available to them in order to protect those rights.

Art. XX Intellectual property rights

1. Indigenous peoples shall be entitled to recognition of the full own-

ership, control and protection of such intellectual property rights as they have in their cultural and artistic heritage, as well as special measures to ensure for them legal status and institutional capacity to develop, use, share, market and bequeath, that heritage on to future generations.

2. Where circumstances so warrant, indigenous peoples have the right to special measures to control, develop and protect, and full compensation for the use of their sciences and technologies, including their human and genetic resources in general, seeds, medicine, knowledge of plant and animal life, original designs and procedures.

Art. XXI Right to development

1. The states recognize the right of indigenous peoples to decide democratically what values, objectives, priorities and strategies will govern and steer their development course, even if they are different from those adopted by the national government or by other segments of society. Indigenous peoples shall be entitled to obtain on a non–discriminatory basis appropriate means for their own development according to their preferences and values, and to contribute by their own means, as distinguishable societies, to national development, and international cooperation.

2. The States shall take necessary measure to ensure that decisions regarding any plan, program or proposal affecting the rights or living conditions of indigenous peoples are not made without the free and informed consent and participation of those peoples, that their preferences are recognized and that no such plan, program or proposal that could have harmful effects on the normal livelihood of those populations is adopted. Indigenous communities have the right to restitution or compensation in accordance with international law, for any damage which, despite the foregoing precautions, the execution of those plans or proposal may have caused them; and measures taken to mitigate adverse environmental, economic, social, cultural or spiritual impact.

Section Six: `General Provisions'

Art. XXII Treaties, agreements and other implied arrangements

Indigenous peoples have the right to the recognition, observance and enforcement of treaties, agreements and other arrangements concluded with States or their successors, according to their spirit and intent, and to have States honor and respect such treaties, agreements and other constructive arrangements. Conflicts and disputes which cannot otherwise be settled should be submitted to competent international bodies (agreed to by all parties concerned).

Art. XIII

Nothing in this instrument shall be construed as diminishing or extinguishing existing or future rights indigenous peoples may have or acquire.

Art. XXIV

Nothing in this instrument shall be construed as granting any right to ignore boundaries between States.

PRINTED AND BOUND
IN BOUCHERVILLE, QUÉBEC, CANADA
BY MARC VEILLEUX IMPRIMEUR INC.
IN SEPTEMBER, 1998